OLDE CLERKIS SPECHE

OLDE CLERKIS SPECHE

Chaucer's *Troilus and Criseyde* and the
Implications of Authorial Recital

WILLIAM A. QUINN

THE CATHOLIC UNIVERSITY OF AMERICA PRESS
Washington, D.C.

Copyright © 2013
The Catholic University of America Press
All rights reserved

Design and typesetting by Kachergis Book Design

Library of Congress Cataloging-in-Publication Data
Quinn, William A., 1951–
Olde Clerkis Speche : Chaucer's Troilus and Criseyde and the implications of authorial recital / William A. Quinn.
  pages cm.
Includes bibliographical references and index.
ISBN 978-0-8132-3568-4 (pbk)
1. Chaucer, Geoffrey, –1400. Troilus and Criseyde—
Criticism, Textual. I. Title.
PR1896.Q56 2013
821'.1—dc23   2013024284

To My One True Love

CONTENTS

Acknowledgments ix

1. Presentation Points 1
2. Book I, Lively Reading or Deadly Silence? 37
3. Book II, Echo Chambers 61
4. Book III, Pillow Talk and Bedroom Eyes 93
5. Book IV, Conjunctions 116
6. Book V, Deceptions and Receptions 137
7. Finishing Touches 173
8. Postscript 201

Bibliography 221
Index 243

ACKNOWLEDGMENTS

As warmly as I can in cold print, I want to thank many people.

I am extremely grateful to all my colleagues and students and friends at the University of Arkansas. For their generous and patient support, I must especially thank my former Dean (now System President) Don Bobbit, Associate Dean Chuck Adams, and my former Chair Joseph Candido. For all her brilliant and tart remarks, I thank Lynda Coon, chair of the Department of History and my sister in medievalist arms. And, most of all, I thank Lyna Lee Montgomery who so benignly corrected this little book in its repeated need. Any remaining errors are entirely to be blamed on my own "negligence and rape."

I am also happy to thank Dean Carolyn Henderson Allen and the entire staff of Mullins Library at the University of Arkansas, especially Anne Marie Candido and Beth Juhl.

My seventh chapter in particular required the expert assistance of so many librarians and staff with whom I never exchanged names but to whom I owe so much. With far too little recognition of their support, I give thanks to all who generously assisted me at the Huntington Library, the Morgan Library, the Green Peace Library of Durham University (with special thanks to A. I. Doyle for his time), the British Library, the Bodleian Library, and the Cambridge University Library.

The start of this project was fostered by an NEH Summer Institute (2005) directed by Steven W. May at the Folger Library, and I must thank all the participants and staff involved, especially Donna Craw-

ACNOWLEDGMENTS

ford, Julia Boffey, and A. S. G. Edwards. The completion of this project was greatly advanced by a visiting fellowship to Wolfson College, Cambridge University (2006–2007). I gladly thank Gordon Johnson, then Deputy Vice-Chancellor, as well as all the Fellows and the entire community of Wolfson College. I also am most eager to acknowledge and thank the English Faculty of Cambridge for their hospitality, especially Helen Cooper.

I am also intensely grateful to Chris Zacher and Pete Wetherbee for their encouragement at certain key moments in this project. I am running out of new ways to say how deeply beholden I have repeatedly been to John Ganim, whom I can never adequately thank for being such a generous scholar and good soul. And I am, once again, deeply indebted to the entire editorial staff and readers of the Catholic University of America Press—to Theresa Walker and Ellen Coughlin, for their conscientious care, and to Trevor Lipscombe, the Editor in Chief, for his courage and constant kindness.

I recall my late parents and their enduring love. I remember all my teachers and their enduring lessons. I want to give a shout out to my distant sisters, Karen and Diane, who are always near to my thoughts. I thank my children, Catherine and Bill, who remind me to think young, and my ever young wife, Tricia, who has now endured decades of my talking to myself.

Finally, Chaucer. As far as I can tell, the poet's last speech-act was a prose prayer ending in a Latin tag. Chaucer's reiteration of an old clerical phrase asks that we pray for the bliss of his soul with Christ "qui vivit" (CT 10, 1091)—and I do.

ОLDE CLERKIS SPECHE

1

PRESENTATION POINTS

This meditacioun
I put it ay under correccioun
Of clerkes, for I am nat textueel.
(*Canterbury Tales* 10. 55–57)

MOST READINGS of Chaucer's *Troilus and Criseyde* already celebrate both its craft and his compassion. Many readers see this text as "Chaucer's greatest poem," "most perfect (in every sense)," perhaps even "the finest long narrative poem in English literature."[1] Since the soul of

---

1. These tributes to the excellence of *Troilus and Criseyde* have, in order, been made by: A. C. Spearing, *Textual Subjectivity: The Encoding of Subjectivity in Medieval Narratives and Lyrics* (Oxford: Oxford University Press, 2005), 68; Stephen A. Barney, Studies in "Troilus": *Text, Meter, and Diction* (East Lansing, Mich.: Colleagues Press, 1993), 1; and John McCall, "Troilus and Criseyde," in *Companion to Chaucer Studies*, ed. Beryl Rowland, 446–63 (Oxford: Oxford University Press, 1979), 446. See Alice R. Kaminsky for a survey of the "few negative notes ... amidst the clamor of idolatrous acclamation," *Chaucer's Troilus and Criseyde and the Critics* ([Athens]: Ohio University Press, 1980), 11. Unless otherwise noted, all citations of Chaucer's texts follow Larry D. Benson, gen. ed., *The Riverside Chaucer*, 3rd ed. (Boston: Houghton Mifflin, 1987), in which *Troilus and Criseyde* was edited by Stephen A. Barney with the assistance of materials provided by Robert A. Pratt and collations provided by Margaret Jennings and Ardath McKee.

PRESENTATION POINTS

Troilus and Criseyde has already been so immortalized, I want instead to dissect its body—to scrutinize the extant book as a corruptible container of Chaucer's imagined intent. The purpose of this study is to excavate what remains of Chaucer's voice in the printed pages of *Troilus and Criseyde* and to restate the corresponding tonal intentions of his own authorial recital. I do not pretend to disclose thereby the text's true meaning at last. Indeed, John V. Fleming doubts that there can truly be "a comprehensive new interpretation—as opposed to a repartition or redistribution of various interpretations already in the public domain."[2] I want instead to read the text of *Troilus and Criseyde* as a broken record of what Chaucer once said aloud—literally speaking.[3]

Chaucer's composition of *Troilus and Criseyde* may have entailed a number of discrete reading stages. Chaucer, having experienced a variety of versions of the story, created therefrom his own rendition, which is a composite of types, tones, and voices. For C. David Benson, "the effect of these different genres in *Troilus*, which like the poem's various styles usually remain distinct from one another, is to challenge our notion of any single reading of the poem."[4] I would like to consider as fully as possible the notion that Chaucer, having read and in some fashion translated Boccaccio's *il Filostrato*, wrote a version of the story for his own viva voce

---

2. John V. Fleming, *Classical Imitation and Interpretation in Chaucer's Troilus* (Lincoln: University of Nebraska Press, 1990), xi. Fleming reads the *Troilus* as "the work of an in*terpres* ... a translator; it may also mean a priest ... a literary critic, also an analyst of dreams. An *interpres* may be a poem; it may also be a pimp" (157).

3. I am using the term *text* in its simplest significance—the transcribed object produced for circulation. Paul Zumthor distinguishes this readable *text* as "a unified linguistic sequence" from its *performance* as "a moment of reception" and from "the simultaneously hearable and visible" work which includes "the totality of performance characteristics" including silence and *forms* ("Body and Performance," in *Materialities of Communication*, ed. Hans Ulrich Gumbrecht and K. Ludwig Pfeiffer, trans. William Whobrey, 217–26 ([Stanford, Calif.: Stanford University Press, 1994], 218–19).

4. C. David Benson, *Chaucer's Troilus and Criseyde* (London: Unwin Hyman, 1990), 42.

PRESENTATION POINTS

presentation.⁵ This script he afterwards—to some highly debatable extent—revised for manuscript circulation. The significance of Chaucer's composing initially for his own public performance is now quite easy to overlook when reading a modern edition of the book; yet, once revived (by the reader's imagination) as an actual event, the interpretive premise of such authorial recital informs all perceptions of the narrating "I" as a real tonal presence.

In the wake of most "progressive" nineteenth- and twentieth-century philosophy, Hans Ulrich Gumbrecht writes:

> If we assume (as indeed I have) that there is no aesthetic experience without a presence effect, and no presence effect without substance in play; if we further assume that a substance in order to be perceived needs form; and, if we finally assume (as I also have in previous reflections) that the presence-component in the tension or oscillation that constitutes can never be held stable, then it follows that, whenever an object of experience emerges and momentarily produces in us that feeling of intensity, it seems to come out of nothing.⁶

I wish I could ask Gumbrecht in person (that is, the "I" within his parentheses) exactly what he means. But most to the point of this study is his observation that "manuscripts provide a path for

---

5. Robert W. Hanning remarks, "The equivocal status of the text as mediating artifact is compounded when the text in question is a translation." ("The Crisis of Mediation in Chaucer's *Troilus and Criseyde*," in *The Performance of Middle English Culture*, ed. James J. Paxson, Lawrence M. Clopper, and Sylvia Tomasch, 143–59 [Cambridge: D.S. Brewer, 1998], 149). See too Rita Copeland, *Rhetoric, Hermeneutics, and Translation in the Middle Ages* (Cambridge: Cambridge University Press, 1991); and Roger Ellis et al., eds., *The Medieval Translator* (Cambridge: D.S. Brewer, 1989). The English text's viva voce "I" is, of course, not merely a verbatim translation of Boccaccio's unnamed "I." Barry Windeatt observes (in his *en face* edition of both texts) that "recurrently, the parallel text shows how Ch's own imagination acts in close response to his original story-line.... Fil provides a pole or core around which Ch's imagination has moved, reacting, accumulating" (*Geoffrey Chaucer, Troilus and Criseyde* [New York: Longmans, 1984], 11). A. C. Spearing observes, "The function of the medieval poet as a reteller and commentator marks a fundamental difference from the role of the novelist" (*Textual Subjectivity*, 22).

6. Hans Ulrich Gumbrecht, *Production of Presence* (Stanford, Calif.: Stanford University Press, 2004), 111.

the undoing of the primary 'theatrical' situation."⁷ In my seventh chapter, I will attempt to trace this "undoing" of Chaucer's own recital of *Troilus and Criseyde* by its textual witnesses. But I do not, therefore, despair of finding some tracks of Chaucer's real (because still perceptible) presence in the tonal record of his text.

The theologically resonant expression "real presence" presents a profound challenge to our now normative conception of the absented author. I would prefer to sidestep this theoretical controversy, but I want to study tone, and a sensing of tone necessarily presupposes the retrievability of authorial intent, and authorial intent has been decreed a dead issue by many, if not by most, modern theorists. Swimming against the current of such skepticism, George Steiner "proposes that any coherent understanding of what language is and how it performs, that any coherent account of the capacity of human speech to communicate meaning and feeling is, in the final analysis, underwritten by the assumption of God's presence."⁸ But how do you argue with someone who insists that the retrieval of authorial intent is merely an act of deluded faith because faith itself is merely a delusion?

Nevertheless, I see no need to hold an auto-da-fé prior to hearing Chaucer's tone as reciter of *Troilus and Criseyde*. In chapters 2 through 6, I will attempt instead to see if my own doctrine works—if authorial recital (as an article of faith) reveals more tonal signals than heretofore believed to exist in the text. There is no real need to belabor further the theory behind this reading premise. For Leonard Koff, a reader's firm grasp of Chaucer's role as the teller of his stories makes his narratives "easy"— albeit in richly complex ways. Real recital motivated all Chaucer's art of rhetoric. But rhetorical studies of Chaucer's compositions

---

7. Ibid., 31.
8. George Steiner, *Real Presences* (Chicago: University of Chicago Press, 1989), 3.

PRESENTATION POINTS

normally focus on his *inventio*—the guts and bones of creativity. A performance-based reading of *Troilus and Criseyde* requires that its tonal surface be skinned. Modern editors initiate this process simply by supplying quotation marks and so determining the cuts in the text's reading surface.[9] One reader may validly question the legitimacy of any other reader's imposition of such punctuation, but some such interpretive, syntactic prompts must be supplied. So, too, whenever dialect variants are regularized or orthographic irregularities are corrected or metrical rough spots are polished, some reader's informed assumptions reimpose Chaucer's corrective voice on the damaged or inadequate manuscript record. It is easy to sound sophisticated by denying the meaning of a text; it is impossible to perceive or impose some tone to the text—"tonelessness" is really just a dull reading.

It is conventionally assumed by editors that Chaucer's final draft of *Troilus and Criseyde*, the one he intended for manuscript circulation, provides the target text for reconstitution of a "best reading." My primary contention is that remnants of a no less hypothetically plausible recital version of *Troilus and Criseyde* can likewise be found in subsequent (so contaminated) transcriptions and contribute to a richer reading of the edited text. Chaucer's recital intentions come to us filtered through an indefinite number of authorial, scribal, and editorial reworkings. What results from these discrete efforts to produce and then reproduce *Troilus and Criseyde*

---

9. Howell Chickering, "Unpunctuating Chaucer," *The Chaucer Review* 25 (1990): 96–109, and Alan Gaylord, "Reading Chaucer: What's Allowed in 'Aloud'?" *Chaucer Yearbook* 1 (1992): 87–109, have both promoted the pedagogical advantages of reading manuscript transcriptions without the imposition of editorial interpretation. For the nature and extent of scribal punctuation itself, see M. B. Parkes, *Pause and Effect: An Introduction to the History of Punctuation in the West* (Berkeley: University of California Press, 1993), and Elizabeth Solopova, "The Survival of Chaucer's Punctuation in the Early Manuscripts of the *Canterbury Tales*," in *Middle English Poetry: Texts and Traditions*, ed. A. J. Minnis, 27–40 (York: York Medieval Press, 2001).

is the present, polyphonic text that contains echoes of all its previous stagings, including Chaucer's intentions as reader, translator, redactor, reciter, and reviser. I hope to increase the volume of only the currently most neglected track in the surviving composite text—the one that preserves indications of Chaucer's apparent attitudes while reciting *Troilus and Criseyde* for its first audience.[10]

I am concerned with the implications of Chaucer's performance of his own composition only in the simplest, most commonplace sense of the term *perform*.[11] I am especially interested in the language of the poem that does not look especially purposeful or poetic. I am not primarily concerned with the art of Chaucer's imagery or plotting or characterization per se. I intend instead to attend to the dynamics of all of Chaucer's small talk. I want to foreground Chaucer's hard-to-justify because difficult-to-explicate remarks. I wish to emphasize the positive performance effects of

---

10. See Beryl Rowland, "Chaucer's Speaking Voice and its Effect on His Listeners' Perception of Criseyde," *English Studies in Canada* 7 (1981): 129–40, and "*Pronuntiatio* and its Effect on Chaucer's Audience," *Studies in the Age of Chaucer* 4 (1982): 33–51. Detailed instructions for actual recitation were largely ignored by classical and medieval rhetoricians; its strategies were considered rather intuitively obvious, and the talent to recite was associated with the less respected skill of actors.

11. In line with the "ordinary language philosophy" of J. L. Austin, John Searle, Stanley Cavell, et al., I do maintain the real referentiality of Chaucer's discourse. I take for granted that there once existed a genuine, if now largely forgotten, frame of reference for Chaucer's initial recital of the *Troilus*. I do not attempt in this particular study to induce a detailed reconstitution of Chaucer's *performatives* defined as his habitual reiterations of behavior, the ritualized rhetoric by which a familiar Chaucer reinvented himself as the new subject in a particular recital context. Nor does my study of the text's *performability* deal in any detail with Chaucer's class identity or gender *performativity*, such as examined by Judith Butler, although the decorum of his presence in court surely dictated the actual choreography of such ethnographic issues. Nor does this study explore *performance study* in Richard Schechner's usage of the term as the web of make-believe which includes theatrical production, ritual, game, and sport. This application of the term *performativity* evaluates the viability of any given theatrical iteration, often without regard to historical authenticity, sometimes with a deliberately subversive agenda. For a survey of the term *performative* as applied to Chaucer, see my "Presenting 'the' *Legend of Good Women*," in *New Approaches to Chaucer's Legend of Good Women*, ed. Carolyn Collette, 1–32 (Cambridge: D.S. Brewer, 2005). For an excellent introduction to the term's phylogeny, see James Loxley, *Performativity, New Critical Idiom* (New York: Routledge, 2007).

his nonce phrasing, his non-narrative interjections apparently addressed to a familiar audience, expressions that most readings ignore as tonally insignificant filler produced by medieval ineptness. In sum, I want to amplify any indication of Chaucer's apparent attitude as he hears himself reading his own story to others.[12] I have come to the conviction that there are no vacuous remarks, no odd rhymes, no metrical missteps, no narrative gaffes in *Troilus and Criseyde*—every apparent flaw served some deliberate tonal function during its authorial recital. We misread Chaucer's roughness if we read him exclusively in terms of print-based conceptions of reading—as Dryden did.

Donald Howard once tried to defend what others considered Chaucer's clumsy authorial intrusions in *The Canterbury Tales* as his "unimpersonated artistry." These moments when "we read the tale as a dramatic monologue spoken by its teller but understand that some of Chaucer's attitudes spill into it" seem violations of the (novel-defined) protocols of fiction.[13] In *Troilus and Criseyde*, however, Chaucer's trespassing seems far more insistent. Indeed, the reciter never fully disappears into the roles of the characters he quotes. Rather, all the dialogue in *Troilus and Criseyde* needs to be read as direct quotation of Chaucer too. As Leonard Koff has put it: "Now declamation necessarily gives to the performer one irresistible quality—omnipresence."[14] And, although Chaucer frequently

12. A. C. Spearing sees *deixis* as the "primary means" that speech uses "to encode subjectivity.... Deitics are terms that have no objective referential meaning but are used to describe objects or events in their spatio-temporal (and, by extension, emotional) relation to the person who uses them—*I, you, here, there, this, that,* and so on" (*Textual Subjectivity,* 5). Spearing subsequently adds, "This large metanarrative element might be expected to have a distancing effect, deflecting attention from the love story to its teller's consciousness, but in practice this is not so" (84). I contend that drawing attention to himself by this phrasing was precisely Chaucer's intended effect during recital.
13. Donald R. Howard, *The Idea of the Canterbury Tales* (Berkeley: University of California Press, 1976), 231.
14. Leonard Michael Koff,. *Chaucer and the Art of Storytelling* (Berkeley: University of California Press, 1988), 13.

renounces omniscience as a narrator, his "I" remains always immanent as the narrative's reciter.[15] What were once the fully realized signals of Chaucer's tonal intent survive now as only vaguely recorded prompts. If correct (that is, convincing), then declarations of Chaucer's recital intentions dispel ambiguity and fix the received text's tone. But the very indefiniteness of Chaucer's recital tone more often than not destabilizes our default assumptions regarding the bare text's tone. It is only a slight exaggeration to say that the printed text has no tone except that induced by each reader from its presumed context of presentation.

Ruth Crosby, who first surveyed the "signs of oral delivery" in Chaucer's poetry, considered his entire canon a homogenous field of evidence.[16] I do not. I do see that there are numerous equally compelling signs of the *textuality* in Chaucer's works. But a real deterrent to imagining Chaucer's oral delivery as tonally beneficial for modern readers has been the deficiency theory which "depicts prelection as the make-do phase of early literacy."[17] I do not think so. The real critical challenge is to reassess even the seemingly most drab elements of *Troilus and Criseyde* as part of its recital brilliance.[18] My running commentary in the following chapters

---

15. A. C. Spearing considers the intrusive "presence of others (Pandarus, the poet, his readers) at supposedly private moments" (*The Medieval Poet as Voyeur* [Cambridge: Cambridge University Press, 1993], 121). Barry Windeatt observes a significant difference in this regard between il *Filostrato* and the *Troilus*: "Comparison of the poems reveals that Ch consistently draws a society that allows much less privacy to his lovers, while at the same time he gives to his characters a much increased sense that their affair must be secret" (*Geoffrey Chaucer, Troilus* [1984], 10).

16. See Ruth Crosby, "Oral Delivery in the Middle Ages," *Speculum* 11 (1936): 88–110, and "Chaucer and the Custom of Oral Delivery," *Speculum* 13 (1938): 413–32.

17. Joyce Coleman, *Public Reading and the Reading Public in Late Medieval England and France* (Cambridge: Cambridge University Press, 1996), 53. Alice Miskimin, for example, rejected "various modern oral-formulaic perspectives" that "all presuppose an originally illiterate audience" (*The Renaissance Chaucer* [New York: Yale University Press, 1975], 105).

18. Moses Hadas explains that works of Silver Age Latin poetry and prose com-

asks that our textual perception of these signs of recital be read as histrionically beneficial to an appreciation of the text's tonal play. Derek Brewer has calculated that Chaucer would have required about six hours to read all of *Troilus and Criseyde* aloud.[19] I think its division into five books may preserve some shadow of its five recital installments.[20] But any straightforward affirmation of the "orality" of Chaucer's composition has become strangely difficult to sustain. Walter J. Ong once famously conceded that every textually implied audience is, in fact, a "fiction." But Fr. Ong did not intend thereby to exterminate the memory of all real recitals.[21] William Nelson

---

posed in the "Pointed Style," deliberately fashioned to invite applause, "are apt to be brilliant in quotation but cloying in extended passages" (*Ancilla to Classical Reading* [New York: Columbia University Press, 1961], 64). Mutatis mutandis, Linda Marie Zaerr has found that the more polished texts of both Chaucer's "Wife of Bath's Tale" and Gower's "Tale of Florent" are in fact "much more difficult to perform at a practical level" than *The Weddynge of Sir Gawen and Dame Ragnell* ("The Weddynge of Sir Gawen and Dame Ragnell: Performance and Intertextuality in Middle English Popular Romance," in *Performing Medieval Narrative*, ed. Evelyn Birge Vitz, Nancy Freeman Regalado, and Marilyn Lawrence, 193–208 [Woodbridge: D.S. Brewer, 2005], 197). Likewise, William Nelson contends that "the inappropriateness of unitary plot to viva voce reading of a lengthy work is clearly the lesson that Bernardo Tasso learned" ("From 'Listen, Lordings' to 'Dear Reader,'" *University of Toronto Quarterly* 46, no. 2 [1976/7]: 110–24, 119).

19. Brewer considers a single "session of some six hours" conceivable (*Chaucer in His Time* [London: Longmans, 1973], 198). Brewer's example of Froissart reading *Meliador* every night after supper to Gaston Phoebus, Count of Foix, may document (*Chroniques* II. 26) a more closeted, less histrionic type of authorial recital—with a quite different pace therefore—than Chaucer's performance of *Troilus and Criseyde*.

20. Boethius's *Consolatio* may have provided a template for the five-book structure of *Troilus*. William Provost finds studies of Chaucer's scene divisions (e.g., Price, Fisher, Meech and Utley) misleading at a basic level; "though the dramatic quality of *Troilus* is great, it remains essentially a narrative, not a drama, and its structural units must be defined accordingly." Provost also dismisses rhetorical analysis (as well as comparison to Boethius) as "invalid or unproductive" (*The Structure of Chaucer's Troilus and Criseyde* [Copenhagen: Rosenkilde and Bagger, 1974], 21).

21. Fr. Walter J. Ong wrote: "Written or printed narrative is not two-way, at least in the short run.... Chaucer, for example, had a problem with the conjectural readers of the *Canterbury Tales*" and, by setting the stories in a frame, "tells his readers how they are to fictionalize themselves" ("The Writer's Audience Is Always a Fiction," *PMLA* 90 (1975): 9–22, 16a). I agree that, insofar as Chaucer anticipated manuscript circulation of the *Canterbury Tales*, the audience must be written into the text. For Joyce Coleman, Ong

modified this idea of the extant text's *intended* audience to factor in a text's form of address to an *anticipated* audience: "Direct address to that audience is therefore not merely a residual trace of an outworn manner.... In the Renaissance the author continues to speak as though real people, not hypotheses, were listening to him."[22]

However plausible the proposition that Chaucer recited *Troilus and Criseyde* himself may or may not be, the hope that his voicing of the extant text can still be retrieved might seem merely a naive revival of New Criticism strangely masquerading as oral performance theory. At bottom, both critical approaches do share a common concern with "how does the text work?" rather than with "what does it mean?" Yet, both labels also currently invite a good deal of reflexive rather than reflective resistance. The "text itself" is no longer a sufficient critical focus.

In the wake of an "essentially sibling" rivalry between the (naively ahistorical) New Critics and the (dogmatically medieval) Robertsonians, Lee Patterson insists "the Exegetical challenge can be met only on its own historicist grounds—specifically in terms of the history of reading."[23] However, the archaeology of reading seldom digs beneath the surface of the manuscript page; so historicized readings of *Troilus and Criseyde* usually begin with evidence derived from records of its fifteenth-century reception. Any attempts to retrieve Chaucer's own words (including editorial efforts) confront this alleged terminus of writing-defined interpretation.[24] The protocols of reader-response are thereafter

---

assumed too rigid an opposition between "oral" and "literate" consciousness, however. C. David Benson notes that Robert Payne in *The Key of Remembrance* anticipated Ong's discussion of reading as a role to play (*Chaucer's Troilus*, 48).

22. Nelson, "From 'Listen, Lordings' to 'Dear Reader,'" 117.

23. Lee W. Patterson, *Negotiating the Past* (Madison: University of Wisconsin Press, 1987), 3, 115.

24. Questioning the critical advantages promised by the Cambridge CD-ROM editions, Joseph A. Dane asks (and answers), "In what sense is it meaningful to claim that

restricted to the evidence of the copied page conceived as a box containing only its own self-referential space.

As an advocate of a performance-based reading, I simply disagree. There is no way to finesse this impasse. The premise of an authorial recital of the text invites, indeed requires, that the printed page be approached instead as a platform for re-staging the fullest possible enactment of a real performance event. The premise that Chaucer himself once recited *Troilus and Criseyde* aloud allows evidence "within the text" to be read as historical evidence of its own prior enactment. The manuscript evidence as such is subsequent to (and so external from) the recital event. Reading the text as a record of Chaucer's voice is more problematic than reading it as a faithful copy of Chaucer's own handwriting—but not completely an exercise in futility. Insofar as the text still preserves the center of its own recital context, a performance-based reading should render every syllable of Chaucer's poem more nuanced. Read as a monopolylogue, *Troilus and Criseyde* seems inherently theatrical even if it does not fit our standard definitions of drama.[25] Most often Chaucer

---

late twentieth-century readers have a better understanding of these authors than did their fifteenth-century counterparts simply because their editors do?" ("Two Studies in Chaucer Editing," in *The Myth of Print Culture: Essays on Evidence, Textuality and Bibliographical Method* [Toronto: University of Toronto Press, 2003], 114–42, 142). As an alternative to using (Lachmannian) recension to edit toward a presumed archetype, the Cambridge CD-ROM project (directed by N. F. Blake with Elizabeth Solopova as principal transcriber and Peter Robinson as executive officer) uses "cladistic analysis" to generate an initially "unrooted" tree of ancestral analysis among manuscript variants. Peter Robinson contends that "electronic editions may be much less of the authoritarian editor handing down the definitive text, and much more of a partnership between editor and reader" ("The Computer and the Making of Editions," in *A Guide to Editing Middle English*, ed. Vincent McCarren and Douglas Moffat, 249–61 [Ann Arbor: University of Michigan Press, 1998], 261).

25. According to T .R. Price's sorting of lines, *Troilus and Criseyde* consists of 64 percent dialogue, 18 percent monologue, 14 percent group scenes, and 4 percent scenes with three speakers ("A Study of Chaucer's Method of Narrative Construction," PMLA 2 [1896]: 307–22.) In *Chaucerian Tragedy* (Cambridge: D.S. Brewer, 1997), Henry Ansgar Kelly observes: "The main kind of 'theatrical' activity Chaucer knew was the sort of mummings,

PRESENTATION POINTS

simply indicates that a character's lines were spoken "thus" with no further qualification of "how" (for example, "sadly," "angrily," "happily," "sarcastically," "deceptively"). Every direct quotation must thus be imagined as performed by the quoter.[26] It is the act of telling the story rather than the plot of the story being told that once required Chaucer to play his specific role as authorial reciter.

Unfortunately—that is, as a result of historical accident—no surviving evidence proves that Chaucer was ever rewarded for his service as a court performer.[27] Glending Olson, therefore, concedes that "although always a court-poet in one sense, Chau-

---

interludes, and other court entertainments described in the *Franklin's Tale*" as well as "the biblical plays of his time" (58). Chaucer understood the term *tragedy* to mean a type of narrative, "a certeyn storie" (*CT* 7, 1973), the performance of which might entail "a vigorous public recitation of the sort he himself must have engaged in" (*Chaucerian Tragedy*, 56). Of course, whatever its tonal connotations, the denotation of *tragedy* is neither Aristotelian nor theatrical in Chaucer's normal usage, but it does require a recitable memory from an old book (cf. *CT* 7, 1974–75). With specific regard to *Troilus and Criseyde*, Monica McAlpine clarifies the thematic (i.e., philosophical) significance of "the narrator's late and solemn designation of his book as a tragedy"(*The Genre of Troilus and Criseyde* [Ithaca, N.Y.: Cornell University Press, 1978], 18).

26. Reading aloud is easy to equate with "dramatic interpretation," but such declamation need not suppose authorial recital. George Lyman Kittredge, R. M. Lumiansky, and John Dryden all assumed that some "dramatic" quality informed Chaucer's storytelling. Francis Ferguson called for a "histrionic" reading that fully engaged the imagination of a silent reader conventionally conceived. E. Talbot Donaldson's highly influential conception of the Chaucerian persona did not insist upon the term's original meaning in Greek drama. For Richard Axton, Saul Brody, et al., "drama" provides an important motif within Chaucer's work but does not necessarily indicate Chaucer's initial type of publication. Nancy Harvey considers how Chaucer plays with his audience's awareness of sources but does not employ "play" specifically in terms of oral enactment. For John Ganim theatricality does not mean "a study of the drama ... narrowly conceived, or even an affiliation between Chaucer's poetry and the forms of medieval theater" except as part of far more expansive study of stylistics (*Chaucerian Theatricality* [Princeton, N.J.: Princeton University Press, 1990], 5). Leonard Koff insisted on imagining Chaucer's actual presence as a storyteller and its tonal implications; see especially "Irony, Declamation, and Chaucer's Presence in His Own Work," chapter 1 of his *Art of Storytelling* (7–36) .

27. Richard F. Green explains the void: "Despite the wealth of material in the Public Record Office, we lack for the whole period from 1361 to 1491 those accounts which might reveal the minute daily expenses of the king himself" (*Poets and Princepleasers* [Toronto: University of Toronto Press, 1980], 5).

cer ... did not produce much work that can be directly linked to specific instances of royal or magnate patronage."[28] No one occasion of Chaucer's recital of *Troilus and Criseyde* can be specified; no setting for its performance can be described in detail; we cannot furnish the parlor, give an exact date, or name the members of the audience. We can at best only guess Chaucer's kinesics while reciting.[29] This lack of circumstantial evidence devalues the self-evident centrality of the author's anticipated performance presence to his compositional consciousness. Without substantial and unambiguous documentation that Chaucer performed *Troilus and Criseyde* at a specific time in a specific place—something equivalent to surveillance tapes—some readers will insist that the premise of oral recital remains unprovable and so banned from further critical discussion. However, unproven does not mean disproved.

In this study of *Troilus and Criseyde*, oral presentation means simply "intended for authorial recital," and textual means only "intended for manuscript or print circulation."[30] Derek Brewer has

28. Glending Olson, "Geoffrey Chaucer," in *The Cambridge History of Medieval English Literature*, ed. David Wallace, 566–88 (Cambridge: Cambridge University Press, 1999), 569. Olson concedes that the records of Chaucer's early service as a valet and squire offer no indication of courtly performance. However, Martin M. Crow and Virginia Leland speculate that the £10 life annuity granted by Gaunt in 1374 "may have been rewarding the author of *The Book of the Duchess*" (*Riverside*, xix).

29. John Hermann studies Chaucer's particular attention to the semiotics of gesturing defined as "any expressive bodily sign" in "Gesture and Seduction in *Troilus and Criseyde*," in *Chaucer's Troilus and Criseyde "Subgit to alle Poesye": Essays in Criticism*, ed. R. A. Shoaf with the assistance of Catherine S. Cox, 138–60 (Binghamton, N.Y.: Medieval and Renaissance Studies and Texts,1992), 139. See too Barbara Korte, *Body Language in Literature* (Toronto: University of Toronto Press, 1997) and J. A. Burrow, *Gestures and Looks in Medieval Narrative* (Cambridge: Cambridge University Press, 2002).

30. The putative orality of *Troilus and Criseyde* has nothing to do with the "strong thesis" of formulaic composition as pioneered by Milman Parry and Albert B. Lord. Chaucer never composed orally in that sense, and Chaucer's audience could read perfectly well for themselves. If Chaucer ever did read *Troilus and Criseyde* aloud in court, he did so with script in hand. Richard Firth Green observes that "by the end of the fourteenth century the minstrel had virtually lost whatever claim he had once had to a share in the literary life of the court" (*Poets*, 105). Green affirms that public reading was a courtly pastime

suggested that all of Chaucer's poetry should be considered inherently oral whereas his prose is inherently textual.[31] At any moment in Chaucer's career, a project could be composed with either kind of primary publication in mind, and yet, it seems, Chaucer seldom wrote anticipating only one or the other type of publication. For example, Chaucer may have intended the prose *Boece* and perhaps Fragment A of the verse *Romaunt* for manuscript circulation—texts which may or may not have then been read aloud by others. But, even if *Boece* or the *Romaunt* or the "Tale of Melibee" or the "Parson's Tale" were ever read aloud, even if these texts were once read aloud by Chaucer himself, we need not imagine these texts as ever having been *performed* by Chaucer as "my work." The reader-reciter's "I"—

but warns that it has often and "too easily been assumed to imply an illiterate audience" (100). Froissart records that King Richard read his French text silently and "read out" his presentation copy of poems (*Chronicles* IV, 64). See Paul Saenger's studies of the late medieval "triumph" of silent reading. It is neither necessary, therefore, nor possible to review fully the wide-ranging scholarship and enduring controversy caused by extrapolations from the initial Parry-Lord theory; see John Foley and Ruth Finnegan for overviews. Joyce Coleman provides a more targeted review of the misdirections taken by a binary conception of orality/literacy theory that have "blinkered discussions of late medieval English literature" (chapter 3, "A Review of the Secondary Literature," *Public Reading*, 52–75, at 52). Initial arguments for the formulaic composition of much Old English poetry—notably the studies of Francis Peabody Magoun, Robert Creed, and Donald K. Fry—have been significantly qualified by Katherine O'Brien O'Keefe and Carol Pasternak. The further extension of this compositional paradigm to Middle English poetry—as explored by Albert C. Baugh, Michael Curschmann, Ronald A. Waldron, Ward Parks, Mark Amodio, W. F. H. Nicolaisen, Dolores Frese, Murray McGillivray, Audley Hall, and myself among many others—has proven even more problematic. But none of these composition and/or transmission theories pertains to the authorial recitation of a text such as *Troilus and Criseyde*. More relevant are the studies of L. O. Aranye Fradenburg, "'Voice Memorial': Loss and Reparation in Chaucer's Poetry," *Exemplaria* 2 (1990): 169–202, an exploration of the psychoanalytic implications of oral presence and textual absence; and Nancy Mason Bradbury, "Literacy, Orality, and the Poetics of Middle English Romance," in *Oral Poetics in Middle English Poetry*, ed. Mark Amodio, with Sarah Gray Miller, 39–69 (New York: Garland, 1994), an outline of the aesthetic and critical issues at stake in attributing affective orality to Middle English verse.

31. Derek S. Brewer, "Chaucer's Poetic Style," in *The Cambridge Chaucer Companion*, ed. Piero Boitani and Jill Mass, 227–42 (Cambridge: Cambridge University Press, 1986), and "Orality and Literacy in Chaucer," in *Mündlichkeit und Schriftlichkeit in englischen Mittelalter*, ed. Willi Erzgräber and Sabine Volk, 85–119 (Tübingen: G. Narr, 1988).

acting as a mere (that is, faithful) lector of such texts—defers to the "I" of its absent author. In the text of *Troilus and Criseyde*, however, Chaucer seems frequently front and center; during his proto-recital of this poem, his tonal presence remains always self-evident, never fading into the textual construct of an absent narrator.

For most Chaucerians, it goes without saying that Chaucer should be read aloud—by trained Chaucerians: "Analysis of performance is essential for understanding and appreciating medieval narratives because they are intended for performance."[32] There is no need to argue that prelection of *Troilus and Criseyde* still works. For modern readers to accept that Chaucer himself once held his script in hand and recited it in public is no minor concession, however. It mandates that more than typical attention be paid to the audible signaling of Chaucer's intentions, which the naked page both shows and veils.[33] The implications of such authorial recitation radically loosen conventional restraints on interpretation. Yet, such oral interpretation does not, thereby, license every willy-nilly reading of the text's tone.

Authorial recital (as distinguished from subsequent prelection) is a special case insofar as it requires an appreciation of Chaucer's highly personal concern for the debut of his newest composition.[34] To a certain extent the inherent performability of *Troilus and Criseyde* has been proven by its subsequent perform-

32. Vitz, Regaldo, and Lawrence, *Performing Medieval Narrative*, 5.
33. Fr. Ong described the realization of an oral text in its original context thus: "The spoken word is part of a present actuality and has its meaning established by the total situation in which it comes into being" ("Writer's Audience," 10a); see too Ong's *The Presence of the Word* (New Haven, Conn.: Yale University Press, 1967), 116–17.
34. "Prelection" is a term popularized by Joyce Coleman to designate the reading of "a written text aloud to one or more listeners; a term borrowed from John of Salisbury" (*Public Reading*, 230); she demonstrates that *aurality* endured as a normative reading experience long after my particular focus, the putative event of initial recital by Chaucer himself.

ance.³⁵ But any re-enactment of Chaucer's recital as such must posit the poet's actual *pronuntiatio* and *actio*, stage-setting and costuming, etc. The prompt book for such a dramatization requires a much more speculative detailing of Chaucer's original recital than the textual evidence alone can support. What seems particularly difficult for such productions to achieve is some sense of how Chaucer must have adjusted his tone to the anticipated, collective, varied yet concurrent reactions of his initially anticipated audience. Since "communal reading necessarily breeds communal discussion," a recital-based tracing of the tonal map of *Troilus and Criseyde* as it first unfolded entails consideration not simply of a one-to-one correspondence between authorial intent and an authoritative reading but of the correlation between Chaucer's own often conflicted opinions regarding his text while reciting it and the multiple, concurrent, and mutually qualifying reactions by his listeners.³⁶ The modern audience for any re-enactment of the text's authorial recital must be rehearsed in its role as well.

This study focuses primarily on a consideration of probable (or at least possible) tonal equivalences. Ideally, the intonation of every syllable should be explicated. Once upon a time, there was no need to apologize for such close reading as a worthwhile exercise in itself. I do hope and fear that the historical legitimacy as

---

35. Joyce Coleman has produced *Troilus: Reading in a Paved Parlor* (University of Oklahoma, 2006) http://www.nyu.edu/projects/mednar/file.php?id=1027, a theatrical interpretation of *Troilus and Criseyde* 2, 78–119 in two parts: first, a dramatization of the scene in which Criseyde and her friends are reading; and then a representation of how medieval audiences received Chaucer's recited poem.

36. Nelson, "From 'Listen, Lordings' to 'Dear Reader,'" 121. Carl Lindahl reads *The Canterbury Tales* as Chaucer's chirographic adaption of the "act of community self-definition" fulfilled by oral tale-telling; the mutually familiar performer and audience both recognize and reaffirm their social context "not in terms of precise events and person, but in conjunction with social patterns representative of his age" (*Earnest Games* [Bloomington: Indiana University Press, 1987], 19); concordantly, the fictional audience of the *Canterbury Tales* reflects an anticipated audience "as multivocal as the city" (172).

well as the dramatic viability of each of my tonal assessments will be challenged.³⁷ Reading the text in terms of authorial recital does generate optional competing tones that agree only in challenging more normative, flat readings of *Troilus and Criseyde* (that is, readings which tend, by habitual default, to be "neutral" and so not voiceless but tedious).

The last fifty years have seen a remarkable shift in critical assumptions regarding Chaucer's career as a court performer and so radical reconceptions of what *reading* Chaucer's extant texts both entails and permits. Until the late 1960s, there was a fairly widespread conviction that Chaucer did indeed recite his own poetry before an aristocratic audience.³⁸ In days of yore, Gervase Mathew could assert without blushing that:

> there was a court public for narrative poems. There was now a large and sophisticated audience of women as well as of men.... *Troilus and Criseyde* and *The Legend of Good Women* are easily serialized.... The dancing and the storytelling could have taken place between vespers (perhaps about three) and the supper and wine and spiced cakes that closed the day.³⁹

---

37. W. B. Worthen offers an analogous consideration of the significance of performances (in addition to editions) as valid iterations of Shakespeare's plays, in "Drama, Performativity, and Performance," PMLA 113 (1998): 1093–1107.

38. John M. Manly proposed a different performance setting for "The Canon's Yeoman's Tale" based on Chaucer's direct address (CT 8, 992–94) to "an audience which included some canons of the church"; however, Manly does "not dare to suggest the tale was read at Windsor" (*Some New Light on Chaucer* [London: Henry Holt, 1926], 247).

39. Gervase Mathew, *The Court of Richard II* (London: John Murray, 1968), 29–30. Mathew does not here state that Chaucer himself did the entertaining, though he subsequently remarks that the loss of several of Chaucer's early works may be attributed to their publication as public reading (66) and that "the manuscript illumination that shows Chaucer declaiming to a court public may represent the way in which it was published" (68). Mathew also acknowledges that *Troilus and Criseyde* was composed for an audience "far wider" than the court (69). Hidekuni Takano considers it "almost certain" that both *Troilus and Criseyde* and the *Legend* "were told to the same audience" ("The Audience of *Troilus and Criseyde*," *Bulletin of the Faculty of Humanities* 8 [1972]: 1–9, 4); Takano doubts, however, that, given Chaucer's social standing, the poet recited *Troilus* before King Richard himself (8).

PRESENTATION POINTS

Most of Chaucer's biographers maintain this seemingly old-fashioned assumption that Chaucer performed in court. Peter Ackroyd, for example, essentially takes for granted that Chaucer's "emphasis upon oration, and the 'covered qualitee' of speech, lends weight to the argument that *Troilus and Criseyde* was indeed designed for oral delivery."[40] The idea that Chaucer recited remains a popular intuition—and suspect therefore as a professional critical premise.

First following but now, as often, reacting against E. Talbot Donaldson's "Chaucer the Pilgrim," most readings of *Troilus and Criseyde* address the narrative strategies of a persona portrayed within the text rather than the recital intentions of its author.[41] Most readings of *Troilus and Criseyde*, therefore, translate what looks like a real reciter's actual anxiety into narrative complexity. More recently, even this acknowledgment of authorial subjectivity has started to disintegrate. A. C. Spearing, for example, observes that:

40. Peter Ackroyd, *Chaucer: Brief Lives* (London: Chatto and Windus, 2004), 107. Derek S. Brewer assumes that "Chaucer published a poem in two ways: either by reading it aloud or by allowing copies to circulate" (*Chaucer*, 2nd ed. [London: Longmans, 1960], 124). Donald Howard likewise considers reading aloud normal as courtly entertainment (*Chaucer and the Medieval World* [London: Weidenfeld and Nicolson, 1987], 57–58) and particularly relevant to picturing the audience of *Troilus and Criseyde* (346–49). Derek Pearsall also does concede: "The early poems, we may presume, were composed primarily to be read aloud to congenial groups on suitable occasions, or to be circulated on a very limited basis in written copies" (*The Life of Geoffrey Chaucer* [Oxford: Blackwell, 1992], 185). But Pearsall accepts the legitimacy of critical denials of real recital: "Chaucer's references to his audience in *Troilus*, present and listening 'in the place,' are not necessarily to be taken literally, but they do figure an importantly imagined reality" (178–79).

41. Rejecting outright the Donaldson-derived conception of the narrator's persona as a fourth fictional character, David Lawton identifies Chaucer's self-consciousness primarily within a compositional rather than a recital context: "It is the voice of an apocryphal author commenting on his own composition, almost the voice of the poem itself speaking from the time and continuum of its own performance" (*Chaucer's Narrators* [Cambridge: D.S. Brewer, 1985], 89).

Ben Kimpel offered an early (and largely ignored) denial of Donaldson's charac-

the notion that every text must have its speaker, every narrative its narrator, may be beginning to dissolve; for late medieval writers, far from being the received idea it has been for twentieth-century criticism, it was a new discovery, just beginning to crystallize.[42]

Chaucer's "I" thus escapes containment as a fictional construct as well as a self-referential pronoun.

New Criticism had largely dismissed the relevance of biographical information for narrative interpretation. For example, as early as 1966, G. T. Shepherd took one step back from affirming the modern reader's need to know Chaucer's vita as a significant context for reading *Troilus and Criseyde:*

> The Narrator is an I, a mask worn by the person who speaks the script. This public apparition of an I is not, of course, Chaucer the man, not even Chaucer the poet: it is the mask made by Chaucer, originally perhaps ... for Chaucer the performer to wear as he delivered the poem to a court audience ... the norm of composition for a vernacular poet was still the actual speaking of the story, the *narratio*.[43]

The voice of Chaucer himself was thus tacitly absented from the reading process by the possibility of another reader's recitation. Dieter Mehl attributed what may now be seen as the first phase of

---

terization of a narrative persona in *The Canterbury Tales* ("The Narrator of the Canterbury Tales," ELH 20 [1953]: 77–86). C. David Benson rejects the notion that the narrator of *Troilus and Criseyde* should be considered a fourth major character; on the contrary, "he never becomes a fully developed, independent human character ... and it is often impossible to distinguish his statements from those of the poet. The narrator in *Troilus* is better seen as a flexible literary voice than as a human personality" (*Chaucer's Troilus*, 112). John Fleming remarks: "Many of Chaucer's recent readers appear to believe that the poet's greatest achievement of characterization in the *Troilus* is his invention of the narrator. There is perhaps a touch of historical overcompensation in this judgment— few readers before E. T. Donaldson noticed there *was* a narrator.... We know remarkably little about this central character" (*Classical Imitation*, 155). A. C. Spearing charts the rise to critical prominence of Chaucer's narrator-persona as a reading premise in *Textual Subjectivity*, 68–77.

42. Spearing, *Textual Subjectivity*, 30.
43. Geoffrey T. Shepherd, "Troilus and Criseyde," in *Chaucer and the Chaucerians*, ed. Derek S. Brewer, 65–87 (University: University of Alabama Press, 1966), 71.

this interpretive shift to a generation of critics deeply influenced by Wayne Booth's *Rhetoric of Fiction*.[44] In a series of essays, Mehl himself de-emphasized the importance of Chaucer's listening audience, but he also maintained the reader's impression of the "exhilarating sense of being in the company of" Chaucer.[45]

Dieter Mehl observed that "one of the most remarkable things about the narrator is that he seems to be at the same time an entertainer, telling the story to a circle of acquaintances, and a scholar, translating a written source and producing a decidedly literary work of art."[46] Chaucer's sources provide the matter but often lack the liveliness of Chaucer's narratives. For example, as authors, Boethius and Boccaccio sound much more aloof than Chaucer. The persona of Boethius as a character in *De consolatione* acts primarily as a listener. Although in his *Proemio* Boccaccio informs readers of *il Filostrato* that *Troilo* was created in its author's own image,[47] the text's narrating "I" does not present himself as the text's rehearser here and now.[48] No less so than imprisoned Boethius, Boc-

---

44. Mehl, in Boitani and Mann, eds., *Cambridge Chaucer Companion*, 213.

45. Mehl, "The Audience of Chaucer's *Troilus and Criseyde*: Afterword, 1979," in *Chaucer's Troilus: Essays in Criticism*, ed. Stephen A. Barney, 211–29 (London: Scolar Press, 1980), 228.

46. Mehl, in Boitani and Mann, eds., *Chaucer Cambridge Companion*, 220. Spearing distinguishes two frequently confused conceptions of the "narrator" and largely dismisses the interpretive significance of the "origin ... of an oral narrative" when reading the words of "a 'narrator' who is allegedly 'an inherent feature of narrative itself'" (*Textual Subjectivity*, 18).

47. Charles Dahlberg analyzes the fundamental distinction between Boethius's third-person narrator and the "I" of Chaucer's dream visions in "The Poet of Unlikeness: Chaucer," chapter 6 in *The Literature of Unlikeness* (Hanover, N.H.: University Press of New England, 1988), 125–48. Since Chaucer does not present the narrative's male protagonist as his own alter ego (as Boccaccio did), there is also a substantial difference in the resulting characterization of Troilus: "Although not wholly passive in all respects, the English Troilus is nevertheless made more passive in pursuing his love affair" (Windeatt, ed., *Geoffrey Chaucer, Troilus* [1984], 8).

48. Barry Windeatt summarizes the pervasive tonal contrast: "When TC is compared line by line with Fil, one of the most emphatic and consistent features is that added vehemence with which Ch has re-expressed his original in English" (Windeatt,

caccio anticipates that manuscript circulation will provide the primary means for publishing his writing: "The narrator introduces himself, states the purpose of his work, and then largely retreats behind the story."[49] Chaucer, however, seems (sounds) far more directly engaged with presenting his tale (and himself) to his readers (audience) in *Troilus and Criseyde*.

Monica McAlpine considered the notion of a "speaking voice" that "would be heard as always in control of the many meanings of its speech," but she argues instead that this intermittent effect does not fully counter the critical need to read Chaucer's creation of a narrator's persona into the text.[50] David Lawton goes one step further in the separation of authorial voice from textual tone: "We may take it that in most later medieval performances the speaker (or reader) was not the writer. This gap between reader and poet marks an important stage in the development of narrators. Intonation becomes a feature of writing."[51] This full entextualization

---

ed., *Geoffrey Chaucer, Troilus* [1984], 5). Winthrop Wetherbee III proposes, however, that "though the *Troilus* is unquestionably a very different poem from the *Filostrato*, there are good grounds for supposing that Boccaccio, or at the very least a somewhat older Boccaccio, would have readily understood Chaucer's enterprise and found himself largely in sympathy with it" (*Chaucer and the Poets: An Essay on Troilus and Criseyde* [Ithaca, N.Y.: Cornell University Press, 1984], 57).

49. Mehl, in Boitani and Mann, eds., *Cambridge Chaucer Companion*, 215. Karla Taylor distinguishes Chaucer's subjective and objective modes of reading (*Chaucer Reads "The Divine Comedy"* [Stanford, Calif.: Stanford University Press, 1989], 6) in terms of Emile Benveniste's differentiation of two complementary subsystems of language: *l'énonciation du discours* and *l'énonciation de l'histoire*. In terms of claims to poetic authority, it usually seems easy to distinguish the vatic confidence of Dante from the reticence of Chaucer, who explicitly refused to play the "divinstre" in both the *Troilus* and (his romance to be reissued as) "The Knight's Tale." Yet, Dante too often represents himself as a highly engaged "I" reciting the *Commedia* because Dante too anticipated his own real recital of his composition as well as its more widespread circulation in manuscript.

50. McAlpine, *The Genre*, 37. She asserts, in particular, "The purposiveness of the silences cannot be assigned to the speaker" (39); yet, reticence (or apparent obtuseness) can be enhanced by performance—perhaps, can only be observed as such by the reader as gaps in some imagined speech.

51. Lawton, *Chaucer's Narrators*, 10.

of Chaucer's "I" is now more or less taken for granted by modern readers although "orality remains a narrative pose."[52]

The burden of proof now falls upon any arguments for rather than against Chaucer's actual recital. Therefore, there is a strong disinclination to see even the frontispiece of Corpus Christi College, Cambridge, MS61 as a valid recollection (never mind snapshot) of such a performance event. Barry Windeatt, for example, accepts that this extraordinary image depicts only "the myth of delivery that Chaucer develops so carefully in the poem."[53] Elizabeth Salter has demonstrated that this supposed portrait represents "a compilation of motifs drawn from earlier and contemporary exemplars."[54] Salter and M. B. Parkes did, nevertheless, grant some evidentiary significance to the *Troilus* frontispiece; though "we cannot accept it as a historical document, there is nothing to prevent us from accepting it as a moving expression of historical

---

52. Seth Lerer, "'Now holde youre mouth': The Romance of Orality in the *Thopas-Melibee* Section of the *Canterbury Tales*," in Amodio, ed., *Oral Poetics*, 181–205, 184 n. 6.

53. Windeatt, *Oxford Guide*, 15. M. B. Parkes and Elizabeth Salter have observed, "No other Chaucer manuscript contains such an elaborate prefatory miniature" (*Troilus and Criseyde, Geoffrey Chaucer, A Facsimile of Corpus Christi College MS 61* [Cambridge: D.S. Brewer, 1978], 15).

54. Parkes and Salter, *Facsimile of Corpus Christi College MS 61*, 17; Salter shows the special influence of illustrators of Guillaume de Deguilleville's *Pèlerinage de la vie humaine*. Montague Rhodes James, the manuscript's cataloger, simply (perhaps naively) observed "a prince in a gold robe and a lady in a diadem. The listeners intent on the speaker" (*A Descriptive Catalogue of the Manuscripts in the Library of St. John's College* [Cambridge University Press, 1913], 126). Laura Kendrick compares the frontispiece to Lydgate's description of a theater in his *Troy Book* in "The Troilus Frontispiece and the Dramatization of Chaucer's *Troilus*," *The Chaucer Review* 22 (1987): 81–92. Joyce Coleman offers an overview of current critical thinking and proposes herself that "the iconography of Genius's sermon" in the *Roman de la Rose* "lies behind the placement of Chaucer in Corpus 61," ("Where Chaucer Got His Pulpit: Audience and Intervisuality in the *Troilus and Criseyde* Frontispiece," *Studies in the Age of Chaucer* 32 [2010]: 103–28, 117). The Magliabachiano MS II. II. 38 of *il Filostrato* reputedly preserves the earliest known portrait of Boccaccio; it is a rather crude pencil drawing of the author holding his book and pointing to the following text. None of the earliest images of Chaucer represent him as such a book presenter though both the Ellesmere (HL EL 26 C9 f 153v) and the Hoccleve (BL MS Harl. 4866 f 88) pictures do show the poet pointing to text.

PRESENTATION POINTS

respect."[55] And, as such, the frontispiece offers a nostalgic staging of what the poem's second generation of readers thought the inherited text preserved.[56]

It is still sometimes acknowledged that Chaucer composed his early pieces for specific occasions; it is less often conceded that Chaucer recited such pieces aloud to the court; it is least often granted that this possibility matters as an interpretive context.[57] The single most influential re-definition of Chaucer's anticipated audience has been that of Paul Strohm in *Social Chaucer*. Strohm himself appreciated that "*Troilus and Criseyde* exemplifies a dazzling array of situations of address" and that "within this one poem we encounter a plethora of temporary (and presumably fictional) addressees";

55. Parkes and Salter, *Facsimile of Corpus Christi College MS 61*, 23.

56. Anita Helmbold thinks the Corpus Christi image represents a Henrician appropriation of the text commissioned by "someone to whose cause Chaucer was more important than Richard" ("Chaucer Appropriated: The Troilus Frontispiece as Lancastrian Propaganda," *Studies in the Age of Chaucer* 30 [2008]: 205–34, 224). Whereas the Corpus Christi image posits an a priori recollection of Chaucer reciting this now copied text in court, the Ellesmere illustrations of *The Canterbury Tales* show the fully entextualized event of the pilgrims (including Chaucer) reciting from horseback; "the oral fiction of the *Canterbury Tales* is not that it is heard, but that it is overheard" (Ganim, *Theatricality*, 21). Mary C. Olson observes that "while the pilgrim portraits" of the Ellesmere manuscript of *The Canterbury Tales* "emphasize orality, the rest of the contents of the graphic field emphasizes the fact that the orality is fiction" (*Fair and Varied Forms: Visual Textuality in Medieval Illuminated Manuscripts*, Studies in Medieval History and Culture [New York: Routledge, 2003], 160). See too Martin Stevens, "The Ellesmere Miniatures as Illustrations of Chaucer's *Canterbury Tales*," *Studies in Iconography* 7–8 (1981–82): 113–34, M. B. Parkes, "The Planning and Construction of the Ellesmere Manuscript," in *The Ellesmere Chaucer: Essays in Interpretation*, ed. Martin Stevens and Daniel Woodward (San Marino, Calif.: Huntington Library, 1995), 41–47; and Richard K. Emmerson, "Text and Image in the Ellesmere Portraits of the Tale-Tellers," in Stevens and Woodward, eds., *The Ellesmere Chaucer*, 143–70.

57. Even when the possibility of Chaucer's court recital is conceded, it tends to be done so only most grudgingly. Tim William Machan, for example, allows that "on some occasions ... Chaucer may have recited his poems before a court gathering ... and on many others one member of court probably read aloud to several others.... Already by 1400, however, this original courtly audience was expanding"("Texts," in *A Companion to Chaucer*, ed. Peter Brown, 428–42 [Oxford: Blackwell, 2000], 434). Maura Nolan sees this change as "a simultaneous narrowing and broadening of the audience" (*John Lydgate and the Making of Popular Culture* [Cambridge: Cambridge University Press, 2005], 5).

nevertheless, Chaucer is actually writing manuscripts to be enjoyed primarily by a society of near-equals—a coterie of New Men, liberal-minded humanists, who like Chaucer himself (and like most Chaucerians) read texts to themselves.[58] The new orthodoxy, "as scholars currently believe," is that Chaucer was not in fact a court poet.[59] Laurel Amtower, for example, all but takes for granted that, "indeed, it is even unlikely that the court predominantly comprised Chaucer's audience, which seems much more apt to have been made up of the lesser gentry and intellectuals with whom he was known to associate."[60] The premise that Chaucer once read many of his own works aloud before a familiar audience of social superiors has been dismissed as illusory and, worse, "old-fashioned."

Mostly on the basis of fifteenth-century book inventories, it has been repeatedly argued that Chaucer and John Gower "were hardly essential reading among the aristocracy"; rather, both wrote primarily for "career diplomats, civil servants, officials and administrators."[61] Anne Middleton describes the resulting implicated speaking "position" of Gower, Langland, and Chaucer as

58. Paul Strohm, *Social Chaucer* (Cambridge, Mass.: Harvard University Press, 1989), 55. Nicholas R. Havely suggests that "one of the attractions of Boccaccio's work" for Chaucer "would very possibly have been its concern to make sense of the relationship between the worlds of the merchant, the courtier and the clerk" (*Chaucer's Boccaccio: Sources of Troilus and the Knight's and Franklin's Tales* [Cambridge: D.S. Brewer, 1980], 12). Anne Laskaya affirms, "Clearly, Chaucer's text is homosocial—written by a man, primarily about men, and primarily for men" (*Chaucer's Approach to Gender in the Canterbury Tales*, Chaucer Studies 23 [Cambridge: D.S. Brewer, 1995], 4); however true this conviction may be for reading the *Tales*, reading Chaucer's precedent court recitals must occasionally account for the tonally significant presence of socially superior women.

59. Helmbold, "The Troilus Frontispiece," 225.

60. Laurel Amtower, *Engaging Words: The Culture of Reading in the Later Middle Ages* (New York: Palgrave, 2000), 145.

61. V. J. Scattergood, "Literary Culture at the Court of Richard II," in *English Court Culture in the Later Middle Ages*, ed. V. J. Scattergood and J. W. Sherbourne, 29–43 (New York: St. Martin's, 1983), 36–38. Derek Brewer reckoned that the king's tutor Sir Simon Burley (whose 1388 will preserves the earliest record of the possession of secular books in English) "just had time to read or hear Chaucer's *Troilus*, which was completed about 1385–6" before being beheaded (*Chaucer in His Time*, 60).

much the same thing. These poets did not speak to an immediate audience; "their poetry, and Ricardian public poetry generally, speaks 'as if' to the entire community—as a whole and all at once rather than severally—rather than 'as if' to a coterie or patron."[62] And this interpretative filter does seem valid—in reference to Gower and Langland and much of *The Canterbury Tales*, "a written work whose central fiction is that of oral performance"—but not *Troilus and Criseyde*.[63]

Strohm's now prevailing re-conception of Chaucer's anticipated audience as a distanced readership is strongly buttressed by most post-structuralist theorizing. The identity per se of an author came to be seen, according to Michel Foucault, as a social construct.[64] Although medieval rhetoricians do not concur with any utter erasure of the author per se, such concepts as the *jouissance* of Roland Barthes, the *undecidability* of Paul de Man, and the *aporia* of Jacques Derrida emancipated modern readers from the interpretive dictates of authorial intent.[65] Broadly speaking, the text came to be perceived as an insulated expression rather than as a transferral of meaning (and of emotional experience) from one author to many readers.[66] C. David Benson celebrates this absence:

62. Anne Middleton, "The Idea of Public Poetry in the Reign of Richard II," *Speculum* 53 (1978): 94–114, rpt. in Stephanie Trigg, ed., *Medieval English Poetry* (Harlow: Longmans, 1993), 27.
63. Seth Lerer, "The Canterbury Tales," in *The Yale Companion to Chaucer*, ed. Seth Lerer, 243–96 (New Haven, Conn: Yale University Press, 2006), 245.
64. Josué V. Harari questions this rather reductive reading of "Qu'est-ce qu'un auteur?" citing Foucault's response to Roland Barthes's "The Death of the Author" as a rejection of imaging writing as absence (*Textual Strategies: Perspectives in Post-Structuralist Criticism* [Ithaca, N.Y.: Cornell University Press, 1979], 145).
65. Three magisterial studies of the medieval reader's conception of authorship are Janet Coleman's *Medieval Readers and Writers, 1350–1400* (New York: Columbia University Press, 1981), J. A. Burrow's *Medieval Writers and Their Work* (Oxford: Oxford University Press, 1982), and Alastair J. Minnis's *The Medieval Theory of Authorship* (Philadelphia: University Pennsylvania Press, 1988).
66. A. C. Spearing offers a self-deferential but magisterial "ramble through the theoretical landscape" (*Textual Subjectivity*, 4), exposing the critical presuppositions that

PRESENTATION POINTS

"Barthes's hope was that the death of the author would stimulate a new birth of the reader, and so it has come to pass.... The doubts raised in *Troilus* about the reliability of the poet and of his materials have the effect of empowering readers."[67]

H. Marshall Leicester Jr., one of the first Chaucerians to champion deconstruction, felt impelled to refute Donald Howard's seemingly straightforward idea of "unimpersonated artistry" precisely because this compositional strategy merely masked a reiteration of the "'dramatic' model" derived from H. Lyman Kittredge. Leicester contends that such readings disregard "the poem's constant and intermittently insistent *textuality*." Leicester, therefore, completely rejects "the confusion of *voice* and *presence*," insisting "that there is nobody there, that there is only the text."[68]

Seth Lerer reads Chaucer as an "invention" of fifteenth-century scribes, imitators, and readers. Although "it is central to the fifteenth-century literary system to imagine Chaucer as a public, and publicly patronized, poet," the fifteenth century's conception of Chaucer as "father" and "laureate" also generates "the fictional persona of the subjugated reader/imitator."[69] The text of Chaucer talks down to its "infantilized" fifteenth-century readership—an imposed rapport very much at odds with the deferential familiarity of Chaucer reciting to his contemporaries.

---

valorize but also restrict modern readings; Spearing offers a radical challenge to "the doctrine of the speaker or narrator" in some medieval texts (31).

67. C. David Benson, *Chaucer's Troilus*, 43–44. Lee Patterson has remarked: "One of the great achievements of Augustinian hermeneutics is to make the preemptive nature of interpretation explicit.... To imply that Augustine prefigures Barthes is a mischievousness that most medievalists will doubtless be unwilling to tolerate. But the point is not meant frivolously" (*Negotiating*, 151).

68. H. Marshall Leicester Jr., *The Disenchanted Self: Representing the Subject in the Canterbury Tales* (Berkeley: University of California Press, 1990), 8–9. Leicester would replace the term *self* (and all its synonyms) with *subject*. Focusing primarily on Chaucer's representations of the Knight, Pardoner, and Wife of Bath, Leicester maintains the *Tales* "are not written to be spoken, like a play, but written to be read *as if* they were spoken" (13).

69. Lerer, *Readers*, 17–18, 5.

PRESENTATION POINTS

Even more emphatically than Lerer, Joseph A. Dane renounces any and all notions of voice as a critical premise, including the work of Jesse M. Gellrich, Barbara Nolan, and Robert Jordan as well as Donaldson, Howard, Patterson, and even Leicester. Dane finds that most modern readings simply posit some other name to designate little more than John Dryden's appreciation of "a psychological center for aspects of the text"; Dane objects most intensely to performance-based readings when "an *actor* takes over from the *auctor*."[70] This warning is most necessary: arbitrarily histrionic reading can grossly distort the tone of Chaucer's text, but to so argue must posit that the text conveys some alternative, more compelling tone. It is equally ludicrous to refuse to play at all. A self-inflicted blindness to Chaucer's own *lectio* completely mutes consideration of his possible *pronuntiatio*, which provided a sort of tonal *ennaratio* concurrent to the act of recital itself. In a very real sense, any modern reader's radical refusal to hear Chaucer's tonal intentions actualizes one of his greatest fears; such reading is an act of infidelity.

The very act of reading, "the seduction and betrayal of the reader," is a much discussed central focus of *Troilus and Criseyde*.[71] Laurel Amtower reads *Troilus and Criseyde* as "in many ways" almost "entirely about reading."[72] For Carolyn Dinshaw, *Troilus and Criseyde* "provides a powerful analysis of reading—of masculine reading ... dominated at last by a desire to contain instability, carnal appetite—those things that ... medieval writers (and their descendants, modern critics) associate with *femina*." A tonal manifestation of this anxiety is Chaucer's habit of speaking as if

---

70. Joseph A. Dane, *Who Is Buried in Chaucer's Tomb? Studies in the Reception of Chaucer's Book* (East Lansing: Michigan State University Press, 1998), 160–61.

71. J. Ganim, *Style and Consciousness* (Princeton University Press, 1987), 79.

72. Laurel Amtower, "Authorizing the Reader in Chaucer's 'House of Fame,'" *Philological Quarterly* 79 (2000): 273–91, 273.

he were the victim of his sources: "And trewely, as men in bokes rede, / Men wiste nevere womman han the care" (V, 19–20). Jennifer Summit hears Chaucer "sounding much like the female medieval mystics who claimed to be the media, rather than the originators, of texts written through them by God, the narrator refers to himself merely as a 'sorwful instrument' (I. 10) who is remarkably passive in the act of writing."[73] Lisa J. Kiser finds "one of the ways in which the narrator most consistently resembles Criseyde is his inability to discern with any accuracy who (or what) is responsible for certain occurrences in the poem's plot—even when his narrative source is clear on the matter."[74] The tonal implications of these feminized expressions become only more intense if imagined as spoken before the queen.

The interpretive implications of Chaucer's authorial recital and subsequent revision may have a profound impact on even the most foundational level of reading *Troilus and Criseyde*—its textual editing. The nuts-and-bolts job of selecting best readings from extant textual witnesses has not itself been immune to deconstructive doubts.[75] But a more matter-of-fact controversy troubles every effort to print a definitive critical edition of *Troilus and Criseyde*.[76] The manuscript variants of *Troilus and Criseyde* are so complicated that R. K. Root (following William S. McCormick)

---

73. Jennifer Summit, "Troilus and Criseyde," in Lerer, *The Yale Companion*, 213–42, 220.

74. Lisa J. Kiser, *Truth and Textuality in Chaucer's Poetry* (Hanover, N.H.: University Press of New England, 1991), 93.

75. Derek Pearsall discusses to what extent a current neglect of the idea of authorial revision—or, the attribution of manuscript variations to scribal practice instead—has been driven by deconstructive theory, in "Authorial Revision in Some Late-Medieval English Texts," in *Crux and Controversy in Middle English Textual Criticism*, ed. A. J. Minnis and Charlotte Brewer, 39–48 (Woodbridge: D.S. Brewer, 1992). Cf. H. Marshall Leicester Jr., "Oure Tonges Différance": Textuality and Deconstruction in Chaucer," in *Medieval Texts and Contemporary Readers*, ed. Laurie A. Finke and Martin B. Schichtman, 15–26 (Ithaca, N.Y.: Cornell University Press, 1987).

76. There does exist a very fundamental disagreement regarding editorial principles among three broadly defined schools: "recensionist" (Lachmann and Paul Maas),

PRESENTATION POINTS

believed Chaucer must have revised his composition perhaps more than once after some version of it had already been circulated.[77] If so, then the apparent *mouvance* of *Troilus and Criseyde* was, at least in part, the author's own fault.[78] Barry Windeatt argues, however: "There is little support from the Troilus MSS that clearly differentiated and self-sufficient versions of the poem existed at significantly distinct periods in time."[79] Ralph Hanna III has termed Root's hypothesis "foolish brilliance."[80] And M. C. Seymour also affirms that the variants can be adequately explained in terms of scribal activity alone.[81] But Stephen Barney, N. F. Blake, and Charles Owen—though all conceding that Root's original hypothesis went too far—defend his basic premise: *Troilus and Criseyde* does seem to have been significantly revised by Chaucer himself. Owen, in particular, has been concerned with the artistic reasons for Chaucer's additions and transpositions. However, Barney largely shares Windeatt's skepticism regarding a planned second circulation of Chaucer's radically revised manuscript.[82]

I am more interested in Chaucer's motivation for revising the

---

"optimist" (Joseph Bédier), and "eclectic" (George Kane). All three labels are somewhat pejorative. See Barney, *Studies* (1993), 50–55.

77. Stephen A. Barney summarizes the debate as "whether, by the classic techniques of recension, manuscript families and their hyparchetypes can be determined, and whether we have evidence in the manuscripts of Chaucer's revision" (*Riverside*, 1161b).

78. Paul Zumthor's seminal idea of *mouvance* in *Essai de poétique medievale* (Paris: Éd. du Seuil, 1972) assumes a history of transmissions prior to the surviving manuscript record. Alterations are not seen as ipso facto contaminations of some pristine original version.

79. Barry Windeatt, "The Text of the *Troilus*," in *Essays on Troilus and Criseyde*, ed. Mary Salu, 1–22 (Cambridge: D.S. Brewer/Rowman & Littlefield, 1979), 21.

80. Ralph Hanna III, "Robert K. Root," in *Editing Chaucer: The Great Tradition*, ed. Paul G. Ruggiers, 191–205 (Norman, Okla.: Pilgrim, 1984), 196.

81. M. C. Seymour, accepting neither Root's concept of revision nor Windeatt's layering, maintains that only the Corpus Christi and Pierpont Morgan MSS and their affiliates "substantially record Chaucer's poem ... all other manuscripts with the exception of MS. Rawlinson poet. 163 offer ... inferior and posthumous versions" ("The Manuscripts of Chaucer's Troilus," *Scriptorium* 46 [1992]: 107–21, 108).

82. Barney, "Owen on Windeatt and Hanna on Root: A Counterblast," chapter 6 in *Studies* (1993), 155–63.

text at all. I think Chaucer fully perceived his need to refashion his own recital for subsequent silent reading. My extraneous evidence for considering this authorial motivation to revise *Troilus and Criseyde* so plausible includes the "Cecil Fragment" of *Troilus* and the F-Prologue to *The Legend of Good Women*. The Cecil Fragment preserves merely a scrap of the oldest known copy of *Troilus and Criseyde* (in the hand of Adam Pinkhurst); it apparently supports Root's conviction that Chaucer substantially revised the poem.[83] I myself have argued that Chaucer reworked his original recital Prologue to *The Legend of Good Women*, the "livelier" F-version, into a more polished G-version for subsequent circulation.[84] But my real reason for promoting the survival of Chaucer's recital voice within our revised texts of *Troilus and Criseyde* is that it works for me—that is, this reading premise increases my enjoyment of Chaucer's artistic achievement, including the decentralized subjectivity of his narrating "I."

The main editorial debate is about how much revision of an already "published" version of *Troilus and Criseyde* Chaucer did himself. Windeatt perceives some "in-eching" to Chaucer's composition as a "series of layers—perhaps physical layers—of writing."[85] Stephen Barney bluntly asks: "What is the difference between a 'layered' text and a revision?"[86] Kevin K. Cureton, while rejecting overstated assertions on both sides of the debate, favors Barney's "agnosticism" (though differing in many details). Barney himself

---

83. Jackson J. Campbell, "A New Troilus Fragment," *PMLA* 73 (1958): 305–8.

84. William A. Quinn, *Chaucer's Rehersynges: The Performability of the Legend of Good Women* (Washington, D.C.: The Catholic University of America Press, 1994), 23–60.

85. Windeatt, *Geoffrey Chaucer, Troilus and Criseyde*, 36. Windeatt takes the term "in-eching" from 3, 1329: "in whatever form his draft exactly developed, the range of his proven sources suggests that Chaucer's composition of the poem was in practice a series of layers—perhaps physical layers—of writing" ("The Text of the Troilus," in Salu, *Essays*, 2).

86. Barney, *Studies* (1993), 158

very precisely summarizes what is now known and not known about the text of *Troilus and Criseyde:*

> We are left with an agreement that the manuscripts preserve what look like Chaucerian revisions, but they do not preserve evidence of distinct stages of revision, versions published as such. I am not convinced that Chaucer deliberately "published" his poem in more than one state, although I certainly grant—as would anyone—that the composition of the poem was not done of a piece, and that the manuscripts may reflect that Chaucer composed some stanzas—especially some that intrude into the sequence of the *Filostrato* and that derive from a separate source—"independently" (as Cureton says). How else? But this is draft work; the term "revision" in this use should not imply belated, post-publication afterthoughts.[87]

And for most readers, who simply wish to enjoy *Troilus and Criseyde,* this whole editorial controversy may not matter much after all: "Editors generally agree in fact on the readings, whatever their hypotheses."[88]

Print publication necessarily foregrounds a preferred reading among manuscript variants. Awareness of the limitations of this transmission process both requires and allows, in A. S. G. Edwards's words, "a clearer recognition than has sometimes obtained that the critical edition is not the only form of editorial activity that is possible and profitable."[89] So, too, manuscript publication necessarily omits numerous features of authorial recital, and again a reader's awareness of such a transcription's limita-

---

87. Ibid., 163.
88. Barney, *Riverside*, 1162a. Similarly, Derek Pearsall says of Windeatt's edition: "Whether it is true or not, no great harm is done to the poem, which evidently has an achieved integrity, whatever the stages by which it was brought to that state" ("Editing Medieval Texts: Some Developments and Some Problems," in *Textual Criticism and Literary Interpretation*, ed. Jerome J. McGann, 92–106 [Chicago: Chicago University Press, 1985], 98).
89. A. S. G. Edwards, "Chaucer from Manuscript to Print: The Social Text and the Critical Text," *Mosaic* 28, no. 4 (1995): 1–9, Pro-Quest Document ID 9156451.

tions both allows and requires a richer consideration of what may have been Chaucer's preferred reading on the basis of what the page records. Yet, not surprisingly, editors seldom consider authorial recital as a significant stage in the publication of *Troilus and Criseyde*.[90] Modern editors must and do seek to reconstruct a corrected version of Chaucer's final composition.[91]

But apparently the Old Adam of imperfect transmission contaminated even this lost alpha-text of *Troilus* as well. In his "Wordes unto Adam, His Owne Scriveyn," Chaucer both vehemently and comically rebukes the scribe for his mistakes in copying *Troilus* and the *Boece*. But Chaucer also anticipates giving Adam Pinkhurst a second chance "if ever it thee bifalle ... for to wryten newe" (1–2). Precisely by seeing the flaws of transcription, the author reaffirms the effort to retrieve his own intent; he wants a copy "after my makyng" (4). And so Chaucer promptly edits Adam's bad copy, rubbing, scraping, and renewing his own voice.

Paradoxically, there now remains more evidence "within the text" that Chaucer once recited *Troilus and Criseyde* than indications among its textual witnesses that a holograph copy ever circulated. Chaucer's initial anticipation of recital (that is, his apparent indifference regarding immediate manuscript circulation) may also

---

90. Robert K. Root desired this "book" that represents "so far as the evidence will permit, a text of the poem, purged from scribal corruption, which shall incorporate all the revisions which represent the poet's final preference as to the reading of his work—such a text as might have received his own final sanction" (*The Book of Troilus and Criseyde by Geoffrey Chaucer* [Princeton, N.J.: Princeton University Press, 1945], lxxxi).

91. Developing the ideas of R. K. Root's "Publication Before Printing," PMLA 28 (1913): 417–31, and H. S. Bennett's "The Production and Dissemination of Vernacular Manuscripts in the Fifteenth Century," *The Library* 1 (1946–47): 167–78, Peter J. Lucas has distinguished as many as ten "conditions" or "stages" from first draft till "when the work was received by the *destinaire* or patron it was effectively published" (*From Author to Audience: John Capgrave and Medieval Publication* [Dublin: University College Dublin Press, 1997], 8); yet, this stage may be followed by two types of post-publication (authorial and/or scribal) revision.

help to explain the significant gap between the putative composition of *Troilus and Criseyde* (ca. 1385) and the earliest surviving copies of the poem (ca. 1399–1425).[92] Beverly Boyd has proposed that Chaucer's work first became well known to a small but highly influential listening audience for whom "he was under no particular pressure to finish things to a state of polish for official presentation."[93]

We no longer have Chaucer's own recital copy of *Troilus and Criseyde*; he may never have thought his revision of it fully done— not even Adam Pinkhurst's less than fair copy. As a result, many of Chaucer's self-referential lines in our reconstructed editions of imperfect recordings of his unfinished project are left in a tonal limbo—a narrative voice floating between present performer and absent author. The fictional setting of *Troilus and Criseyde* is primarily a place of recalled voices. The rooms where they converse all seem quite cozy, however. And the recital setting for *Troilus and Criseyde* was probably just such a parlor, not the prison of a strictly self-referential text.

Both the need to read and the benefits of reading *Troilus and Criseyde* as if it were originally intended for authorial recital are one and the same. This interpretive premise, if valid, demands closer attention to the tonal possibilities of the text as performed even if the text itself does not explicitly state the narrator's tone. If close scrutiny of the text then produces a more nuanced and cu-

---

92. Linne R. Mooney's identification of Adam Pinkhurst as Chaucer's scribe ("Chaucer's Scribe," *Speculum* 81 [2006]: 97–138) has significantly narrowed the gap between Chaucer's composition of *The Canterbury Tales* and its earliest surviving transcriptions. The Cecil Fragment of *Troilus and Criseyde* is acknowledged to be the work of the same scribe. Jackson Campbell argues that "the ancestor of the manuscript of which CF [the Cecil Fragment] formed a part was derived from Chaucer's 'foul papers' at some intermediate stage in the successive derivations" ("New Troilus Fragment," 307).

93. Beverly Boyd, *Chaucer and the Medieval Book* (San Marino, Calif.: Huntington Library, 1973), 115.

mulatively a more convincing interpretation of otherwise unnoted tonal features of *Troilus and Criseyde*, such a reading ipso facto provides inductive confirmation of the legitimacy of this premise—I hope you agree. This is not circular reasoning—well, yes, it is, but at least no more so than arguing from effect to cause, or from fruit to tree.

I hope to have called into question the prevailing critical orthodoxy that the reception-context which Chaucer anticipated for reading *The Canterbury Tales* (that is, by means of manuscript circulation) need be imposed as the reading-context supposed for all of his earlier compositions as well. I want to read each of the five "books" of *Troilus and Criseyde* as a revised (and so frequently blurred) record of some previous recital installment. By means of "close reading," I seek a "nearer hearing." But I have no intention of reproducing Chaucer's proto-script, nor do I intend to direct a restaging of his performance. Though the idea of authorial recital does, no doubt, tempt one to imagine the event itself, I doubt that Chaucer's own recital of *Troilus and Criseyde* can truly be duplicated because his audience too provided such an integral component of its tonal context. To say that a full comprehension of Chaucer's recital presence cannot be absolutely discerned by any one reader is not to say, however, that its supplemental implications should not be considered at all.

Therefore, I mean my own responses to be suggestive, not definitive; provocative, not privileged interpretations of Chaucer's intentions; more exhausting than exhaustive, I fear.

It is, however, somewhat consoling to read that Chaucer himself explicitly and repeatedly shared my fears of infidelity or inadequacy. Confronting the challenge of repeating what Troilus once said, and how, Chaucer lines up these excuses:

PRESENTATION POINTS

> But now, peraunter, some man wayten wolde
> That every word, or soonde, or look, or cheere
> Of Troilus that I rehercen sholde,
> In al this while unto his lady deere—
> I trowe it were a long thyng for to here—
> Or of what wight that stant in swich disjoynte,
> His wordes alle, or every look, to poynte. (III, 491–97)

A rehearser can detail far too much and still not clarify enough. Furthermore, Chaucer notes that his source text has already obliterated much data:

> For sothe, I have naught herd don er this
> In story non, ne no man here, I wene;
> And though I wolde, I koude nought, ywys;
> For ther was som epistel hem bitwene,
> That wolde, as seyth myn autour, wel contene
> Neigh half this book, of which him liste nought write.
> How sholde I thanne a lyne of it endite? (III, 498–504)

Nevertheless, Chaucer's speech conveys a general impression of his author's tone:

> But to the grete effect: than sey I thus ...
> As I have told, ...
> That it bifel right as I shal yow telle. (III, 505–11)

The authorial intentions of this *telling* must be retold in every subsequent reading of *Troilus and Criseyde*.

In "The Squire's Tale," Chaucer again dramatizes (far more comically) the most basic problems of reproducing a recital event as such. With rhetorically conventional modesty, the Squire apologizes for the limitations of his own rendition of the strange knight's speech before the Mongolian court:

> And for his tale sholde seme the bettre,
> Accordant to his wordes was his cheere,
> As techeth art of speche hem that it leere.
> Al be that I kan nat sowne his stile,
> Ne kan nat clymben over so heigh a style,
> Yet seye I this, as to commune entente:
> Thus much amounteth al that evere he mente,
> If it so be that I have it in mynde. (CT 5, 102–9)

Although the Squire cannot "sowne" the speaker's style exactly, he does claim to be able to recount its "commune entente." Strangely, Chaucer then has his Squire quote the strange knight's speech verbatim. But our text of the tale does not fully record how the Squire's voice accorded to his own "cheere"—or to Chaucer's fictionalized rehearsal of it. The tone of this direct quotation needs to be intuited by the reader, nevertheless.

It has been objected (and no doubt will be again) that any performance-based interpretation of *Troilus and Criseyde* is both arbitrary and self-indulgent. If so, I do not think it is peculiarly so because the performing art of reading always indulges some level of vocalizing the text's tone—the prefatory debate is really: how much, and who says?[94]

---

94. In *Chaucer Aloud: The Varieties of Textual Interpretation* (Philadelphia: University of Pennsylvania Press, 1987), Betsy Bowden has described what amounts to an oral heritage among highly influential Chaucer scholars—that is, the process of transmitting by means of classroom recital certain tonal interpretations.

2

BOOK I, LIVELY READING OR DEADLY SILENCE?

IT IS NO longer easily affirmed that Chaucer wrote much of his poetry for authorial recital. But even when it was, this proposition seldom proved significant to further interpretation of his texts in hand. Everyone enjoys reading Troilus and Criseyde aloud, and the sort of recitation commonly given in class serves as a more or less equivalent reproduction of Chaucer's voice. Chaucer's revision of Troilus and Criseyde does valorize such public re-reading. But such prelection of a dead language usually remains far too sanitized, more worried about philological accuracy and metrical regularity than about Chaucer's own performance vitality in court.

From the very start of Troilus and Criseyde, Chaucer states that he intends to maintain an appropriate tone: "For wel sit it, the sothe for to seyne, / ... to a sorwful tale, a sory chere" (I, 12–14). In order to revive some echo of Chaucer's own now sorry, now cheery tone, it is necessary to ponder the poet's *pronuntiatio* as a concurrent *ennaratio*.[1] The reciter's apparent emotions (whether genuine

---

1. Ennaratio traditionally starts as a simple glossing (i.e., "providing a tongue") to

or feigned) provide a simultaneous show as the story proper is told. At times, the reader must attempt to recall Chaucer's performance simply to enliven otherwise dead moments on the surviving page. At times, the page invites multiple, equally plausible readings as alternative rehearsal possibilities.[2] Yet, at these very moments when the tone of *Troilus and Criseyde* is clearly not clear, when the text records an equivocalness that Chauncey Wood calls "the heart of the debate," the reader's interpretive choice posits a recital determination of tone.[3]

At least twice within *Troilus and Criseyde*, Chaucer provides exactly the sort of performance notes that we would like to have for his first recital of the entire text.[4] Chaucer narrates in some detail how Troilus performed his *cantus* (I, 400–420) and his *canticus* (III, 1744–71).[5] The sources of these embedded lyrics have long been identified as a sonnet by Petrarch and a *metrum* by Boethius respectively.[6] It has also often been noted that Chaucer completely

---

the literal meanings of transcribed difficult words. The "running" (*concurrens*) metaphor is now normatively used in reference to a sporting event, though the OED cites Charles Lamb's description (1811; *Reflector* IV. 342) of lively storytelling as its first usage (s.v. "running," ppl. a., def. IV. 16.e.).

2. Beryl Rowland proposes that Chaucer's *pronuntiatio* would have eliminated a good deal of controversy regarding apparent indeterminacy.

3. Chauncey Wood, *The Elements of Chaucer's Troilus* (Durham, N.C.: Duke University Press, 1984), x.

4. Something akin to Charles Dickens's own prompt-copy of *A Christmas Carol* in the New York Public Library, available in facsimile, *A Christmas Carol: The Original 1843 Manuscript* (Del Ray, Fla.: Levenger Press, 2009).

5. William Provost considers the lyrics among six types of "structural devices" including proems, elaborate temporal references, dreams, letters, and the epilogue. Provost maps thirteen "structurally important lyrics" (*The Structure of Chaucer's Troilus*, 100), the first of which is the "Cantus Troili." James I. Wimsatt observes that the "regular recurrence" of such embedded texts "imparts lyricality to Chaucer's entire work" (*Chaucer and His French Contemporaries: Natural Music in the Fourteenth Century* [Toronto: University of Toronto Press, 1991], 142).

6. Thomas C. Stillinger, for example, sees the *cantus* as a special opportunity to study verse-for-verse "Chaucer's deployment of a prior text" (*The Song of Troilus: Lyric Authority in the Medieval Book* [Philadelphia: University of Pennsylvania Press, 1992], 2)— an intertextual appreciation that recital presumably does not foster. Patricia Thomson

BOOK I, LIVELY READING?

redressed the interpretive contexts for responding to each poem. Chaucer makes both translations fit his own rhyme royal pattern, and this formal continuity seems to invite a consistent reading tone. But the tones of Chaucer's *cantus* or *canticus* are not necessarily so fixed by their new recital contexts. As lyric interludes within a performance, Chaucer's tone of voice could have been sympathetic (a faithful impersonation of Troilus's sincerity) or mocking (a subversive parody), or one and then the other. A straightforward or "neutral" prelection of the first "cantus Troili" seems adequate. The second "canticus," however, requires a much more enthusiastic type of reiteration—actual singing, perhaps.[7] For both retrievals of Troilus's tonal intentions, Chaucer felt required to address at some length the integrity of his own acts of rehearsal. Chaucer never mentions that his translations are accurate renditions of the texts of Petrarch and Boethius. Chaucer does claim, however, to re-present Troilus's true voice now.

Preparing to repeat the first *cantus*, Chaucer reflects in tranquility yet aloud upon the compositional challenge of translating such a distant text. He does not ready himself for a full blown re-

---

considers the ways in which Chaucer could have become acquainted with the sonnet in "The 'Canticus Troili': Chaucer and Petrarch," *Comparative Literature* 11 (1959): 313–28. But the more immediate question is when does a reader's awareness of Chaucer's source become an integral component of valid responses to the "cantus Troili" itself. Skeat provided the Italian original in his edition of *The Complete Works of Geoffrey Chaucer*, 2nd ed., 7 vols. (Oxford: Clarendon Press, 1899, rpt. 1972), vol. 2, 464 n. 394. But such a context for reading Chaucer's "canticus" was apparently not at all commonplace prior to the twentieth century. For example, "J. M. B." found it necessary to correct an assertion by Nicholas Harris in his brief "Life of Chaucer" for the Aldine edition of Chaucer (1845) that Chaucer was unfamiliar with Italian poetry.

7. "Sing" probably means simply "recite" in reference to Chaucer's longer narrative poems, by analogy to *cantare*, which David Wallace (following Vittore Branca) defines as primarily "intended for piazza recitation" (*Chaucer and the Early Writings of Boccaccio* [Woodbridge: D.S. Brewer, 1985], 76). This metonymy does not preclude the possibility of Chaucer's embedded lyrics having been truly sung, however. Derek Brewer proposes that Chaucer may have played a psaltery, and "he must himself have learned to sing" (*The World of Chaucer*, 2nd ed. [Cambridge: D.S. Brewer, 1992], 47).

BOOK I, LIVELY READING?

enactment of Troilus's emotional overflow. He claims only that his translation offers both a form-to-form and a sense-for-sense equivalence of what Lollius recorded of Troilus's song:[8]

> And of his song naught only the sentence,
> As writ myn auctour called Lollius,
> But pleinly, save oure tonges difference,
> I dar wel seyn, in al, that Troilus
> Seyde in his song, loo, every word right thus
> As I shal seyn; and whoso list it here,
> Loo, next this verse he may it fynden here. (I, 393–99)

Chaucer introduces Lollius as a Trojan eyewitness to some transcript of Troilus's words. Chaucer's remark that the text is to be found *here* suggests that his translation was meant to be read in manuscript—a subsequent recital of which one may *hear* if one pleases. Chaucer seems willing to dissemble in order to guarantee that his rendition seems faithful. Chaucer wants primarily to assure "whoso list" that his English repetition can be true—and this "one self-referential statement capable of probation turns out to be a blatant lie."[9]

The first "cantus Troili" is indeed, if read in isolation from its narrative context, "a fairly close rendering" of "S'amor non è."[10] David Wallace has remarked that this unique pre-sixteenth-century translation of a Petrarchan sonnet is "introduced with considerable fanfare."[11] Literary historians have come to see Chaucer's three

---

8. Cf. Chaucer's assurances to little Lewis at the start of *A Treatise on the Astrolabe* that an English translation can serve his education as well as a Greek or Latin text (ll. 25–40).

9. Fleming, *Classical Imitation*, xiii and 155. Deanne Williams claims that "even if Chaucer believed that Lollius was a genuine authority ... he knows perfectly well that he's never read a word of him" ("The Dream Visions," in Lerer, ed., *The Yale Companion*, 147–78, 166). Unlike "Boccaccio," the sound of "Lollius" provides a convenient rhyme, including one for "Troilus," but then so would "Anonymous."

10. Petrarch's sonnet is number 88 in his *Vita*, number 132 in the *Canzoniere*.

11. Wallace in Peter Brown, *A Companion*, 228.

BOOK I, LIVELY READING?

stanzas as the moment when "English Petrarchan love poetry begins."[12] Although it seems highly unlikely that Chaucer's audience would have recognized his distortions of the Italian source as such, authorial recital could make Chaucer's intended tonal variations immediately clear without further research.

Mirroring his own struggles as an author anticipating a very specific target audience's reactions, Chaucer sympathetically recounts the lonely labor of Troilus as he first tries to translate his love into words. Troilus's compositional "experience is presented again and again in terms of a sequence of roles borrowed from other poems."[13] So, too, the diction of Chaucer's prelude to Troilus's song is invested with studied craft: "Thus took he purpos loves craft to suwe" (I, 379); Troilus ponders "what to arten hire to love" (I, 388); he edits "what for to speke, and what to holden inne" (I, 387). The preliminary drafts of this compositional process remain hush-hush, however: "And thoughte he wolde werken pryvely" (I, 380), keeping his *making* secret "from every wight yborn" (I, 382).

Troilus starts "on a song anon-right to bygynne" (I, 389), and his struggle to compose apparently also entails some practice recitals. Chaucer is particularly attentive to Troilus's "loude" volume while expressing his sorrow. Stephen Barney glosses "for to wynne" (I, 390) as either "overcome(?)" or "complain(?)." John Fleming observes that Chaucer's addition of the line "For ay thurst I, the more that ich it drynke" (I, 406) combines echoes of both Narcissus's complaint and Jesus' admonition to the Samaritan woman at

---

12. Patricia Thomson, "The 'Canticus Troili,'" 315. Thomas C. Stillinger remarks further that "the first *Canticus Troili* has always been recognized as a moment of literary achievement.... Placed next to this poetic monument—an unfair setting, perhaps, but one suggested by the text—the second *Canticus Troili* seems unremarkable and somewhat awkward" (*The Song*, 166).

13. Wetherbee, *Chaucer and the Poets*, 45.

41

BOOK I, LIVELY READING?

the well.[14] Since the Christian reference implicitly contradicts the pagan allusion, only some assumption regarding a recital tone can specify what Chaucer meant "right thus" (I, 397) by the sincerity of his impersonation of Troilus's mood or by his subversion thereof—or somehow, ironically, both.

The oscillation of Troilus's moods as he "possed to and fro" (I, 415) between the *sic et non* of his contraries (I, 418) is perhaps especially vulnerable to a performer's mockery. Even the syntax of Troilus's rumination does seem a bit seasick. Recital can impose a kind of affectionate scorn on Chaucer's textually tacit attitude, a tone soon echoed when Chaucer quotes Pandarus: "How hastow ... / Hid this fro me, thow fol?" (I, 617–18). But if Chaucer completely ridiculed Troilus as a love-poet, he would have simultaneously sabotaged his own success as a poet-translator of Lollius (Petrarch).

Since Troilus's *cantus* is half again as long as Petrarch's sonnet, Chaucer's translation has often needed to be defended against an impression that "the result of the expansion is often puffy."[15] This critical feeling presupposes that Chaucer intended simply to duplicate Petrarch's tone, which Chaucer may indeed have once sincerely wished to do as translator of a stand-alone lyric. While reciting *Troilus and Criseyde*, however, Chaucer may have simply wished to impersonate an intense amateur at work. Chaucer's three stanzas do conform "with the traditional three-stanza format of French ballade."[16] Nevertheless, the narrative context demands that Chaucer be imagined as reading this transcribed lyric without music.

---

14. Fleming, *Classical Imitation*, 185, identified as I, 405 [for 406].

15. Thomson, "The 'Canticus Troili,'" 319.

16. Wallace in Peter Brown, *A Companion*, 229. The triple ballade format maintains strong memories of singing: Chaucer's "'Fortune' and 'Complaint of Venus,' as well as the triple rondeau 'Merciles Beaute,' were perhaps designed for musical settings" (Wimsatt, *Natural Music*, 300, n. 75).

BOOK I, LIVELY READING?

Chaucer's restrained prelection, thus, interposes a certain emotional detachment between Troilus's "song" and Book I's audience. Chaucer presents Troilus's final text but not his true voice which, in any event, Criseyde did not hear, so "al was for nought" (I, 544). Insofar as the transcribed *cantus* does speak for itself in its narrative context, Chaucer's first audience and future readers can sense both the absence of Troilus's "pitous vois" (I, 422) and the aloofness of Chaucer's presentation.

Chaucer's performance of the second "canticus Troili" (III, 1744–71) is apparently quite a different matter.[17] The text informs us that this *canticus* was actually sung by Troilus as he held hands with Pandarus in a garden (III, 1737–38). Mirroring this narrative scene, the reciter too can sing and hold the hand of a friend in the audience. Nothing in the text mandates such a performance possibility, nor does anything preclude it. Without reference to its sources,[18] Troilus's *canticus* sounds very much like a reprise of the poet's own invocation to Venus in this same book's proem.[19] If part of the original recital, such an audible coincidence seems a ripple effect of Chaucer's pervasive (because immediately relevant) fascination with hearsay. If added as part of the revision process, the proem still serves as an authorial prolepsis of his character's *canticus*.

Troilus's honor has circulated throughout the world as a

---

17. The *canticus* is omitted in MS Harley 3943 (H2) and appears as a flyleaf inserted in MS Huntington Library HM 114. So there is some possibility that the lyric circulated in isolation and/or was added to a revision of the original text, a suggestion made by Root that Windeatt does not support.

18. Except for a bit of Dante, Troilus's *canticus* is a partial translation of Boethius's *Consolation of Philosophy* (Bk. 2 met. 8)—presumably a far more familiar text at the time than Petrarch's *Canzoniere*. Chaucer presents this translation as a stand-alone lyric, not as an excerpt per se. It substitutes for a much longer song by Troilo in il *Filostrato* (Bk. 3, sts 74–89), which itself alludes to the same Boethian metrum. Chaucer instead presents in propria persona part of Troilo's lyric in the proem to Book III.

19. Barney notes Chaucer again echoes this invocation at the end of the installment and thus "consciously encloses and sets off his third book" (*Riverside*, 1044, nn. 1811–13).

"vois" and as a "stevene" (III, 1723). Chaucer recognizes that reputation is largely a matter of mouth-to-mouth repetition. He explicitly attends to the excellence of Troilus's singing voice: "It was an hevene his wordes for to here; / And thanne he wolde synge in this manere" (III, 1742–43). The "here/manere" couplet specifically asks the reader to imagine Chaucer himself now singing too. Chaucer assumes what he imagines to be the closest approximation of Troilus's intended tone: "That in his herte he demed, as I gesse" (III, 1727). All subsequent readings should harmonize with this mood. After five stanzas of impersonated infatuation, singing Chaucer returns to retelling a history "but if that bokes erre" (III, 1774). Voice is thus translated into text and vice versa, and each act of translation both attempts fidelity and allows distortion, and so Chaucer's own struggle to read *Troilus and Criseyde* presents its most engaging *agon*.[20]

The extant text starts with Chaucer introducing himself with the declaration that he intends "to tellen" (I, 1) the double sorrow of Priam's son "er that I parte fro ye" (I, 5). In the first twenty-one lines of Book I, "the narrator stakes his confident claim to knowing his story and judging it aright."[21] Chaucer asks his audience to hearken "now ... with a good entencioun" (I, 52). But Chaucer also appeals to Tisiphone to help him "endite" (I, 6), weeping "as I write" (I, 7) right now. Several references to Chaucer's voice—"to the clepe I" (I, 8) or "as I kan, to pleyne" (I, 11)—are readily overlooked as merely vestigial phrasing.

20. For Thomas C. Stillinger, "the second *Canticus Troili* is an image for this book: its very failure, as it drifts uncertainly between interpretive contexts, is an image for the success of the *Troilus*, a work that finally bases its claim to stature on instability—a work that, rather than finding a new and better constitution for its relations between lyric and narrative, makes the dismantling of the lyrical book a (lyrical) book" (*The Song*, 188).

21. Leonard Koff, "Ending a Poem Before Beginning It, or The 'Cas' of Troilus," in *Chaucer's Troilus and Criseyde "Subgit to alle Poesye": Essays in Criticism*, ed. R. A. Shoaf, 161–78 (Binghamton, N.Y.: Medieval and Renaissance Studies and Texts, 1992), 168.

BOOK I, LIVELY READING?

It is possible to dismiss the tone of Chaucer's entire proem as merely conventional too. His invocation of a Fury (rather than Venus or a Muse) should, however, sound somewhat disturbing. Is Chaucer suggesting that his poem be read as epic (like that of Statius) or as satire (like that of Matheolus) or as something peculiarly tortured (like the experience of reciting this particular romance)? Tisiphone's name itself suggests sound (*phoné*), and Chaucer's first three invocations all imply the author's desire to have his writing vocalized.[22] He calls upon Cleo (II, 8), who may be glossed as "domina eloquentiae" (as in BL Harley MS 2392), and upon Calliope, "meaning 'bona vox' or 'optima vox,'" to speak again, "thi vois be now present" (III, 45).[23] The proem to Book IV, we shall see, instead presents the poet with pen in hand calling upon Tisiphone and her sisters to help him *show* this story inspired by other books. Chaucer ends his pagan prayer with a papal epithet (I, 15). It is difficult for the modern reader to say whether Chaucer's pose as *servus servorum* (*Amoris*) sounds comically pompous or sincerely subservient. It was easy for Chaucer to say (or to imagine saying) the line one way or the other, and the text does preserve an image of Chaucer as odd man out "for myn unliklynesse" (I, 16) in a court full of lovers. Even if he wrote the proems of *Troilus and Criseyde* exclusively for manuscript circulation, Chaucer maintains a twin conception of *showing* his tonal intent, both seeing the story as a text to be written (I, 49) and hearing its current recital (I, 52). In either type of reading, Chaucer's "travaille" (I, 21) requires a responsive sympathy. "Any" reader/listener must be favorably predisposed as a "lovere" (I, 20) to re-

---

22. According to John McCall, "Chaucer read somewhere or learned somehow that she was the voice or sound" of tragedy (*Chaucer Among the Gods* [University Park: Pennsylvania State University Press, 1979], 29).

23. Ibid., 16.

45

BOOK I, LIVELY READING?

call an analogous experience: "If any drope of pyte in yow be, / Remembreth yow on passed hevynesse" (I, 23–24).

The resonant anaphora (I, 29, 36, 43, 50) that informs the rest of this rapport-defining proem may be played aloud or read silently (as if so recited) with full liturgical pomp—that is, "echoing the form of the 'bidding prayer'" and enacting a tone consistent with Chaucer's initial pose as Cupid's Pope.[24] As mock-celebrant before his congregation, Chaucer asks "us" to pray "that I have myght to shewe, in som manere" the pain of Love. If this petition is performed sincerely, then our prayers should be addressed to the One, True, though textually Unclear "God so dere" (I, 32–33).

Book I of *Troilus and Criseyde* is by far the shortest. It is 1,092 lines, whereas the other four books all approach or exceed 1,800 lines. The very brevity of Book I may indicate that it best preserves Chaucer's recital version, the one least revised and amplified for subsequent manuscript circulation. If its proem was an act of revision, Chaucer's recital of installment one begins at line 57, not so draped in purple.

Once recital of the action begins, Chaucer's references to his "text" can be read as comments about his own prior reading—for example, "as I rede," (I, 159). Chaucer frequently mentions his authorities, mostly when he finds them inadequate or irrelevant or whenever he anticipates some resistance from his literally present audience (or then his metaphorically present reader). For example, Chaucer cannot "rede" (I, 133) whether Criseyde had children or not. Boccaccio had, in fact, specified that part of her amorous appeal was her infertility. Nor is Chaucer interested in the history of the Trojan War—"a long digression" (I, 143). Go read *Homer, Dares,* and/or *Dictys* "as they write" (I, 147)—but not now.

---

24. Windeatt, ed., *Geoffrey Chaucer, Troilus and Criseyde* (1984) 87, nn. 29–46.

BOOK I, LIVELY READING?

On the other hand, no direct quotations and not all references to speech in *Troilus and Criseyde* need be read as signs of Chaucer's own oral delivery. For example, the first threat of "rumour" (I, 85) which Criseyde "alday herd at ere" (I, 106) causes her to beg Hector for mercy "with pitous vois" (I, 111). This reported event provides no indication of Chaucer's recital voice, though it does exemplify his consistent concern with gossip and news and indeed with the transmission of both true facts and true feelings as a speech-act.

Criseyde is so vulnerable to rumor precisely because Calkas has already heard the conclusion of Troy's story (I, 76). Calkas can read the future "by calkulynge" (I, 71)—an audibly deflating pun, I think—because Calkas has listened to Apollo's "answer" (I, 72). Having been so abandoned by her absentee father, Criseyde seeks silence (I, 126). But men insist on talking about her. In Book I, they speak well of her (I, 131). Chaucer then first shows Troilus talking to himself.

Chaucer can voice Troilus's scorn as his own, as mocking his own audience: "I have herd told ... Ye loveres" (I, 197–98)—but safely in jest. Blind Cupid has been listening to sincere Troilus, however, and retaliates with the sight of Criseyde. Whether or not this *contrapasso* satisfies Aristotle's definition of true tragedy, Troilus recognizes the ironic relevance of an aphorism—"Ther nys nat oon kan war by other be" (I, 203). Troilus's self-applauding skepticism sounds a bit hubristic: "Loo! is this naught wisely spoken?" (I, 205). His *sententia* that no lover can learn from another's folly may in truth sabotage the didactic usefulness of Chaucer's tragic text (V, 1786) but not the emotional impact of its recital.

Troilus falls "sodeynly" (I, 209), and Chaucer is moved—as suddenly—to intrude. Chaucer exclaims that, like Cupid, the world is blind, and so is "entencioun." Chaucer uses this recital moment,

BOOK I, LIVELY READING?

the time-out of his apostrophe, to consider the text's *peripety*—"the effect contraire" (I, 212)—that inevitably follows Troilus's "surquidrie and foul presumpcioun"(I, 213). The tragic finale of *Troilus and Criseyde* having been predicted, Chaucer insists that we "wise, proude and worthi folkes alle" (I, 233) listen to the lesson: "Forthy ensample taketh of this man" (I, 232), even though Chaucer thus contradicts his own repetition of Troilus's aphorism. Chaucer then contradicts himself again, it seems, by affirming—what he thinks his audience already knows (I, 240)—that resistance is futile, so "refuseth nat to Love ... I yow rede" (I, 255–58). Chaucer's recital tone must somehow express sycophancy (I, 233), blasphemy (I, 232), clichés (I, 257–58), and even raw sarcasm: "To folowen hym that so wel kan yow lede"(I, 259).

Chaucer then sounds embarrassed by his own excess:

> But for to tellen forth in special
> Of this kynges sone of which I tolde,
> And leten other thing collateral,
> Of hym thenke I my tale forth to holde,
> Both of his joie and of his cares colde;
> And al his werk, as touching this matere,
> For I it gan, I wol therto refere. (I, 260–66)

Chaucer returns to the show in the temple.

Although Troilus had mocked anyone who spied upon the ladies in attendance (I, 192–93), he too seems guilty of "scoping" them out (I, 186–87) as if they were a pile of boring books ... until his crowd-piercing sight (I, 271–72) spots ink-like Criseyde: "She, this in blak ... he stood for to biholde" (I, 309).[25] Troilus must then conceal the text of his heart; he resists being

---

25. "Scoping" is Sarah Stanbury's term ("The Lover's Gaze in *Troilus and Criseyde*," in Shoaf, ed., *Chaucer's Troilus and Criseyde "Subgit to alle Poesye,"* 224–38, 229).

BOOK I, LIVELY READING?

rightly read himself: "but what he mente, / Lest it were wist on any manere syde, / His woo he gan dissimilen and hide" (I, 320–22), "And al his chere and speche also he borneth" (I, 327). For the eavesdropping entertainment of Chaucer's real audience, Troilus addresses "Ye [frustrated] loveres" (I, 331), the misunderstood (and so chaste) monks of Love (I, 336–40). Chaucer, and therefore Troilus, is particularly concerned with the misinterpretation of his tonal intent as a female failing:

> But take this: that ye loveres ofte eschuwe,
> Or elles doon, of good entencioun,
> Ful ofte thi lady wol it mysconstruwe,
> and deme it harm in hire oppynyoun. (I, 344–47)

If Chaucer's voice makes Troilus seem ridiculous, then this sarcasm sounds rather pathetic. If Chaucer plays this direct quotation straight, Troilus (and so frustrated Chaucer, too) can command the audience's sympathy.

Troilus holds his peace (I, 352) and his tongue, and retreats to his restless bedroom. He fabricates a waking dream, "a mirour of his mynde" (I, 365), by means of which he retrieves the presence of Criseyde: "Right of hire look, and gan it newe avise" (I, 364). Chaucer interjects a quick reminder that woe is "comynge," but "ful unavysed" Troilus (I, 378) continues to speculate. Troilus desperately hopes that Criseyde will be compassionate. This expectation makes her worth his travail (I, 372; cf. I, 21), and his pursuit of this "purpos" (I, 379) requires rhetorical strategy: "What for to speke, and what to holden inne" (I, 387).

The *cantus* that Troilus then composes does not win Criseyde, but it does woo its own author's full "assente" (I, 391). Troilus seduces himself. The inherent narcissism of Troilus's song resides primarily in its pronouns. Fifteen of its twenty-one lines use some

BOOK I, LIVELY READING?

form of the first-person pronoun. If the God of Love is actually being spoken to at all, he seems a moving target in the lover's imagination: sometimes "he" (I, 401, 405), sometimes "it" (I, 403), sometimes "the" (I, 412). After his reiteration of this lyric's *quaestio de amore*, Chaucer has Troilus attempt to speak in a supposedly more impromptu fashion to Cupid "thus" (I, 421).

Like Palamon in the Knight's tale—an analogy which Chaucer's familiar audience might have quite readily made—Troilus wonders in retrospect whether he saw a "goddesse or womman, iwis" (I, 425). This hyperbole may sound hackneyed, but Troilus then renounces his princely status with a startling impetuousness: "I here resigne / Into hire hond" (I, 432–33). The solitary reader quite easily shares a comfortable bed with Troilus in the privacy of "his owene thought" (I, 442), "a space from his care" (I, 505), in "his chambre thus allone" (I, 547). Spoken vehemently in a royal court, however, the tone of Troilus's abdication would shock.

With what looks like a throw-away line qualifying a mere cliché, Chaucer then somewhat nervously confesses that he does not know if Troilus was near or far from the fire as yet (I, 451). But Chaucer does "dar" to "sey this" (I, 451): that, from Troilus's point of view, Criseyde was *sans pareil*—which is actually a not-so-daring comment. Troilus sees what he wants to see with the "brestez yë" (I, 453). Troilus thus personifies the strong reader, blind to any alternative interpretations: "N'yn him desir noon other fownes bredde, / But argumentes to his conclusioun" (I, 465–66). There is then a lull in the middle of the already minimal action of Book I.

Meanwhile, Hector's war with its "sharpe shoures felle of arms" (I, 470) has been raging.

Troilus excels in combat, but his companions-in-arms com-

BOOK I, LIVELY READING?

pletely misread his motives. Troilus does not care if the siege is lifted; he does not hate the Greeks (I, 477–78). He fights "but only, lo, for this conclusioun"(I, 480)—to impress his love. The fire of that love "shewed in his hewe" (I, 487) which Troilus would disguise so he invents a cover story: "And seyde he hadde a fevere and ferde amys" (I, 491). He borrows the "title . . . / of other siknesse" (I, 488–89) that fictionalizes the show of his face. With a somewhat dizzying sally of negations, Chaucer then says that he cannot say how Criseyde interpreted Troilus's unreported actions because his sources say she took no note or pretended not to:

> But how it was, certeyn, kan I nat seye,
> If that his lady understood nat this,
> Or feynede hire she nyste, oon of the tweye;
> But wel I rede that, by no manere weye,
> Ne semed it that she of hym roughte,
> Or of his peyne, or whatsoevere he thoughte. (I, 492–97)

Once again, Troilus is reduced to talking to himself, "O fool" (I, 507).

Troilus talks himself to the brink of suicide (I, 526–27). Chaucer here impersonates an impersonation that dreads sarcasm—that is, he quotes Troilus quoting what he imagines other lovers will say about him (I, 514–18). Troilus fears being mocked by a versifier: "I shal byjaped ben a thousand tyme / More than that fol of whos folie men ryme" (I, 531–32).[26] Chaucer's scene-ending remark confesses the futility of Troilus's verbosity, "Thise wordes, and ful many an other to, / He spak ... / Al was for nought: she herde nat his pleynte" (I, 540–44)—a realization that only mul-

---

26. Chaucer's "poetic license"—i.e., his liberty to satirize—has been compared to that of a court fool, but Richard F. Green warns against "underestimating the awe in which members of the *familia regis* held their superiors" (*Poets*, 21).

BOOK I, LIVELY READING?

tiplies Troilus's woe and words "a thousand fold" (I, 546). And then Pandarus makes his entrance.

Like Chaucer in the *Book of the Duchess*, Pandarus eavesdrops (I, 549). But, instead of simply playing dumb, Pandarus probes his patient with a series of sarcastic misdiagnoses. Pandarus accuses Troilus of cowardice (I, 552). Alternatively, he suspects that Troilus suffers remorse for some unnamed sin (I, 554–57) which he should now confess. Bitter tongue in cheek, Pandarus even blesses the Greeks for scaring us lusty Trojans into holiness (I, 558–60). After performing this mocking interlude, Chaucer then states the tonal and medical rationale for Pandarus's opening act. To purge Troilus of melancholy with anger: "thise wordes seyde he for the nones alle" (I, 561). Pandarus knows well Troilus's true worth "as fer as tonges spaken" (I, 565). So recital should sugar all the text's verbal abuse with friendly concern (and curiosity).

To speak or not to speak—that is the question for Troilus: "But though that I now telle it the ne leste, ... I hide it for the beste" (I, 580–81). Pleading for candor, Pandarus promises to be an invincibly supportive (or completely unobjective) listener:

> I have, and shal, for trewe or fals report,
> In wrong and right iloved the al my lyve:
> Hid nat thi wo fro me, but telle it blyve." (I, 593–95)

Pandarus's petition for Troilus's full disclosure combines a defiance of hearsay with an odd echo of the marriage vow. Troilus anticipates that his complete refusal to speak may be misinterpreted by Pandarus as distrust (I, 601); so he ornately admits that he is in love—without naming with whom (I, 602–9). Troilus intends this confession to satisfy and silence Pandarus's friendly inquisition: "Suffiseth this, my fulle frend Pandare, / That I have seyd ... / So hide it wel—I tolde it nevere to mo" (I, 610–13). Instead, Pandarus

BOOK I, LIVELY READING?

calls the prince a fool to his face (I, 618). Reading and re-reading the tonally obscure text induces a genuine rapport between two fictional characters, but Chaucer's recital could make real all the tonal maneuvers of this dialogue.

Pandarus calls Troilus an unkind friend. Tit for tat, Troilus questions Pandarus's credentials as a lover. In his own defense, Pandarus repeats proverbial wisdom (at some length); he firmly (if only for the nonce) believes that bad experience can make a good teacher (I, 625–37), a conviction that affirms Chaucer's authority but contradicts Troilus's prior despair regarding the efficacy of negative examples.

Pandarus makes a very good guess about the key omission in Troilus's confession: "Peraunter thow myghte after swich oon longe, / That myn avys anoon may helpen us" (I, 619–20).[27] Listeners can recognize the dramatic irony of Pandarus's speculation as readily as readers—as does embarrassed Troilus. Troilus responds with a verbal irony: "How[,] devel[,] maistow brynge me to blisse? [!]" (I, 623), but Chaucer's voice must provide the emphases indicated by my italics and punctuation.

Pandarus then provides a prolonged apology for the anticipated role he must play "as frend" (I, 680) in the plot to come. The tour de force of this quasi-monologue (I, 625–722) starts with an equivocal excursus on contraries. Pandarus proposes a comparison between himself and Paris about whom Oënone composed a letter of complaint that has been circulating in manuscript. Troilus admits he has not himself read this supposedly popular text as yet. Never mind, Pandarus claims he can recite the shepherdess's "compleyente" from memory—"herkne, it was thus" (I, 658). But Chaucer has Pandarus perform only one stanza of her lyric (I,

---

27. I think it an unlikely but irresistible opportunity for the reciter to mispronounce "myn avys" in a fashion that suggests "my niece."

659–65), and the ventriloquist moves his lips: "Quod she" (I, 660; cf. CT VII, 582). Our transcript of the last line of this excerpted lyric does not scan; recital thus misremembers the author's measure, or the poet intends the reciter to trip.[28]

Chaucer plays Pandarus as either a caring jokester or an unscrupulous pimp. The tone attributed here to the extravagance of Pandarus's speech influences (and is influenced by) one's interpretation of all his subsequent actions. Pandarus promises to help Troilus pursue even Helen, "thi brother wif" (I, 678), but assures Troilus that he has only the purest intentions "to speke as now" (I, 685). He explains that "a preve / of trouth" requires the act of speaking to someone (I, 687–93)—as in the sacrament of confession.

Furthermore, speech is purgative (I, 702).

Besides, sharing secrets would be only fair because Troilus already knows the name of Pandarus's lady—though we never hear (I, 717).

But, "for al this," Troilus "no word seyde / But longe he ley as stylle as he ded were" (I, 722–23). Chaucer quite explicitly assures his audience that Troilus too has been listening with care, "to Pandarus vois he lente his ere" (I, 725). But, in response to Pandarus's closing invitation to "tel me somwhat," Troilus can only start upright, sigh, and roll his eyes—body language that Pandarus interprets (perhaps rightly) as "frenesie" (I, 727) or worse.

The loss of the ability to comprehend the intent of human speech signifies the loss of human nature itself:

Or artow lik an asse to the harpe,
That hereth sown whan men the strynges plye,

---

28. Ovid had Oënone begin her complaint by questioning whether his new (and predictably faithless) wife would allow Paris to read her epistle (*Heroides* V. 1, 99). The "complaint" seems to have been Chaucer's favorite lyric type.

BOOK I, LIVELY READING?

> But in his mynde of that no melodie
> May sinken hym to gladen, for that he
> So dul ys of his bestialite? (I, 731–35)

Such resistance to the tonal implications of recital makes the dull page brutish, "and with that, Pandare of his wordes stente" (I, 736), but Troilus still refuses to reply "for-why to tellen nas nat his entente / To nevere no man" (I, 737). The text quotes a proverb to explain Troilus's silent caution: "For it is seyd ... as this wyse treten" (I, 740–42).

Chaucer must fill the dead air by explicating Troilus's inarticulate dilemma "namelich in his counseill tellynge" (I, 743): Love dictates that love should be kept "secree" (I, 744). Like Pandarus, Chaucer can "crye"—quite loudly—"Awake!" (I, 751, 729), forcing Troilus to cup his ears and say:

> Frend, though that I stylle lye,
> I am nat deef. Now pees, and crye namore,
> For I have herd thi wordes and thi lore. (I, 752–54)

Troilus wants to terminate the conversation with his minimal response, but "'No,' quod Pandarus, 'therfore I seye'" (I, 761); reciting these same words, Chaucer cannot stop till he has achieved his intended tonal effects, even against any audience's or reader's predisposition to the contrary.

Some special identification of Chaucer with Pandarus has been often proposed in various contexts.[29] As a recital feature, Chaucer does become Pandarus at times, achieving what may be thought of as the medieval equivalent of method acting. But Chaucer can also back off at will. Chaucer like Pandarus knows when to

---

29. That such a self-projection explains why Chaucer made his Pandarus older than Boccaccio's Pandaro is an "opinion advanced by Rossetti and often assented to" (Riverside, 1023b)—though not textually demonstrable.

BOOK I, LIVELY READING?

shout (I, 729) and when to whisper (I, 767). It is a bit more challenging to imagine Chaucer performing the stychomythia of lines 770–75. Perhaps, the sight of Chaucer's rapid vacillation between two voices provided an amusing representation of the exchange. Pandarus grants the severity of Troilus's woe; even so, the pain of Tityus "as bokes telle" (I, 788) seems a rather grandiose (and so perhaps mocking) analogy, however. Strangely, Chaucer indulges his own interest in a strange word, "volturis" (I, 788), suggesting that curious diction fascinates him more than true love.[30]

Troilus would still refuse to "tellen ... as muche as speke" (I, 794–96) and so die. Pandarus predicts the absent and still unnamed Criseyde's reaction. Assuming the demeanor of an urbane woman, Pandarus pooh-poohs the passion of Troilus—and any reciter can easily voice the same scorn in quotation marks: "Thus wol she seyn, and al the town attones, / 'The wrecche is ded, the devel have his bones!' (I, 804–5) for the folly of loving "allone" (I, 806) without an audience. Chaucer writes a Ciceronic triplet for Pandarus to flourish in conclusion:

> But love a womman that she woot it nought,
> And she wol quyte it that thow shalt not fele;
> Unknowe, unkist, and lost that is unsought. (I, 807–9)

Better to serve unrewarded than unheard (I, 810–19)—"Of that word took hede Troilus" (I, 820).

Troilus concedes silently to himself "how that soth hym seyde Pandarus" (I, 822). Now, well on the road to real communication, Troilus moves from mere sighing (I, 827) to a question, "What is me best to do?" (I, 828). Pandarus's simple imperative needs to be

---

30. See MED s.v. "vultur(e". The only recorded uses of "vulture" that predate manuscript publication of a complete *Troilus* are those of Trevisa, the earliest being 1387. Chaucer may again be offering a (self-mocking) auto-citation of his somewhat clumsy identification of "The foul that highte voltor" in *Boece* III. m. 12. 42.

BOOK I, LIVELY READING?

spoken with increasing intensity—speak! (I, 830, 862, 864, 870). First and last, Pandarus desires to coax Troilus's ejaculation of a name—the performance climax of Chaucer's first recital installment: "'Criseyde' ... the word" (I, 873–74). Pandarus rejoices "whan that" the "name" of his niece is spoken (I, 876)—a release concurrently experienced by both Chaucer and his audience.

All too forgiving Pandarus states that Troilus's sins against Love have so far been only venial, only "in cogitatione" and "in verbo" rather than "in opere."[31] Troilus used to call Love "Seynt Idiot" (I, 910) and to label his servants "Goddes apes" (I, 913)—and all the rest "thow seydest" (I, 916), "so seydestow ful ofte" (I, 919) "and told" (I, 920), "thus seydestow" (I, 924), and "yet seydestow" about what lovers "wolden speke in general" (I, 925–26). Pandarus cannot resist some mild ridicule, "Now may I jape of the" (I, 929), which simultaneously can be voiced as affection. Troilus needs to repent these speech-acts (I, 933–34), his "nyce japes" (I, 911) committed before seeing Pandarus's niece. The reciter too may strike his breast (I, 932), a light-hearted sacrilege. Troilus prays for forgiveness with a firm resolution to jape no more (I, 937–38), and hopeful Pandarus (I, 939) imposes no further penance on Troilus: "'Thow seist wel,' quod Pandare" (I, 939). This is not to say that Chaucer's tone of voice concurs, nor has the God of Love absolved Troilus.

The text then quotes Pandarus speaking without interruption for nine more stanzas (I, 946–1008). It is very difficult to determine the tone of this speech with any certainty. Such talking at

---

31. Arthur E. Hutson reads Book II, 506–74 in terms of the sacrament of penance ("Troilus' Confession," *Modern Language Notes* 69 [1954]: 468–70). Lawrence Besserman sees Chaucer's diction throughout *Troilus and Criseyde* as investing both Pandarus and his narrator with priestly roles ("'Priest' and 'Pope,' 'Sire and Madame': Anachronistic Diction and Social Conflict in Chaucer's *Troilus*," *Studies in the Age of Chaucer* 23 [2001]: 181–224); here, Chaucer as *servus servorum* (cf. I, 912) recites Pandarus's act of absolution.

length can itself signal a certain anxiety, and Chaucer's recital may have only intensified the uncomfortable tone of Pandarus's subtext by making clear that there is more to the meaning of these words than meets the eye. First, a somewhat avuncular Pandarus celebrates contraries—the rose grows next to the nettle, dawn follows the dark, etc.—all promising that sorrow turns to joy. Pandarus invites Troilus "now" to "be" lusty, free, true yet hidden, "and al is wel" if Troilus remains single-minded "as writen clerkes wyse" (I, 961). Pandarus warns Troilus against hastiness—good, conventional advice that can be recited to make Pandarus sound as if he is stalling. Progressing so slowly from general remarks to particulars may be played primarily as nervousness: "And wostow why I am the lasse afered / Of this matere with my nece trete?" (I, 974–75).

Pandarus has "herd seyd of wyse lered" (I, 976) that everyone answers to love somehow (I, 977–79). Furthermore, "And for to speke of hire in specyal, / ... It sit hire naught to ben celestial" (I, 981–83). Since the young widow Criseyde is no nun, Pandarus defines her chaste *daunger* as "vice" (I, 987). Promising to serve the pleasure of both Troilus and Criseyde, Pandarus's slightly too clever wordplay—"wyse ... wyse ... wiser" (I, 991–93)—invites a winking recital. So too Chaucer can make Pandarus's preemptory approval "by my trouthe" of his own wit "as I gesse" (I, 995–96) sound conceited if not smarmy when actually said aloud.

After all this oratory, Troilus has heard only what he wants to hear—that Pandarus has "assented / to ben his help" (I, 1009–10). The text specifies that Troilus prays to Venus "with sobre chere" (I, 1013), but Chaucer quickly baffles Troilus (and us) by anticipating the tonal complexities of Pandarus's solicitation of Criseyde: "ek telle me this: / How wiltow seyn of me ... and ek for the manere / Of the, hire em, she nyl so swich thyng here" (I, 1017–22).

BOOK I, LIVELY READING?

Pandarus silences Troilus's simple-mindedness with sarcasm (I, 1023–25) and counters by wondering whether the prince's hesitation should be interpreted as honor or fear (I, 1026).[32] Chaucer's recital can favor either tone; Chaucer's recital could also and more probably did hold this tonal determination in suspense.

Pandarus then asks Troilus a real question. He requests a specified boon (I, 1027). Intending all the "beste" (I, 1028), he wants solitary control of the script. Troilus says I do, with one tonal qualification: "herke, ... o word" (I, 1030). Troilus intends only "that that myghte sownen into goode" (I, 1036). Pandarus laughs because every seducer says he means well (I, 1037–38). Pandarus adds, "I roughte naught though that she stood and herde / How that thou seist" (I, 1039–40), a concession that can be played to sound opportunistic or dismissive. He expects Criseyde would respond the same to Troilus's declaration whether faked or earnest. Pandarus foretells that his own business (I, 1042) will achieve her sweet response irrespective of sincerity.

Troilus falls to his knees in excessive gratitude: "I kan no more seye, / But, thow wis, thow wost, thow maist, thow art al!" (I, 1051–52), again too readily abdicating his true rank (I, 1053). A sympathetic reader or a very good actor might be able sustain the tonal integrity of Troilus's intensity, but it would probably have seemed an awful strain for Chaucer in the Ricardian court. Chaucer contrives to have Troilus speak a rime riche as his last couplet in Book I (1056–57). Pandarus promises to get to work (I, 1071), and Troilus is quickly up and about again, being happily heroic, though not yet truly healed. And then this book ends.

---

32. I, 1026 is glossed by Barney as an exclamation with the conventional meaning of "entremette" as "meddle with, worry about" (*Riverside*, 487, n. 1026). See MED s.v. "entermeten" def. 1 "To intervene." But "entremette of" seems in this context to be an odd use of "entremette" (< Fr. "metre") and "of" to mean "put off"; if so, Pandarus is asking a rhetorical question: "Why put off what you have to do?"

BOOK I, LIVELY READING?

Recital of the text requires no scribe's *explicit*. Chaucer announces, "Now lat us stynte of Troilus a stounde" (I, 1086). Exiting, Chaucer calls for our ("us") collective disengagement from the narrative event so far ("now"). Every solitary owner of the book is, of course, free to proceed immediately to the next book. But Chaucer's first audience had to wait for a (now indeterminate) "stounde."

3

BOOK II, ECHO CHAMBERS

CHAUCER begins Book II of *Troilus and Criseyde* with a narrative transition, an invocation, and his excuses. Editorial identification of its "prohemium" as such encourages readers to ponder both the formatting of this discrete segment and the overall design of Chaucer's entire book in hand.[1] A reader's grasp of that text permits page-flipping, which uncovers that Book I had no proem; neither will Book V. Perception of these twin absences then poses the mystery of an intriguing symmetry—a modern reader's observation of the author's first and last omissions, which probably went utterly unnoticed during recital.

---

1. Chaucer did have the specific precedent of Boccaccio's *Filostrato*, but all three of Chaucer's proems differ substantially from "il Proemio." Boccaccio had finished composing his entire poem prior to writing its one prose preface. Boccaccio's *Proemio* specifically addresses his book's initial recipient, la Fiametta. Chaucer also uses the term "prohemye" in his "Prologue" to the Clerk's tale (CT 4, 43); the pilgrim-narrator criticizes (in his own somewhat prolix fashion) Petrarch's prolonged preliminary remarks as "a thyng impertinent" (CT 4, 54h). James J. Murphy identifies "prohemium" as one of the "traditional rhetorical names for introductions" in *Rhetoric in the Middle Ages* (Berkeley: University of California Press, 1974), 323; the term maintains a strong expectation of addressing a listening audience. Cassiodorus (ca. A.D. 490–585), for example, explains that the primary function of a proem is to prepare listeners "ante ingressum rei, de qua dicendum sit," cited in Carolus Halm, *Rhetores Latini Minores* (Leipzig: Teubner, 1863), 501–2.

BOOK II, ECHO CHAMBERS

Perhaps Chaucer planned to write two more proems someday. More probably, Chaucer's revision of each recital installment entailed a substantial modification of each book's opening remarks, which scribes subsequently (and inconsistently) designated "proems."

In all three proems, Chaucer spotlights his own role now: in Book IV, as writer (13–14, 17); in Book III, as speaker (47); and in Book II, as both. Chaucer begins his second recital installment as if it were part of a still ongoing and "personal experience of the process of writing"—and indeed it may have been when first performed as the recently finished part of a work in progress.[2] To enhance this proem's composition-centered (or simply egocentric) permutation of the *in media res* convention, Chaucer struggles, it seems, to include an epic simile regarding his current "travaylle" (II, 3; cf. I, 21).[3] The vehicle of his nautical and perhaps Dantean metaphor for book-writing is a "boot,"[4] which he steers with "my connynge" (II, 4).[5] Chaucer's immediate audience seems to be the air, "O wynd, o wynd" (II, 2). But a change in the weather suits a change in the story's "matere" and a change in Chaucer's tone.

As reciter of his own experience as writer, Chaucer welcomes the first day of happy hope "now" (II, 7). He prays "fro this forth" that Cleo will speed him "to ryme wel this book til I have do" (II, 9–10). He must chart a fixed plot, not explore terra incognita. He will "endite" no new "sentement" (II, 13).

---

2. Windeatt also remarks that "Ch omits B's 'autobiographical' proem and makes little use of Fil for his own proem. Fil is presented by its poet as an elegant self-projection" (*Troilus* [1984], 7).

3. Meaning "hard physical labor" though perhaps punning (if audibly so emphasized) with "travel"; see MED s.v. "travail" defs. 1a and 4.

4. This possible echo of the start of Dante's *Purgatorio* (*Riverside*, 1030, nn. 1–4) also anticipates the shipwreck motif beginning Book III.

5. Windeatt's edition omits Barney's comma separating "Of my konnyng" from "swych trauaylle" (II, 3–4).

62

BOOK II, ECHO CHAMBERS

Chaucer's professed modesty as a mere translator—"but out of Latyn in my tonge it write" (II, 14)—also shields him from hostile reviews. He refuses all "thank" in order to avoid any "blame" (II, 15). He promises to give "yow" (II, 16) as tonally faithful a reading of his source as he can: "For as myn auctour seyde, so sey I. / Ek though I speeke of love unfelyngly" (II, 18–19). Handicapped by a lack of personal experience, Chaucer sees his own failure as reader to sympathize with the sentiment of his source as partial blindness—"A blynd man kan nat juggen wel in hewis" (II, 21).

Digressing in order to consider his own true love, Chaucer then worries us about words:

> Ye knowe ek that in forme of speche is chaunge
> Withinne a thousand yeer, and wordes tho
> That hadden pris, now wonder nyce and straunge
> Us thinketh hem, and yet thei spake hem so. (II, 22–25)

It is primarily the "usages" (II, 28) of various ages and distant lands that separate "them" from "us" and "then" from "now" and the author from his future readers. Any lover "here ... in this place / That herkneth ... / Or wondreth on his speche or his doynge" (II, 30–34) witnesses and so shares Chaucer's anxiety about being misread.

Chaucer then anticipates that his present listeners' concurrent responses will vary from one another's and differ from his own. Hoping for harmony, Chaucer translates a familiar saying, "*omnes viae Romam ducunt*," in the proem's next-to-last stanza. However, Chaucer's rendition emphasizes the diversity of approaches—"not o path, or alwey o manere" (II, 37)—rather than a common destination. Chaucer addresses a gathering of real individuals individually:

> Ek scarsly ben ther in this place thre
> That have in love seid lik, and don, in al;

For to thi purpos this may liken the,
And the right nought. (II, 43–46; my italics)

It is quite impossible to read Chaucer addressing one "thee" as distinguished from another "thee" without imagining his real presence in front of familiar listeners for whom "yet al is seid or schal" (II, 46) within the immediate experience of this recital event.

Having seen his distant author's words for what they are and are not, Chaucer sounds less than thrilled to continue: "But syn I have bigonne, / Myn auctour shal I folwen, if I konne" (II, 49). His boat-book must try to follow tracks at sea. His fictional time frame moves from the gloomy April of Book I (156) to May "that moder is of monthes glade" (II, 50). The very specificity of Chaucer's reference to "Mayes day the thridde" teases modern readers, but this *reverdie* may have once simply referred to his recital's *now, today*, "as I shal synge" (II, 56).[6]

As a fellow insomniac, Chaucer seems to seem sincere in his sympathy for Pandarus, who suffers despite "al his wise speche" (II, 57) and even though "koude he nevere so wel of lovyng preche" (II, 59). The sad text preserves a pathetic pun, however—one that can be played as part of a more humorous peek at green Pandarus: the "sorowful lay" of a swallow's matins wakes him from unpleasant dreams as he "lay" (II, 64, 66). Dozy Pandarus is a bad audience; so the swallow sings louder, "so neigh hym made hire cheterynge" (II, 68). Pandarus hears only the "noyse" (II, 70) of Procne's song (but no ominous implications to Chaucer's allusion).

Pandarus's first action when fully awake is "to calle" (II, 71) for action. When he arrives at Criseyde's palace, he first locates her company by sound (II, 80), that of a maiden reading in

---

[6]. Cf. CT KnT 1, 1462–63 and NPT 7, 3189–90. Barney notes that this day's association with escapes has possibly inauspicious connotations (*Riverside*, 1031, n. 56, and 832, nn. 1462–64).

a "paved parlour" (II, 82). For Joyce Coleman, "the entire scene breathes elegance and refinement; this is a court (a small one) *being* a court—sharing a pleasurable activity in a way that unites the members while it entertains them."[7] The ladies are rehearsing a "geste / Of the siege of Thebes" (II, 83–84)—a tantalizing adumbration of Troy's future fall (and, even more provocative in a recital context, of King Richard's).

Pandarus blesses the presently joyful scene "with youre book and all the compaignie!" in the name of a god imagined to be the omnipresent spectator (II, 85–86). Criseyde sees the arrival of her uncle as the happy fulfillment of a dream, and "with that word" (II, 91) she sits him down for a chat. Pandarus intends to lead this conversation again, as he had done with Troilus. But, rather than probing for a secret, Pandarus will now stimulate Criseyde's curiosity by withholding information. He first apologizes for having inserted himself between his niece's company and their text: "But I am sory that I have yow let / To herken of youre book ... what seith it? telle it us!" (II, 94–96). Pandarus suggestively asks if the "romaunce" (II, 100) is about love. The ladies laugh at his plausible, leading, but false intuition regarding the tone of the text that "we rede" (II, 100). Pandarus, like many a know-it-all (II, 106), claims to have read the unabridged edition—"For herof ben ther maked bookes twelve. / But lat be this" (II, 108–9) book-talk. Pandarus would entice the ladies to dance rather than read, and such an "observaunce" (II, 112) may indeed have been scheduled for Chaucer's audience as well.

Pandarus would have Criseyde put her veil away as well as her book (II, 110–11). Although his printed lines hardly seem to "rave" (II, 116), Criseyde hears Pandarus's proposal as wildness.[8] Chau-

---

7. Joyce Coleman, *Public Reading*, 165.
8. Windeatt does read Chaucer's revision of Boccaccio as supportive of a reading

cer has the widow perhaps protest too much when she claims she is better suited to sit "ay in a cave / To bidde and rede on holy seyntes lyves" (II,117–18); such "love celestial" seeks the security (or solitude) of silent reading. Though Criseyde dismisses the invitation to dance (and any double entendre), her audible tone may desire a contradictory compliment regarding her age (II,119). Pandarus knows how to "telle a thyng to doon yow pleye" (II, 121), how to tease Criseyde's desire (II, 126, 128).

Chaucer expresses Criseyde's simultaneous fascination and frustration as a reader of Pandarus's intent:

> For al this world ne kan I reden what
> It sholde ben; some jape I trowe is this;
> And but youreselven telle us what it is,
> My wit is for t'arede it al to leene.
> As help me God, I not nat what ye meene. (II, 129–33)

Pandarus pretends to find Criseyde ill-disposed to listen because of her pride—a ploy that only makes her more attentive: "For nevere, sith the tyme that she was born, / To knowe thyng desired she so faste" (II, 143–44). Chaucer too is toying with his audience's appetitive curiosity.

Chaucer elides "many wordes glade, / And frendly tales, and with merie chiere, / Of this and that they pleide, and gonnen wade / In many an unkouth, glad, and dep matere" (II, 148–51). All this erased conversation precedes Criseyde's hint regarding her hidden infatuation with Hector (I, 113), which Pandarus detects and promptly redirects. About Hector "nedeth it namore

---

that attributes such raving to Pandarus: "Ch's P speaks first and then makes as if to leave at the climax of his much wilder speech, with its added assertions of good faith, threats of death, and recriminations" (Troilus [1984], 173, nn. 429–48). Chaucer's recital could amplify the intensity of Pandarus's "Do wey" on first hearing (i.e., without reference to the text's source) and so validate Criseyde's otherwise prissy first response.

for to telle" (II, 176); instead, by the way, "and ek" (II, 157), "dar I seye" (II, 173), Troilus is as worthy. The tone of Criseyde's response—indicating her attraction to this second-best prince—is measured, at most. She is certain of the "sooth" of Hector's glory; she concedes only "the same thyng trowe I; / ... men tellen" (II, 183–85) of Troilus's merits. Recital could make her implicit lack of enthusiasm more conspicuously understated. But Pandarus hears Chaucer's meiosis as Criseyde's agreement: "Ye sey right sooth, ywys" (II, 190). Pandarus amplifies yesterday's report of Troilus's performance on the battlefield, a rehearsal that still reverberates "in everi wightes eere" (II, 195). Trojans and Greeks obviously have radically opposed readings of Troilus's persona. "And with that word" (II, 208), Pandarus fakes a premature exit.

Criseyde retains him with a tongue-in-cheek question about his fatigue "namelich of wommen" (II, 212). She wants to continue speaking "of wisdom" (II, 214), a word that must be invested with some discernible though secret significance because the sound of it causes the rest of the courteous company to withdraw: "And everi wight that was aboute hem tho, / That herde that, gan fer awey to stonde, / Whil the two hadde al that hem liste in honde" (II, 215–17; my italics). Criseyde first recounts for Pandarus a "tale" (tally?) of her personal finances (II, 218–19). This confidential exchange makes quite plausible for Chaucer's audience Criseyde's later credence in Pandarus's cover story that a certain Poliphete has filed "advocacies" against her (II, 1469).

Pandarus again pretends to leave, only to continue his plotting: "But yet, I say" (II, 221). Although Chaucer's audience knows where he is headed, Criseyde fails to fully follow Pandarus's directions: "Shal I nat witen what ye meene of this?" (II, 226). Pandarus knows timing is everything and tells her "this thing axeth leyser"

(II, 227) without defining "thing" or footnoting "leisure."⁹ To tease Criseyde further, Pandarus dwells upon his worry that further recital of an unwelcome "truth" might falsely displease her:

> If I it tolde and ye it toke amys.
> Yet were it bet my tonge for to stille
> Than seye a soth that were ayeyns youre wille. (II, 229–31)

Chaucer thus has Pandarus here echo his own most fundamental anxiety: his current audience might not yet (or ever) want to hear what Lollius had to write. Before speaking further, Pandarus swears by wise Minerva and loud Jupiter and blissful Venus that he loves his niece best among women—excepting paramours, and maybe some dead women. The syntax of Pandarus's "wyttynge" (II, 236) sounds a bit befuddled, but he assumes Criseyde knows what he means (II, 238).

In reply, Criseyde sounds implicitly guarded though explicitly trusting: "I am to no man holden, trewely, / So muche as yow" (II, 241–42). She grants that she has not as yet "quyt" Pandarus sufficiently. Not only will she not be offended by Pandarus's continued rehearsal, but she repents her own past offences, firmly resolving to "amende" (II, 245) her failures as a friend.¹⁰ Presumably absolved, Criseyde asks Pandarus to speak more straightforwardly and renounce the "fremde manere speche, / And sey ... what yow liste" (II, 248–49).

Licensed to speak freely, Pandarus first tries to control the anticipated response(s) of Criseyde and Chaucer's listeners: "Tak it for good, that I shal sey yow here" (II, 252). Then, clearing his throat with oratorical aplomb, Pandarus allows Chaucer to deliver a mini-disquisition on the teleology of composition:

---

9. Leisure acts as porter to the Rose; cf. "Faire Idelnesse" in *The Romaunt of the Rose*, Fragment A, 1273–80.

10. Listeners can recall Troilus's penance in Book I; re-readers can see a later parallel in the shriving of Pandarus (II, 440 and 525–29).

And seyde, "Nece, alwey—lo!—to the laste,
How so it be that som men hem delite
With subtyl art hir tales for to endite,
Yet, for al that, in hire entencioun
Hir tale is al for som conclusioun.

And sithe th'ende is every tales strengthe,
And this matere is so bihovely,
What sholde I peynte or drawen it on lengthe
To yow...." (II, 255–63)

Enchanted by the mirror of his listener's face (II, 265), Pandarus hopes for a welcoming response to his authorial desire but pauses to anticipate Criseyde's possibly negative reaction: "If I my tale endite / Aught harde, or make a proces any whyle" (II, 267–68). Chaucer then describes an author's ability to adjust his recital tone to accommodate his audience's expected mood: "Forthi hire wit to serven wol I fonde" (II, 273).

Pandarus is concerned primarily about being seen through; he worries about being discovered as a beguiler more than about the act of beguiling itself. He suspects that the innocent are most suspicious: "For tendre wittes wenen al be wyle / Theras thei kan nought pleynly understonde" (II, 271–72). The dramatic delay of this introspective stanza is sufficient for Criseyde to become self-conscious: "And she was war that he byheld hire so" (II, 275). Pandarus continues to hem and haw about Criseyde's "goodly aventure" (II, 281, 288)—a circumlocution supposedly spoken with "good entencioun" (II, 295). Her uncle's hesitation either piques Criseyde's interest or exhausts her patience: "come of, and telle me what it is! / For both I am agast what ye wol seye, / And ek me longeth it to wite, ywis" (II, 310–12). Chaucer's recital determines which of her two possible feelings should surface more clearly.

BOOK II, ECHO CHAMBERS

Pandarus finally obliges his niece's need for clarity: "now harkeneth! I shall telle" (II, 315). He says bluntly that Troilus loves her—"Lo, here is al! What sholde I moore seye?" (II, 321). Yet, Pandarus keeps talking passionately, indeed with suicidal intensity, for eleven more stanzas. He regrets her beauty; he guarantees her independence; mostly, he just whines "Wo ... Wo ... Wo ... Wo" (II, 344–47). But this emotional outburst has a specific rhetorical purpose. Pandarus would reveal himself to be no "baude" (II, 353). Acting on behalf of *alto amore*, Pandarus would move Criseyde to respond with some "bettre chiere" (II, 360) and so save Troilus—"This al and som, and pleynly, oure entente" (II, 364). Chaucer's recital intent, however, would be to display the fraud or self-deception of Pandarus's self-defense.

Pandarus justifies his own mission to Criseyde as "naught but skylle, ywys" (II, 365). But, anticipating her skepticism or timidity, he poses "the worste" (II, 367) possible outcome: nosey tattletales might see. Pandarus (rather disingenuously) assures Criseyde that "every wight," unless he be a "fool of kynde," will assume that she and Troilus share only an innocent "love of frendshipe in his mynde" (II, 370–71); Chaucer's end-rhyme somewhat wrenches Pandarus's reassurance. The sarcastic tone of Pandarus's quasi-Wycliffite image of eating images in a temple (II, 372–73) approaches sacrilege, at least for the more orthodox members of Chaucer's audience.

The much anticipated response of Criseyde sounds surprisingly muted at first. She thinks to herself, "I shal felen what he meneth, ywis" (II, 387). This line of caution looks more cold-blooded than cold-hearted. She states she will listen further—"what wolde ye devise? / What is your reed I sholde don of this?"—which Pandarus takes at face value as her consent: "That is wel seyd" (II, 389–90).

BOOK II, ECHO CHAMBERS

Pandarus anticipates Criseyde's old age—a *carpe diem* ploy that would be more persuasive if it were less clichéd. Pandarus quotes proverbs and then four lines "The kynges fool is wont to crien loude" (II, 400), and Chaucer too could shout: beware "crowes feet" (II, 401–5)! Chaucer too could wish all ladies here present "namore sorwe" (II, 406). And Chaucer too can nod and pause when Pandarus drops his head and "with this he stynte" (II, 407).

Pandarus's intent completely backfires—apparently. Criseyde bursts into suicidal tears (II, 409). She acts outraged that her deceptive uncle's definition of "friendship" should so bluntly mean "go love" (II, 396). She discards all the rest of his rhetorical art: "Is al this paynted proces seyd—allas!—/ Right for this fyn?" (II, 424–25). Pandarus seems to answer with equal intensity and at more length. The high melodrama of this written text seems oddly dispelled by Criseyde's body language, however, when Pandarus threatens to go (for a third time) and she "agayn hym by the lappe kaughte" (II, 448). In recital, the integrity of their perceived distress with each other depends entirely upon the intervention of Chaucer's observable reactions to it.

It seems crucial that at this very moment Chaucer intrudes to excuse Criseyde as "the ferfullest wight/ That myghte be" (II, 450–51). Readers who see "brotilnesse" as Criseyde's *hamartia* may read Chaucer's confession of her timidity as a reluctant condemnation. To some, this sentence seems irrevocably judgmental. To others, Chaucer's aside sounds more sympathetic than condemnatory. Meanwhile, Criseyde herself has rather quickly revised her reading of Pandarus's petition based on her present perception of his intent; she "herde ek with hire ere ... And in his preier ek saugh noon unryght" (II, 451–53).

Criseyde's pity for Pandarus precedes her (com)passion for Troilus (II, 455). She speculates that her wild uncle might indeed

BOOK II, ECHO CHAMBERS

commit suicide "here ... in my presence" (II, 459–60). Criseyde worries most specifically about reactions to such a spectacle: "What men wolde of hit deme I kan nat seye" (II, 461). She plans, therefore, to act her part too: "It nedeth me ful sleighly for to pleie" (II, 462); otherwise, there may be "no solas" (II, 460). A patently unsympathetic recital can mimic all Criseyde's precedent sighs and then quickly terminate her weeping (II, 469) here as if it were all a patent sham.

Criseyde's conversation with Pandarus turns into a discussion of semantics. On the printed page, such code-speak as "maken hym good chere" (II, 471), "holden hym in honde" (II, 477), and "han other routhe" (II, 489) should probably be italicized by editors. Having come to terms, Criseyde concedes that, had she understood from the start what Pandarus pretends he meant, "therto nolde I nat ones han seyd nay" (II, 481). And Pandarus then reinterprets Criseyde's concession as an oral contract:

"But may I truste wel to yow," quod he,
"That of this thyng that ye han hight me here,
 Ye wole it holden trewely unto me?"
"Ye, doutelees," quod she, "myn uncle deere." (II, 491–94)

Pandarus is not entirely convinced; he asks for confirmation that there will be no reneging:

"Ne that I shal han cause in this matere,"
 Quod he, "to pleyne, or ofter yow to preche?"
"Why, no, parde; what nedeth moore speche?" (II, 495–97)

The reciter of these lines must convey some suspicion of Criseyde's voice—a performed tone that becomes crucial to subsequent assessments of her broken promises.

Presently satisfied with their exchange of "trowthe" (II, 490,

493), Pandarus and Criseyde turn to "other tales glade" (II, 498). They talk primarily about talk. Even if the reader ignores all the "he saids" and "she saids" of Chaucer's text, their conversation repeatedly calls attention to the activity of talking itself: "Tel me" (II, 501), "Kan he wel speke of love" (II, 503), "Tel me" (II, 504), "By my trouthe, I shal yow telle" (II, 506), "'Gan he and I ... / Right for to speken'" (II, 509–10), "'Til that I herde'" (II, 517), "'And sikerly, the soothe for to seyne'" (II, 520).

Criseyde asks Pandarus to recount how he acquired his privileged insight into Troilus's secret: "how first ye wisten ... / Woot noon of it but ye?" (II, 501–2). His candid answer is: subterfuge—"Tho gan I stalke hym softely behynde" (II, 519). The phrasing of Pandarus's reply recalls that memory itself is a re-*calling*: "As I kan clepe ayein now to mynde" (II, 521). His present account (II, 518–71) contradicts in some crucial details the textual record and the audience's recollection of Troilus's somewhat embarrassing behavior in Book I, however. There was no talking in a garden by a well (II, 508–10); there was no playing with javelins (II, 513); there was no napping on the lawn (II, 515). All these added vignettes present a more attractive (and so seductive) portrait of Troilus, who did certainly complain (II, 522), and there was a pseudo-sacramental confession or two (II, 525–29, 579–80), and there was some head-smiting and muttering, no doubt, and Pandarus did play dumb, and the lovesickness of Troilus was both intense and loud—"so soore grone / Ne herde I nevere" (II, 557–58)—and Pandarus did need to outdo himself rhetorically, "And God woot, nevere sith that I was born / Was I so besy no man for to preche" (II, 568–69). But Pandarus suppresses any mention of Troilus's "coward herte" (I, 792):

> But now to yow rehercen al his speche,
> Or alle his woful wordes for to sowne,
> Ne bid me naught, but ye wol se me swowne. (II, 572–74)

It would be a showstopper if the reciter were now really to swoon; if Chaucer only started to swoon, however, mimicking Pandarus's make-believe gesture, the tonal effect would be only momentarily amusing.

Pandarus again prompts Criseyde to grant Troilus "cheer" (II, 578). And again Pandarus defends the innocence of this proposition: "And sith ye woot that myn entent is cleene, / Take heede therof, for I non yvel meene" (II, 580–81). Pandarus wants them simply to meet, but Criseyde apparently reads too much into his past participle "*ymet*" (II, 586; mated?)—"'Nay, therof spak I nought, ha, ha!' quod she; / 'As helpe me God, ye shenden every deel!'" (II, 589–90)—but perhaps no more than Chaucer intended to imply aloud.[11] Insisting one more time that "what so I spak, I mente naught but wel" (II, 592), Pandarus finally does make his exit (II, 596).

Left alone, Criseyde reviews her conversation with Pandarus, like a solitary reader reflecting upon the text:

> ... streght into hire closet wente anon,
> And set hire doun as stylle as any ston,
> And every word gan up and down to wynde
> That he had seyd, as it com hire to mynde. (II, 599–602)

This silent reiteration "right for the newe cas" astonishes Criseyde herself (II, 603–4). "But as she sat allone and thoughte thus"

---

11. As part of his more general consideration and the controversial ambiguity of Chaucer's puns (i.e., D. W. Robertson's reading of "quaint"), John Fleming validates Thomas Ross's reading of sexual innuendo of Pandarus's puns (hool, ring, ruby) by reference to the fifteenth elegy of the second book of Ovid's *Amores*; "given our moral and linguistic distance from the fourteenth century, our misreadings are quite as likely to be underreadings as overreadings" (Fleming, *Classical Imitation*, 8–9).

BOOK II, ECHO CHAMBERS

(II, 610), her study is disturbed by shouts calling everyone ("we") to see the grand (and somewhat Freudian) entrance of Troilus through the city gates (II, 615–16).

Criseyde then beholds Troilus himself as "a knyghtly sighte" (II, 628). Chaucer apparently shares Criseyde's excitement as a spectator of this show: "And ek to seen hym ... so weldy semed he/It was an heven upon hym for to see" (II, 635–37).[12] For one stanza, Chaucer shows us, "the peple," a glimpse of war-battered Troilus. Troilus sees himself being seen and blushes and soberly "caste down his yën" (II, 648) like a modest maiden on display. It is this "chere" that causes Criseyde to recite to herself (II, 651) what Isolde would say in a future book.[13]

With the exception of a three-stanza aside, a one-stanza digression about astrology, a one-line transition, and a two-line footnote, lines 651 to 812 of Book II all present Criseyde's solitary reflections, what she spoke aloud (II, 703–63), what she thought silently (II, 771–805). Chaucer describes her body language and her conflict with Thought itself (II, 652, 656, 660, 694, 701, 768, 769, 806). Chaucer's always omnipresent, never omniscient, voice thus invades Criseyde's privacy to reveal her anxieties about being revealed. Chaucer can thoroughly identify with Criseyde's spotlighted performance here as *confabulator* of her own story.[14]

Since Criseyde has fallen in love almost at first sight, she an-

---

12. Chaucer emphasizes both the reader's (II, 632, 635, 637) and Criseyde's (II, 649) pleasure in seeing Troilus.

13. Barney doubts that Criseyde's remark alludes specifically to the love-potion scene of *Tristan and Isolde*. Criseyde's recognition of her own infatuation may signify a more generic sense of "love-drunkenness" as in Gower's *Confessio Amantis* VI, 76–529 (*Riverside*, 1033, n. 651; cf. II, 718, 784). If anyone in Chaucer's audience made the specific association, however, then the factual error becomes a recital effect.

14. Glending Olson considers Chaucer's narrative role in his dream-visions to be highly recollective of a *confabulator* and "typical of the way much medieval literature was presented ... as part of conversational entertainment" (*Literature as Recreation in the Later Middle Ages* [Ithaca, N.Y.: Cornell University Press, 1982], 84).

75

BOOK II, ECHO CHAMBERS

ticipates that "now myghte som envious jangle thus" (II, 666). She then mimics three lines of such mean-spirited chat, "ye, parde" (II, 667–69). In his own voice, Chaucer renounces such sarcasm with a curse: "whoso seith so, mote he nevere ythe!" (II, 670). Here and now (unlike Book V), Chaucer can sound effectively dismissive of suspicious minds: "For I sey nought . . ." (II, 673–79). The heavens may or may not have compelled Criseyde's seemingly sudden choice. Chaucer does observe that the planet Venus has favored speedy Troilus (II, 686), but almost as an afterthought "and also . . . and soth to seyne" (II, 680–84). As translator, Chaucer too must obey certain textually predestined imperatives: "And what she thoughte somwhat shal I write, / As to myn auctour listeth for t'endite" (II, 699–700). But his recital reactions can still rebel freely; Chaucer's tone hardly follows Boccaccio's star. Whereas Criseida "starts off with simple hedonism," Chaucer has Criseyde first praise Troilus's propriety, at least so "seith men" (II, 724).[15] Furthermore, Criseyde predicts she will give Troilus no occasion to "avaunt" (II, 726–27). She grants her attractiveness "so men seyn" (II, 748) and finally concedes to herself that she is "naught religious" (II, 759). She almost surrenders to her own persuasiveness till she remembers (or espies) from the example of other "folk": "Ther loveth noon, that she nath why to pleyne" (II, 775–77).

Criseyde keeps trying to talk herself out of loving, while Chaucer's recital already shows that she truly is so enthralled. She knows that love (even in the Maytime of Book II) is stormy, that Isolde's love potion turns into a drink of woe (II, 784), that men are untrue (II, 786), and especially that people will talk:

---

15. Windeatt, *Troilus* (1984), 187, nn. 694ff.

"Also thise wikked tonges ben so prest / To speke us harm" (II, 785–86)

"How bisy, if I love, ek most I be / To plesen hem that jangle of love" (II, 799–800)

"And who may stoppen every wikked tonge, / Or sown of belles whil that thei ben ronge?" (II, 804–5)

For now, Criseyde surrenders to the inevitability of her tale being told (by Chaucer), and so begins "to pleye" (II, 812, 817).

Criseyde joins her three nieces in their garden where dawn-like Antigone commences "a Troian song to singen cleere, / That it an heven was hire vois to here" (II, 825–26) a song that—coincidentally—answers Criseyde's objections "point for point."[16] Criseyde asks Antigone to identify the author who composed her song "with so good entente" (II, 877).[17] Antigone fails (as does Chaucer) to name, however, "the goodlieste mayde / Of gret estat in al the town of Troye, / And let hire lif in moste honour and joye" (II, 880–82). Criseyde agrees that the excellence of the poem reveals the goodness of its poet, "so it semeth by hire song" (II, 883). This lyric interlude seems a gratuitous delay in Chaucer's plot—unless the song and its author were once familiar to Chaucer's audience,

---

16. *Riverside*, 1034, nn. 827–75. This parallelism has been observed by Sr. M. C. Borthwick. Of course, Criseyde's prior objections have not been heard by Antigone herself. Within the fictional setting, only Criseyde can hear the song's specific though seemingly coincidental relevance. A reader's or an audience's concurrent perception of the song's parallels also recognizes this serendipity as authorial design—her "as I have seyd'" (II, 870) as his reply to what "thei speken" (II, 861).

17. For R. A. Shoaf, this scene serves as an emblem for perceiving Chaucer in the *Troilus*: "The author is not a falsifier, if he and his desires are visible in the construction of his work, as in the case of the maker of Antigone's lyric, then the audience is responsible for its construction of the work. Chaucer, throughout his career in poetry, sought to make himself as visible as possible. Indeed, we see him everywhere—he is no Pandarus with 'wordes whyte' (3. 1567)—and if his visibility often seems to hide him, that is only because we, the audience, are not doing our part" (*Dante, Chaucer, and the Currency of the Word* [Norman, Okla.: Pilgrim, 1983], 132).

making his recital tone immediately clear because his intended compliment was perceived to be immediately relevant.

Antigone assures Criseyde that Cupid's bliss inspires lovers to write fair poetry (II, 885–86). It seems an awkward (so deliberate) accident that at precisely this moment Chaucer strains to rhyme "endite" with "sike" (II, 884, 886).[18] Quoting Antigone's sentiments poses a far more substantial problem for Chaucer's recital tone, however. Anachronism be damned, Antigone insists that sympathy for love poetry requires the listener or reader to have had some personal experience of love:

> Men moste axe at seyntes if it is
> Aught fair in hevene (Why? For they kan telle),
> And axen fendes is it foul in helle. (II, 894–96)[19]

Criseyde herself has nothing to say about the afterlife, "unto that purpos naught answered" (II, 897). Instead, she observes it is getting dark (II, 898), a polite hint that her entourage does not immediately take though Chaucer provides a highly embellished description of the setting sun (II, 904–10).

Criseyde must still spend some unspecified time before "voided were thei that voiden oughte" (II, 912), and so she masks her true reactions to Antigone's recital for a while. But Criseyde has fully imprinted the text of the song in her memory: "every word which that she of hire herde, / She gan to prenten in hire herte faste" (II, 899–900). Criseyde goes to bed, but Chaucer sees no need to explicate her dreamy imagination: "Reherce it nedeth

---

18. Barney notes that this is "the only clear case in Chaucer of an assonance in place of a full rhyme" (*Riverside*, 1034, nn. 884–86).

19. Antigone's analogy sounds like a familiar aphorism in Chaucer's mouth. In his own person (or some textualized surrogate for that "I"), Chaucer at the start of the *Legend of Good Women* questions hearsay testimony that there exists empirical evidence regarding heaven and hell (F- and G-Prologue, 1–16).

noght, for ye ben wise" (II, 917). A nightingale sings vespers about an eagle, the tonal implications of which require no Daniel or Cassandra to interpret.

Chaucer's recital moves on: "Now lat hire slepe, and we oure tales holde / Of Troilus ... of the which I tolde" (II, 932–33). But his *tale* becomes little more than a discussion of how to convey feelings in writing. Troilus's bedroom serves as both a stage and an atelier. Pandarus promises "shorte wordes" (II, 956) to recount his wooing of Criseyde—a rehearsal which Chaucer shortens further: "What sholde I lenger sermoun of it holde? / As ye han herd byfore, al he hym tolde" (II, 965–66). In response to four lines of as many questions (II, 981–94), Pandarus asks his bed-companion for a little more manly calm. Pandarus will coach Troilus to coax Criseyde in writing: "do now as I shal seyn, and far aright" (II, 999).

If he were Troilus, Pandarus "wolde outrely / Of myn owen hand write hire right now / A lettre, in which I wolde hire tellen how," for starters, that "I ferde amys" (II, 1004–7). Pandarus obviously itches to take the quill in hand but tries to restrain himself, instructing Troilus to "now help thiself" (II, 1008) as a letter-writer and lover.[20] Pandarus will settle for the roles of courier (II, 1009) and, more significantly, annotator: "And we shal speek of the somwhat, I trowe, / Whan thow art gon, to don thyn eris glowe!" (II, 1021)

Pandarus is far more concerned with the text's tone than its truth:

---

20. Jonathan Gibson discusses the homosocial bond of secretary and employer ("Letters," in *A Companion to English Renaissance Literature and Culture*, ed. Michael Hathaway, 615–19 [Oxford: Blackwell, 2000], 617). Seth Lerer perceives "the machinations of a voyeur" in the instructor's role in *Courtly Letters in the Age of Henry VIII* (Cambridge: Cambridge University Press, 1997), 7; for Tudor courtiers, Pandarus provided a role model for the "theatrics of minion politics" (Ibid., 37).

> Towchyng thi lettre, thou art wys ynough.
> I woot thow nylt it dygneliche endite,
> As make it with thise argumentes tough;
> Ne scryvenyssh or craftyly thow it write. (II, 1023–26)

The tangible text itself can be enhanced by histrionic touches: "Biblotte it with thi teris ek a lite" (II, 1027). Pandarus warns Troilus to avoid sounding monotonous: "And if thow write a goodly word al softe, / Though it be good, reherce it nought to ofte" (II, 1028–29). Nothing is more tedious than a Johnny-One-Note minstrel (II, 1030–36). Pandarus also condemns mixing tonally disparate patois (with Chaucer's somewhat fishy analogy):

> For if a peyntour wolde peynte a pyk
> With asses feet, and hedde it as an ape,
> It cordeth naught, so were it but a jape. (II, 1041–43)

Troilus apparently listens to this counsel (II, 1044) on tone as a good student should. Chaucer's more sophisticated audience, however, would have more probably been quite amused (if not bemused) by the author's lesson.

Despite all Pandarus's instruction, Troilus suffers writer's block, authorial impotence: "I am ashamed for to write, ywys, / Lest of myn innocence I seyde amys" (II, 1047–48). He is also daunted by the prospect of Criseyde's predisposition as hostile reader, "that she nolde it for despit receyve" (II, 1049). Pandarus warns that only silence makes failure inevitable: "If the lest, / Do that I seye ... I hope of it" (II, 1051–54). Troilus consents to write, confirming the effectiveness of Pandarus's tonal intent—"Sith that the list" (II, 1059).

Troilus begins to write his letter "with good entente" (II, 1060), though all we can read (or hear) is Chaucer's (tonally filtered) paraphrase (II, 1065–84). First, Troilus calls Criseyde "his righte lady" (II, 1065), using pat "termes alle/That in swich cas thise loveres alle seche" (II, 1067–68). Troilus intends to appear suitably humble "as in his speche" (II, 1069). Yet, Chaucer seems a bit bored: "To telle al how, it axeth muchel space" (II, 1071), and "But that was endeles, withouten hoo" (II, 1083). Chaucer compliments Troilus by calling him a liar "ful loude" when he demeans himself too much (II, 1077). And the syntactic choppiness of Chaucer's synopsis might mimic the trepidation of Troilus's expression. But Troilus's rhetoric was reportedly excessive, whereas Chaucer's report is sparse.

Although disinclined to recite Troilus's letter verbatim, Chaucer seems fascinated by the theatrics of its transmission. As its first reader (II, 1085), Troilus makes love to his own text in lieu of its intended recipient (II, 1089–90), but he then becomes jealous of its physical reception (II, 1091–92). Punctual Pandarus serves as postman (II, 1093–94), making sure that his discussion of the letter with Criseyde can be seen but not heard: "he so fer was that the sown/Of that he spak no man heren myghte" (II, 1118–19). As Troilus feared, Criseyde does not welcome the letter: "Scrit ne bille ... Ne bryng me noon ... What sholde I more seye?" (II, 1130–34). Pandarus is forced, therefore, to make a special delivery: "'Refuse it naught,' quod he, and hente hire faste,/ And in hire bosom down he thraste" (II, 1054–55).

The complex tonal significance of this scene resists precise explication. Pandarus uses Criseyde's awareness that they are still in public view to restrict her responses: "Now cast it awey anon,/ That folk may seen and gauren on us tweye" (II, 1156–57). So the full intent of Criseyde's smile remains her secret. She surrenders her right as respondent to the messenger—"Swich answere as yow list, youreself purveye" (II, 1160). And Pandarus promptly exercises that commission. He interprets Criseyde's refusal to "write"

BOOK II, ECHO CHAMBERS

only by the card and so volunteers to act as her amanuensis (II, 1161–62). Readers frequently return to scrutinize the subtext of this exchange. But, during recital, Chaucer's suggestiveness regarding the rapport between uncle and niece must seem what it is: confusing. Some listeners laugh, some smirk, some frown, and the reciter keeps reciting. Criseyde herself laughs at Pandarus's offer to play the scribe. His immediate role, however, is to make her laugh, to play the jester—with himself as the major joke (II, 1163), because such "folye" (II, 1168) is his most tonally effective strategy.

Finding a room of her own, Criseyde reads Troilus's letter as only a solitary reader can: "Ful pryvely this lettre for to rede; / Avysed word by word in every lyne" (II, 1176–77). Her initial review is positive though still reserved. She "fond no lak, she thoughte he koude good, / And up it putte" (II, 1178–79). She snatches instead Pandarus by the hood, who had apparently become distracted in his own "studye" (II, 1180–83). Pandarus then "ful sleighly" (II, 1185) maneuvers Criseyde to a window seat for a pending pageant, unaware that Criseyde has already seen this show. Pandarus covers some delay to Troilus's anticipated entrance with small talk (II, 1191). When he "saugh tyme unto his tale" (II, 1193), Pandarus asks about the letter, claiming—that is, lying that he has not already read it—"I noot" (II, 1197). This discussion of the text physically affects Criseyde more than her solitary reading had. She blushes and hums and so signals to both eye and ear the emotions she would hide (II, 1198–99). Criseyde's copied words reveal only her appreciation of Troilus's writing skills "so I trowe" (II, 1199).

The conversation of Pandarus and Criseyde becomes even more conspicuously enigmatic. Pandarus volunteers to expedite Criseyde's RSVP.[21] If Pandarus's body language seems exuberant,

---

21. Norman Davis explains that the particular significance of a sewn letter is that it "was actually to be sent" (*Paston Letters and Papers of the Fifteenth Century*, Part I [Oxford:

BOOK II, ECHO CHAMBERS

Chaucer's attention to trivial details and possible puns sounds weirder:

> "Myself to medes wol the lettre *sowe*"
> And held his hondes up, and sat on knowe;
> "Now, goode nece, be it nevere so lite,
> Yif me the labour it to *sowe* and plite." (II, 1201–4, my italics)

Criseyde assures she can write: "'Ye, for I kan *so* writen,' quod she tho" (II, 1205), though she does not know what to say. Pandarus says, "Sey nat *so*" (II, 1207). Meanwhile, the real tonal significance of "aquite hym wel" (II, 1200) has been glossed over.

Pandarus prays that Criseyde shall at least thank Troilus (II, 1208). Criseyde claims that she is a virgin letter writer: "God help me so, this is the firste lettre / That evere I wroot, ye, al or any del" (II, 1213–14). Nevertheless, she "sette hire down, and gan a lettre write" (II, 1218) which Chaucer again refuses to read in full: "Of which to telle in short is myn entente / Th' effect as fer as I kan understonde" (II, 1219–20). Recital can make Chaucer's reticence sound like Criseyde's coyness. The gist of this letter is that Criseyde will please Troilus "but as his suster" (II, 1224). Criseyde shuts her reply from view (II, 1226) before handing it over to Pandarus. Having lost her epistolary virginity, she complains about the compulsory assignment: "I nevere dide thing with more peyne / Than writen this, to which ye me constreyne" (II, 1231–32). Pandarus, somewhat tangentially (except to Chaucer), considers the correspondence between the difficulty and the duration of "impressiouns" (II, 1238–41) and then, "Lo ... Lo" (II, 1248, 1284), Troilus appears below.

Clarendon Press, 1971], xxxiv). By offering to sew Criseyde's letter, Pandarus plays a presumably male role as her secretary; however, sewing may also suggest his willingness to undertake a stereotypically feminine chore.

BOOK II, ECHO CHAMBERS

Criseyde tries to part, but Pandarus reminds her she too has a part to play; indeed, they are both now on display "(he seeth us, I suppose)" (II, 1254). Pandarus warns her not to let her body language give the wrong impression. Even without any details about what Troilus in fact sees, the reader can induce the emotional status of Criseyde. Nor does Chaucer here provide a real *descriptio* of Troilus's second procession: "God woot" (II, 1261, 1263), the hero looked as he should. Chaucer focuses instead on the physical effect of his visual attraction upon Criseyde: "What sholde I drecche, or telle of his aray? ... To telle in short, hire liked al in-fere ... To God hope I, she hath now kaught a thorn" (II, 1264–72). With colloquial candor, Chaucer wishes: "God sende mo swich thornes on to pike!" (II, 1274). The audience thus witnesses not Troilus's appearance but Chaucer's delight in Criseyde's impression.

Pandarus insists that Criseyde respond honestly to the moment: "Ye sey me soth / Ye felen wel youreself that I nought lye" (II, 1282–83). He would then have her present her feelings directly to Troilus: "And spek with hym in esying of his herte" (II, 1287). But Chaucer steps forward to speak in defense of Criseyde's reluctance. Intimate conversation is too demanding: "Considered al thing it may nat be" (II, 1290). Furthermore, meeting would make Criseyde appear too easy: "And whi? For speche; and it were ek to soone / To grauntten hym so gret a libertee" (II, 1291–92). Criseyde declares "pleynly hire entente" is to love Troilus "unwist, if she myghte, / And guerdoun hym with nothing but with sighte" (II, 1293–95)—a delight in absence as frustrating as silent reading. Pandarus as plainly ridicules Criseyde's "nyce opynyoun" that Troilus should be satisfied with only visual stimulation for "fully yeres two" (II, 1298). In between their two tones, Chaucer again sounds a bit impatient himself: "What sholde I make of this a long sermoun?" (II, 1299).

BOOK II, ECHO CHAMBERS

Pandarus accepts Criseyde's "conclusioun, / As for the tyme" (II, 1300–1301) and carries Criseyde's letter "homward" (II, 1303) to Troilus, announcing its delivery with a song: "as who seyth, 'Somwhat I brynge,'" (II, 1309)—an *incipit* probably familiar to Chaucer's audience and possibly now sung again before them. Pandarus tries to resurrect "iburied" Troilus (II, 1311) with the promise of a moonlit "charme" (II, 1312–14). But there is nothing truly magical about their joint reading of Criseyde's text:

> And Pandarus gan hym the lettre take,
> And seyde, "Parde, God hath holpen us!
> Have here a light, and loke on al this blake." (II, 1318–20)

Troilus's response to this text vacillates between hope and dread. "But finaly"—because so strongly inclined to do so—"he took al for the beste / That she hym wroot" (II, 1324–25), although the uncertainty of his first reading was Criseyde's intended effect: "Al covered she tho wordes under shield" (II, 1327). But Troilus foregrounds only "the more worthi part" (II, 1328). His desire and hope increase together thereafter–a Procrustean habit "as we may alday oureselven see" (II, 1331).

Both wishful thinking and "Pandarus loore" move Troilus "to preessen on ... and writen" (II, 1341–42) back. Every day, "by Pandare he wroot somwhat or seyde" to Criseyde (II, 1344)—"seyde" here must mean "have Pandarus recite." And every day the perceived (or imagined) tone of Criseyde's reply determines Troilus's mood.[22] With one voice, Pandarus and Chaucer fully commiserate with Troilus's pain "sooth to seyne" (II, 1356), although it truly takes only two days (II, 1362) to convince Criseyde to "here and see" (II, 1372) Troilus in person.

---

22. Windeatt notes that "Troilo is driven to write by his *gran favore* (131/5)" (*Troilus* [1984], 223, n. 1343).

BOOK II, ECHO CHAMBERS

Pandarus imagines Troilus imagining a mini-morality play; "peraunter thynkestow" (II, 1373) Criseyde's *Daunger* will debate her *Kynde* (II, 1374–78). Pandarus promises a positive resolution, a happy catastrophe: "Thenk here-ayeins" (II, 1380) Criseyde will fall for him. Pandarus proposes fast action "now ... now" (II, 1399, 1401). And Chaucer's recital pace seems to accelerate too— "To telle in short, withouten wordes mo" (II, 1405).

To acquire his next set, Pandarus deceives Deiphebus (II, 1404). Pandarus asks Troilus's favorite brother and second-best friend to act as Criseyde's advocate "withouten more speche" (II, 1421): "'Than nedeth,' quod Deiphebus, 'hardyly, / Namore to speke ... I roughte nought though alle hire foos it herde'" (II, 1425–28). Pandarus apparently did not expect this instant consent even from such a favorably disposed listener, and Chaucer must now make his audience hear how he improvises to arrange further consultations: "'But tel me how' ... 'Now lat se'" (II, 1429–30). Pandarus asks Deiphebus to meet Criseyde tomorrow for an interview "hire pleyntes to devise" (II, 1434) and recommends coyly that some "bretheren" (II, 1438) attend this audience. Deiphebus, curiously, perhaps with ulterior motives, proposes Helen first, supposedly because her voice can in turn persuade Paris "as hire leste'" (II, 1449). Deiphebus then conveniently admits that there is no need to trouble Hector (whose presence would only distract Criseyde). Deiphebus finally fulfills Pandarus's original intent when he says, "Spek thow thiself to Troilus / On my behalve" (II, 1457–58).

Pandarus next tells Criseyde a very plausible story about Poliphete's unspecified lies: "Be ye naught war" (II, 1467). Although Criseyde suspects a conspiracy by Aeneas and Antenor, it is Pandarus and Troilus who are truly now conspiring. Criseyde's too-quick concession of the claim (II, 1474–78) catches Pandarus again, as with his appeal to Deiphebus, somewhat by surprise:

"Nay ... it shal nothing be so" (II, 1479). To bolster Criseyde's courage, Pandarus tells the truth about Deiphebus, partly lies about Hector, neglects to name Troilus among "other lordes moo" (II, 1480–81), "and as thei casten what was best to doone," Deiphebus enters as if on cue to deliver his lines "in his propre persone" (II, 1485–87).

Chaucer now sounds almost desperate to pick up the pace:

"To telle in short" (II, 1493)
"But fle we now prolixitee best is / For love of God, and lat us faste go" (II, 1564–65)
"Right to th'effect, withouten tales mo, ... And lat us ... pace" (II, 1566–68)
"But al passe I, lest ye to longe dwelle; / For for o fyn is al that evere I telle" (II,1595–96)
"What shold I lenger in this tale tarien?" (II, 1622)

To accelerate the conclusion of Chaucer's recital, Pandarus must bring stone-still Troilus up to speed, "and al this thyng he tolde hym, word and ende" (II, 1495).

Pandarus shares Chaucer's sense of urgency as the close of Book II draws near. Very soon—"Now is tyme" (II, 1497)—Troilus must take the stage himself; so Pandarus coaches his delivery: "Now spek, now prey, now pitously compleyne ... Somtyme a man mot telle his owen peyne" (II, 1499–1501). Pandarus assures Troilus that "folk" will not see through his masquerade: "For I right now have founden o manere / Of sleyghte, for to coveren al thi cheere" (II, 1511–12).[23] He tells Troilus to seem sick at Deiphe-

---

23. Both Barney and Windeatt neglect to gloss "for to coveren al thi cheere" (II, 1512) probably because the individual words all seem so clear. Pandarus probably intends to be upbeat, promising Troilus "to recover all your happiness," but the phrasing in context also allows a reading that suggests his deceptive means to that happy end, "to camouflage your entire appearance."

bus's house "soth for to seye" (II, 1516). He would help Troilus get in character—"And lat se now how wel thow kanst it make" (II, 1522). Troilus insists that he need not feign a fever since he is "sik in ernest" (II, 1529), which Pandarus takes as a rehearsal remark: "Thow shalt the bettre pleyne, / And hast the lasse need to countrefete" (I, 1531–32). Pandarus approves Troilus's getting in character: "For hym men demen hoot that men seen swete" (II, 1533).

Though he quotes and so must share Pandarus's enthusiasm for the pending action while quoting, Chaucer's asides sound much less than exuberant—"What nedeth yow to tellen" (II, 1541) how Troilus "held forth ay the wyse / That ye han herd Pandare er this devyse" (II, 1546–47). When Deiphebus asks Troilus to befriend Criseyde, he "certayn is," "God woot," willing. "But" Chaucer considers "swich a nede" to ask eager Troilus comparable to asking a madman (or Lancelot) to run wild (II, 1553–54). After guaranteeing that the relationship of Deiphebus and Helen is entirely innocent (II, 1558–60), Chaucer adds, "But God and Pandare wist al what this mente" (II, 1561).

So far, surely, Criseyde remains "al innocent" (II, 1562) of everything going on backstage. Deiphebus's dinner tastes good, but the conversation sounds very gloomy because the host keeps saying "Allas" (II, 1571) and Helen grieves "that pite was to here" (II, 1576–77). Possible cures for Troilus are discussed, but Criseyde knows the correct diagnosis: "But ther sat oon, al list hire nought to teche, / That thoughte, 'Best koud I yet ben his leche'" (II, 1581–82). The tone of Chaucer's remark duplicates the tone of Criseyde's unspoken comment; they share a momentary smirk. Chaucer thus shows his audience what Criseyde hides from the Trojan company. Criseyde's imagination becomes more actively involved in listening: "Herde al this thyng Criseyde wel inough, / And every word gan for to notifie" (II, 1590–91). She reacts ambiguously

BOOK II, ECHO CHAMBERS

and still silently: "For which with sobre cheere hire herte lough" (II, 1592). This textual observation reveals Criseyde's hidden emotions; Chaucer's recital tone allows us to envision her blushing.

After dinner, Pandarus "brak al that speche anon" (II, 1600), telling Deiphebus it is time "as I yow preyde" to change the topic of their conversation, "to speke here" instead about Criseyde's alleged needs (II, 1602–3). Helen "took first the tale" (II, 1605) and leaps to a verdict. Chaucer quotes her sisterly support as a syntactically twisted curse (II, 1607–10). Deiphebus asks Pandarus to speak for Criseyde in this "cas ... for thow kanst best it telle" (II, 1611–12), and Pandarus then gladly takes center stage. Chaucer both admires and derides the effectiveness of this performance: "He rong hem out a proces lik a bel" (II, 1615). The dinner guests intensify one another's responses—"Answerde of this ech werse of hem than other" (II, 1618)—until they achieve the unanimity—"Pleynliche, alle at ones" (II, 1623)—of a lynch mob (II, 1620).

Helen "than" asks Pandarus if her "brother" knows of "this matere"; she must promptly clarify which brother(-in-law) she means—Hector first, then Troilus (II, 1625–27). Chaucer lets Pandarus leap through this opening with tripping politeness:

Ye, but wole ye now me here?
Me thynketh this, sith that Troilus is here,
It were good, if that you [Helen and Deiphebus] wolde assente,
She [Criseyde] tolde hireself hym al this er she wente.
For ...
By cause, lo, ...
And, by youre leve.... (II, 1628–36)

Pandarus then quickly hops from one set to another where he whispers (as should the reciter) to corpse-like Troilus. Panda-

BOOK II, ECHO CHAMBERS

rus kids the slugabed that he has brought a coffin: "ibrought have I thi beere!" (II, 1637–38), which translates in recital as "get ready!" Pandarus returns to Helen and Deiphebus "withouten rekenynge" (II, 1640), a hasty thrill that the reciter should likewise convey. Pandarus warns that Troilus is a fragile audience, "and as he may enduren, he wol here" (II, 1645). Furthermore, his closet, a "chaumbre ... but lite" (II, 1646–47), will become too hot if overcrowded. Pandarus simply wants Deiphebus and Helen to go without Criseyde and then to get out. Pandarus uses flattery (II, 1652) to explain why they should visit first with only himself, "for I kan in a throwe/Reherce hire cas unlik that she kan seye" (II, 1655–56). More importantly, and perhaps even plausibly, Pandarus explains two reasons why Criseyde should not join them: Troilus will clam up because she acts "straunge" (II, 1660), and there are some matters of state "that toucheth [Criseyde] nought to here/He wol yow telle—I woot it wel right now—/That secret is" (II, 1662–64). Only after Deiphebus and Helen exit should Criseyde make her cameo appearance "ones" to state her plea "in short, and take hire leve" (II, 1657–58). Deiphebus and Helen "nothyng knewe of his entente" and "in they wente" (II, 1665–66).

Helen takes center stage for two stanzas (II, 1667–80); her wit comforts Troilus, she commands him to heal. Helen's goodly, soft "wyse" (II, 1667) allows Chaucer briefly "wommanly to pleye" (II, 1668) her lines and gestures as best he could, as she best could (II, 1673). With one of Chaucer's most amusing though literally distasteful conceits, Pandarus then "gan newe his tong affile" (II, 1681). Chaucer's pen mutes this tonally pointless speech, however: "And al hire cas reherce and that anon./Whan it was seyd, soone after in a while" (II, 1682–83).

Not surprisingly, Pandarus convinces Troilus, who promises to support Criseyde's cause "as sone as I may gon" (II, 1684),

BOOK II, ECHO CHAMBERS

pretending not to know of her proximity. Pandarus suggests that Criseyde come herself to take her leave of Troilus. "And with that word" Troilus feels a need "to speke of a matere" (II, 1692–94). Troilus has a prop handy "as hap was" (II, 1696) at his bed's head: "The copie of a tretys and a lettre" (II, 1697) sent to him by Hector regarding the capital punishment of "woot I noot who" (II, 1700). This text's sole function is to accelerate the *exeunt* of Troilus's brother and sister-in-law from the present scene for "the mountance of an houre" (II, 1707). Chaucer asks us to respect the privacy of Deiphebus and Helen as they go to read "into an herber greene" (II, 1705-8)—unchaperoned, but quite all right, no doubt, "now lat hem rede, and torne we anon" (II, 1709).

Chaucer insists Criseyde remains "al innocent of Pandarus entente" (II, 1724) and evidently disinclined to enter Troilus's bedroom. Pandarus anticipates, at first proposes, but then declines Criseyde's desire to have a chaperone other than himself: "take with yow youre nece, Antigone, / [pause] Or whom yow list; [pause] or no fors; hardyly / The lesse prees, the bet" (II, 1716–18). With a magistrate's voice, Pandarus charges—that is, both *conjures* and highly *defends* (II, 1733)—Criseyde to care more about Troilus within than gossips without. Pandarus then dismisses the blind gossip of mere folk by ridiculing its performance:

> In titeryng, and pursuyte, and delayes,
> The folk devyne at waggyng of a stree;
> ... For she, and she
> Spak swych a word; thus loked he, and he! (II, 1744–48; cf. II, 43–46)

In recital, each "she" and each "he" may have been pointed at one member of Chaucer's audience to achieve a present jest equivalent to the text's cajoling tone.

BOOK II, ECHO CHAMBERS

Book II ends with a strangely irresolute *demande des lectuers* (or *auditeurs*) addressed "now to yow, ye loveres that ben here" (II, 1751). What shall Troilus, after listening with us to these whisperings of Pandarus and Criseyde, say next (II, 1757)? After some delay (and much intervening confabulation) and an odd proem, Chaucer answers.

4

BOOK III, PILLOW TALK
AND BEDROOM EYES

THE SUSPENSE achieved by Book II's cliffhanger need last no longer than the turning of a page. Chaucer describes a fictional time gap, "al this mene while" (III, 50), between the April of Book I and the May of Book II, an expression that can also acknowledge some intermission between his first two recital installments—time for the audience to have guessed and chatted and perhaps argued and so caused the author's pronounced "destresse" (III, 46) now. The first forty-nine lines of Book III are the most purely lyrical of Chaucer's three proems. Their very artiness has inspired radically contradictory interpretations of Chaucer's intended tone, however. Donald W. Rowe, for example, reads this proem as an expression of "the narrator's confusion and lack of control, a seeming inability to distinguish the Holy Spirit from Jove the ravisher."[1] But A. C. Spearing maintains that "Chaucer's poetic style reaches its height in a magnifi-

---

1. Donald W. Rowe, *"O Love, O Charite!": Contraries Harmonized in Chaucer's Troilus* (Carbondale: Southern Illinois University Press, 1976), 159.

cently sustained periphrastic apostrophe to Venus."[2] Serving as love's acolyte, Chaucer may have actually chanted this hymn as his introit to this part of the "servyse" (III, 42).

Chaucer celebrates Venus's informing power, the "vapour eterne" (III, 11) that unites all things.[3] Chaucer conceives of the goddess as if she were Anima (III, 15–16) because Boccaccio did, and all this text's singular apostrophes ("ye") are addressed to her.[4] Chaucer's recital, however, can redirect this elaborate praise to thank his principal patron, a certain "lady bryght," here and "now" (III, 39), as well as "hem that serven the" (III, 40). Chaucer addresses Calliope in the seventh stanza on similarly familiar terms ("thi," "sestow"). Thus, Chaucer can voice all this flattery as immediately functional; these compliments enhance his subservient familiarity as "clerc" (III, 40–41)—"For now is nede ... How I mot telle anonright" (III, 46–47).

The story proper restarts with "Troilus / Recordyng his lesson in this manere: 'thus wol I sey, and thus ... That word is good'" (III, 51–54). His *recording* requires anticipation of a convincing *actio* as well as a considered *pronuntiatio*: "and this shal be my cheere; / This nyl I nought foryeten in no wise" (III, 54–55). Chaucer has nothing but sympathy for the task: "God leve hym werken

---

2. Spearing, *Textual Subjectivity*, 80.

3. Chaucer is here invoking "the good Venus," closely associated with Natura, whom George D. Economou finds "more prominent, because of Troilus's devotion to her and the narrator's respect for her, but the wicked Venus has her moments, particularly in the Trojan parliament and with Criseyde in the Greek camp" ("The Two Venuses and Courtly Love," in *In Pursuit of Perfection: Courtly Love in Medieval Literature*, ed. Joan M. Ferrante and G. D. Economou, 17–50 [Port Washington, N.Y.: Kennikat Press, 1975], 40). The hylomorphism of Chaucer's third proem is clearly informed by Boccaccio's conceit; as Thomas C. Stillinger observes, the "Proem of Boccaccio's *Filostrato* describes the discovery of a form. In fact, the word "forma" appears twice, with two very different applications" in reference to both Troilo and the text (*The Song*, 118).

4. If "Venus" is imagined as the *senhal* of some lady present in Chaucer's audience, then "to Venus heryinge" (III, 48) can be played as an audible pun; in addition to denoting "for the sake of praising Venus" it might suggest "for her to hear."

BOOK III, PILLOW TALK

as he kan devyse!" (III, 56). The author then becomes particularly attentive to the mistakes of first impressions.

Pandarus enters, leading Criseyde by the "lappe" (or flap of her skirt) (III, 59; cf. II, 448). Troilus kneels, a gesture of adoration that Criseyde finds excessive: "'O, for the love of God, do ye nought so / To me,' quod she, 'I! What is this to seye?'" (III, 73–74). Criseyde says she has only two reasons for being dragged here in person: to thank Troilus and to ask "of youre lordshipe eke / Continuance" (III, 76–77). Since Troilus takes *lordship* (III, 79) to mean much more than Criseyde truly intends, he completely forgets his prepared lines: "And sire, his lessoun, that he wende konne / To preyen hire, is thorugh his wit ironne" (III, 83–84).[5] Criseyde actually prefers Troilus's choked intensity to "malapert" or "tough" or "bold" suitors who "synge a fool a masse" (III, 87–88). Chaucer sounds a little shaky himself: "His resons, as I may my rymes holde, / I yow wol telle, as techen bokes olde" (III, 90–91). Troilus can speak only "in chaunged vois, ... / Which vois ek quook"; his "verray drede" causes stage fright, or performance anxiety (III, 92–93).

At first, Troilus can say only four words: "Mercy, mercy, swete herte!" Chaucer draws particular attention to his phrasing, "the alderfirste word ... /Was twyes ... / And stynte a while" (III, 97–99). When Troilus recovers enough to utter "the nexte word" (III, 100), he falters (echoed in the rhythm of Chaucer's recital). If what he says "thus muche as now" (III, 106) displeases Criseyde, Troilus promises to kill himself gladly "syn that ye han herd me somwhat seye" (III, 111). Chaucer assures his audience that Troilus's "manly sorwe to biholde" (III, 113) should move even stonehearted spectators, and Pandarus demonstrates by weeping "as

---

5. If not a scribal error—i.e., "and sure"—Chaucer's peculiar interjection "and sire" (or "Oh boy!") must be read like "but Lord" in the preceding line, unless Chaucer actually once did appeal for the special understanding of a specific "sir" in his audience.

BOOK III, PILLOW TALK

he to water wolde, / And poked evere his nece new and newe" (III, 115–16). Unfortunately, Criseyde does not know her lines: "I not nat what ye wilne that I seye'" (III, 121). Pandarus tries to prompt her (III, 122–23), but she first needs to know Troilus's motivation for this scene: "I wolde hym preye / To telle me the fyn of his entente. / Yet wist I nevere wel what that he mente" (III, 124–26).

Troilus does find his voice, taking three stanzas to explain: "What that I mene ... Lo, this mene I" (III, 127–47). The very conventionality of his expressions—for example, "frendly"(III, 130), "don yow my servise" (III, 133), "right as yow list, comfort"(III, 136), "honoure" (III, 139)—keep Troilus's intentions unclear, to Criseyde. Pandarus ridicules her hesitation: "Lo, here an hard requeste" (III, 148). Criseyde remains coy for a moment: "she gan hire yen on hym caste ... and hied nought to faste / With nevere a word, but seyde hym softely" (III, 155–58). She whispers that she will accept Troilus's *honorable* service "and in swich forme as he gan now devyse" (III, 160).

Criseyde admits that she has been pretending standoffishness, promising not to continue "hennesforth, iwys" (III, 167), and she indeed stops referring to Troilus in the third person. She insists on defining her own terms for their relationship (III, 171–72), however, and notes her promise is conditional (III, 180). That said, when it comes to performing a first kiss, Criseyde takes the lead (III, 182). At this sight, Pandarus imagines church bells ringing (III, 187–89; cf. II, 1615). Pandarus must adjust his exuberant tone as soon as he observes Deiphebus and Helen return. Criseyde leaves, and "in hire absence" (III, 214) she becomes an object of conversation. Troilus and Pandarus praise Criseyde so "wonder wel" that "it joie was to here" (III, 217). Yet again, we hear only the reciter's reaction to the unrecorded conversation.

Chaucer invites his audience's attention to leave Criseyde:

BOOK III, PILLOW TALK

"Now lat hire wende ... and torne we to Troilus ayein" (III, 218–19). Troilus only "lightly" glances at the text that has so preoccupied the attention of Deiphebus and Helen. He asks to be excused from further talk "and seyde that hym leste / To slepe, and after tales have reste" (III, 223–24). After less than a stanza's rest, however, Pandarus returns "as lyne right" (III, 228) to entertain tired Troilus again "with mery chere, / To tale" (III, 230–31). A remarkable performance follows, "whan every wight was voided but they two" (III, 232). Chaucer promises "to telle in short, withouten wordes mo" (III, 234) what Pandarus said "in a sobre wyse / To Troilus, as I shal yow devyse" (III, 237–38).

The recital act of direct quotation makes Pandarus's pun and his anxiety as go-between Chaucer's own: "I sey it for no bost, / ... For shame it is to seye: / ... I bigonne a gamen pleye / ... That is to seye ... / Bitwixen game and ernest swich a *meene* ... / Al sey I nought, thou wost wel what I *meene*" (III, 248–56). Pandarus calls upon Chaucer's omniscient god to witness his good intent (III, 260), but his primary concern is to avoid any bad publicity for Criseyde, whose name remains blameless "as yet" (III, 267). Pandarus dreads that, if all his "engyn" were known, "al the world upon it wolde crie" (III, 274–77). So he prays for "privitee ... That is to seyn ... ofte ... To holden secree" (III, 283–86). Chaucer's recital, obviously, ignores this request as Pandarus continues to talk a good deal about not talking.

Pandarus, recalling the woe caused by "avantes, as men rede" (III, 289), warns Troilus not to talk too much: "For which thise wise clerks that ben dede / Han evere yet proverbed ... / That 'first vertu is to kepe the tonge'" (III, 292–94). Such sayings of old still speak to "us yonge" (III, 293). Pandarus renounces prolixity: "And nere it that I wilne as now t'abregge / Diffusioun of speche I could almoost / A thousand olde stories the allegge" (III, 295–

97

BOOK III, PILLOW TALK

97).[6] But, before getting "to purpos" (III, 330), Chaucer grants Pandarus another four stanzas to berate "O tonge" (III, 302–22).[7] Boasters, especially liars, cause women to distrust "us men" (III, 322)—not, of course, Troilus: "I sey nought this for no mistrust of *yow*" (III, 323), whom Pandarus more commonly addresses as "thou." Perhaps, Chaucer also meant to except some other *you* "in the werld is now'" (III, 323–25) as well as singularly trustworthy Troilus—"For wel I woot, *thow* menest wel, parde" (III, 337).

Pandarus has exhausted himself. Chaucer can yawn too: "Have now good nyght" (III, 341), though the text demands that he continue reciting the response of energized Troilus after "herying th' effect" of Pandarus's behest (III, 346). Troilus hopes to die "if I lye" (III, 374).[8] He will swear on every shrine in Troy (III, 384). He vows to serve as Pandarus's slave (III, 391). Such hyperbolic intensity sounds either remarkable or ridiculous as Chaucer pleases.

Troilus then wonders if he has misread Pandarus's misinterpretation of his intentions: "As I shal seyn: me thoughte by thi speche" (III, 395). In defiance of what Chaucer is making common knowledge, Troilus assures Pandarus that he will never be accused of "bauderye"; instead, "calle it gentilesse / Compassioun, and felawship, and trist" (III, 397–403). Intentionality (or self-deception) can distinguish friendship from pimping because "ther is diversite required / Bytwixen thynges like, as I have lered'" (III,

6. Barney glosses "allegge" as "cite" (*Riverside*, 517, n. 297). Windeatt glosses the verb as "adduce. See MED s.v. allegen v. (1)2(a)" (*Troilus* [1984], 301, n. 297). Pandarus and Chaucer may be speaking etymologically and so mean "to read to" in the same lexical context as this verb's rhyme-mate "abregge" (III, 295).

7. Neither Barney nor Windeatt reads "O tonge . . . Hath" as a vocative (Windeatt, *Troilus* [1984], 265, nn. 302–3). It could, however, be recited as "Oh, tongue!" by Chaucer; cf. *CT* 9, 317–62.

8. Chaucer has Troilus anticipate dying by Achilles's spear, a sadly prophetic or darkly ironic nonce phrase (cf. V, 1806). Troilus also somewhat gratuitously denies the immortality of his own soul (III, 375–76), the ultimate disposition of which Chaucer later denies knowing.

BOOK III, PILLOW TALK

405–6). Troilus then offers to procure three of his own sisters by name "or any of the frape—/ ... Tel me which thow wilt of everychone" (III, 410–12). This counteroffer, stripped of any mitigating tone of voice (for example, childish innocence), looks far too rude. But overeager Troilus simply wants Pandarus to "perfourme it out" (III, 417), and "it" means all the remaining buildup to this book's climax. To achieve that "it," Chaucer has Troilus perform white lies, self-excusing dissimulation, public posturing, private suspicion, confident error, professed ignorance, and sometimes studied obtuseness. Troilus's intentions become so encrypted "that al tho that lyven, soth to seyne, / Ne sholde han wist, by word or by manere, / What that he mente ... so wel dissimilen he koude" (III, 430–34).

Chaucer's recital pace itself simulates "al the while" (III, 435) before Troilus gets Criseyde. Chaucer describes his own act of description more than Troilus's actions: "which that I yow devyse, / This was his lif" (III, 435–36). Chaucer hesitates to testify, for example, how "disesed" Troilus actually was: "Nil I naught swere ... For aught I woot ... That kan I deme of possibilitee" (III, 442–48). In order to regain his narrative momentum, the reciter seems to be skipping pages: "But certeyn is, to purpos for to go, / That in this while, as writen is in geeste" (III, 449–50). Troilus and Criseyde "somtyme ... spoken in so short a wise" and only most surreptitiously, "lest any wight ... to it laye an ere"; since Chaucer effectively erases their conversation, he too prevents that "any wight" be able to "devynen or devyse" (III, 451–59) its full significance.

Chaucer, in short, blocks our view but tells us the gate of joy was opened (III, 469). Troilus and Criseyde have prayed together (even if apart) that Cupid "maken of hire speche aright an ende" (III, 462)—that is, a happy conclusion and/or an end to mere talk.

BOOK III, PILLOW TALK

Troilus and Criseyde speak "litel," but they do so most efficiently. Indeed, Criseyde believes in telepathy: "It semed hire he wiste what she thoughte / Withouten word" (III, 465–66).

"And shortly" Chaucer wants to pick up the "pace" of "this process" (III, 470). During this interim, Troilus has proven himself by both "werk and wordes" (III, 471) so "wis" that Criseyde will no longer behave "afered," an assertion which Chaucer quickly qualifies with a nervous pun: "I mene, as *fer* as oughte ben requered," (III, 482–83). If the approaching liaison between Troilus and Criseyde seems overhasty, it is primarily because Chaucer's running remarks make it sound as if he might think so:

> "But to the grete effect: than sey I thus," (III, 505)
> "That it bifel right as I shal yow telle" (III, 511)
> "Right for the fyn that I shal speke of here" (III, 513)
> "Now is ther litel more for to doone / ... and, shortly for to seyne" (III, 547–48)
> "Ye han wel herd the fyn of his entente" (III, 553)
> "And finaly he swor and gan hire seye / By this and that" (III, 556–57)
> and—somewhat belatedly—"But to the point" (III, 604)

It is only the distance of Chaucer's actual voicing that makes such tonally charged remarks look like pointless filler.

"Absent" (III, 488) Troilus too must settle for written communication in lieu of face-to-face suggestiveness. Chaucer especially admires that no one has ever carried letters better than Pandarus (III, 489–90). Chaucer spends some time saying he cannot now repeat what has not been reported.[9] But he assumes Troilus and Criseyde lived "in concord and quiete ... As I have tolde" for some in-

---

9. Lisa Kiser observes that "several of the narrator's deluded assumptions about storytelling are exposed in this single address to the reader" (*Truth*, 57).

BOOK III, PILLOW TALK

definite "tyme swete" (III, 506–8). It goes without saying that they desired more togetherness: "Save only often myghte they nought mete, / Ne leiser have hire speches to fulfelle" (III, 509–10).

Pandarus plans a little get-together "right for the fyn that I shal speke of here" (III, 513). Chaucer shares the maestro's enthusiasm for this "gret deliberacioun" (III, 519): "Now al is wel" (III, 528). His recital "shortly for to seyne" (III, 548) casts us as co-conspirators: "Ye han wel herd the fyn of his entente" (III, 553). With jokes (III, 555) and whispers (III, 566–67), Pandarus invites Criseyde to supper. At first, she simply refuses with a laugh, but they eventually "fille at one" (III, 565)—to concord, though Chaucer adds a strange discord: "Or elles, softe he swor hire in hire ere, / He nolde never comen ther she were" (III, 566–67). The most innocent reading of this compound sentence is that Pandarus will boycott her company if she does not accept this invitation. If voiced as a promise regarding the invitation, darker implications can be heard in Chaucer's whisper. Criseyde whispers back; she asks a completely transparent question: "if Troilus were there" (III, 569). In reply, Pandarus simply lies: "He swor hire nay" (III, 570), but adds, "Nece, I pose that he were; / Yow thurste nevere han the more *fere*" (III, 572). If Chaucer intends to pun "fear" with "fere" ("companion"), he must do so with audible emphasis. Yet, Chaucer clearly intends not to clarify Criseyde's comprehension of her uncle's inference: "Nought list myn auctour fully to declare / What that she thoughte ... / As if he seyde therof soth or no" (III, 575–78). Criseyde remains wary "of goosissh poeples speche, / That dremen thynges which as nevere were" (III, 584–85); nevertheless, she says yes. She trusts her uncle to advise himself regarding the guest list—she tells him so—and accepts the invitation. After happily joining Pandarus's victory dance, Chaucer gathers himself— "what sholde I more telle?" (III, 589–93).

BOOK III, PILLOW TALK

Criseyde comes to dinner with a rather large entourage, who will notice nothing of significance. Chaucer's audience, however, can share Troilus's perspective as a peeping Tom: "who was glad, who, as trowe ye" (III, 599). Antigone plus certain men and nine or ten women (III, 596–98) are entertained but miss the real show. Criseyde would necessarily take her leave. But Chaucer and Fortune intervene; "this mene I now" (III, 621) that Criseyde must stay put. Pandarus invites Criseyde to make herself at home in a house she probably owns (III, 635; cf. II, 1478).[10] Pandarus would be shamed if Criseyde departed now: "I sey it nought a-game" (III, 636). Chaucer claims that Criseyde can be savvy, "which that koude as muche good / As half a world" (III, 638–39). Criseyde claims that she was only kidding all along: "I seyde but a-game I wolde go" (III, 648). Even Pandarus seems a bit confused—"Were it a game or no, soth for to telle" (III, 650)—and, if so sounds Chaucer, so will be his listeners.

Pandarus recommends that Criseyde "dar I seye" (III, 661) take his bedroom to escape the "noyse" (III, 662). He assures her that the women, who block his access, will answer should she call (III, 686). But Chaucer incessantly reminds us that the storm is incredibly loud: "so wondirliche loude, / That wel neigh no man heren other koude"(III, 678–79), "so loude ... / That no wight oother noise myghte heere" (III, 743–44).

Meanwhile, the stage having been set "ther as I have seyd" (III, 689), Troilus has been waiting "stille as stoon" (III, 699). With quick paraphrase, Chaucer tries to help Pandarus "his wirk begynne" (III, 697) by accelerating his own task: "And shortly

---

10. Carolyn Collette discusses the economic independence of Criseyde in "Criseyde's Honor: Interiority and Public Identity in Chaucer's Courtly Romance," in *Literary Aspects of Courtly Culture: Selected Papers from the Seventh Triennial Congress of the International Courtly Literature Society*, ed. Donald Maddox and Sara Sturm-Maddox, 47–55 (Woodbridge: D.S. Brewer, 1994).

BOOK III, PILLOW TALK

to the point right for to gon, / Of al this werk he tolde hym word and ende" (III, 701–2). As direct quotation increases, Chaucer's own recital tone becomes subordinate to genuine impersonation but never completely silent. Troilus (and so Chaucer for a while) sounds like an increasingly verbose virgin, spending three full stanzas on his pathetic bedtime prayers that only postpone "this werk that is bygonne" (III, 715–35). Pandarus reprimands Troilus, dresses him, and then leads the mouse by his "lappe" through a trapdoor (III, 736–42).

Pandarus "with a ful sobre cheere" shuts the outer door and goes to wake Criseyde, and Chaucer's syntax (marked by two pauses per line) tiptoes too (III, 747–49). Criseyde asks "Who goth there?" (III, 751) with a startled voice, or perhaps not. Pandarus hears wonder and fear in her guard-like challenge (III, 753). Pandarus identifies himself "and seyde hire in hire ere, / 'No word[!]'"; he wants no one else to "heren of oure speche" (III, 754–56). He anticipates and prevents her (supposed) first impulse to call for her attendants who "myghte demen thyng they nevere er thoughte" (III, 763).

Chaucer's voice can again easily appropriate Pandarus's second-person pronouns to work as genuine vocatives addressed to an audience: "ye shul wel understonde, / ... so as ye wommen demen alle ... I meene ... Now wherby that I telle yow al this: / ye woot youreself, as wel as any wight" (III, 771–79). Pandarus has a story "right platly for to seyn" (III, 786) that he has heard from Troilus, who has heard it from a friend. This hearsay about Horaste seems to have far less credibility for Criseyde than had the story about Poliphete. When she had "al this wonder herde" (III, 799), she rebukes both Troilus's gullibility regarding such a friend "whoso tales tolde" (III, 802) and the tattletale's motives: "what wikked spirit tolde hym thus?" (III, 808). His extended response includes lamentation, phil-

103

BOOK III, PILLOW TALK

osophical consolation, and cursing. She chops off her uncle's first attempt to explain this "cas" and challenges him instead to name her accusers: "who tolde hym this?" (III, 841–42). She will give Troilus a talking-to tomorrow (III, 809, 848, 889), perhaps.

Pandarus argues against any such delay as "thus writen clerkes wise" (III, 852). Chaucer punctuates his point with a tongue twister: "For al among that fare / The harm is don, and fare-wel feldefare!" (III, 860–61). The conversation of Pandarus and Criseyde then becomes a duel or a duet. Criseyde reiterates "lief" twice (III, 869, 870) to rebuff Pandarus's pun on "lif" (III, 864, 868)—a wordplay more obvious in recital than print. Since Criseyde's retort recycles his own phrasing, he thinks she means to "make this ensaumple of me" (III, 872), and so he imagines that, in her place, he would not let Troilus suffer all night; only her malice, not folly, would motivate further delay "if that I shal naught lie. / What! Platly" (III, 880). Convinced, a bit, Criseyde offers a token at which Pandarus sneers, "A ryng? ... Ye haselwodes shaken!" (III, 890). If we could hear how Chaucer actually "quod" this idiom, there would be far less need to write so much about exactly what it means. But this act of direct quotation sounds certainly sarcastic in context: "that ryng moste han a stoon / That myghte dede men alyve maken; / And swich a ryng trowe I that ye have non" (III, 891–93). Criseyde's response lacks "discrecioun" (III, 894). A jealous fool might be so easily appeased: "feffe hym with a fewe wordes white" (III, 901). But "this thynge"—this lover, this situation, this tonal context—is entirely different, Pandarus says. Troilus will speak no such "jalous wordes" once Criseyde speaks "o word" (III, 907–10).

Pandarus offers to fetch Troilus at once and stay all night as chaperone if required. Chaucer grants the legitimacy of Criseyde's consenting to this (absurd) offer before she actually does: "This accident so pitous was to here, / And ek so like a sooth at prime

BOOK III, PILLOW TALK

face, / ... No wonder is, syn she did al for goode" (III, 918–24). After so successfully impersonating Pandarus's precedent sarcasm and distress, Chaucer takes a brief time out to excuse Criseyde's acquiescence to such an effective performance. Right after this recital pause, Criseyde admits she is confused by the algebra of love and (more weary than won) accepts rather donnish-sounding Pandarus's tutelage. "Than," and not before, Criseyde surrenders, but still not unconditionally: "doth herof as yow list, / But" she would like to get out of bed (III, 939–40); "I am here al in your governaunce" (III, 945), so long as he and Troilus work discreetly. Chaucer gives Criseyde a rime riche "wise/wise" (III, 942–43), an audible toy for her teeter-tottering concerns. Pandarus hears no ambivalence in her consent, however: "That is wel seyd" (III, 946). So he tells her to stay still in bed (III, 948).

Troilus hits his mark "ful soone," again on his knees with a rehearsed line, "in his beste wyse" (III, 953–55), at which "sodeynliche" (III, 956) blushing Criseyde "kouth nought a word aright out brynge" (III, 958). So Pandarus, who "so wel koude feele / In every thyng, to pleye anon bigan, / And seyde ..." (III, 960–61) almost anything to fill the awkward silence caused by his tongue-tied niece. He says "se ... / Now for youre trouthe, se" the spectacle of Troilus still kneeling, "and with that word" he fetches a cushion (III, 962–64), leaving Chaucer to sound curious about Criseyde's failure to bid Troilus rise: "Kan I naught seyn" what she was feeling, "but wel fynde I" Criseyde pleasantly kissed Troilus with a sigh (III, 967–71). Pandarus rearranges their set so "that ech of yow the bet may other heere" (III, 977). He also adjusts the stage lighting and "fond his contenaunce" to depart "as for to looke upon" some other text (III, 979–80).

Chaucer himself buys that Criseyde's truth stands "on a ground of sikernesse," so she understandably seems a bit miffed

BOOK III, PILLOW TALK

about Troilus's jealous credulousness: "Ne sholde of right non untrouth in hire gesse" (III, 981–84). The tone of Criseyde's following speech—"Thus to hym spak she" (III, 987)—puts Troilus and Chaucer on the spot: faking one's reactions to a fiction is not for amateurs. Criseyde replies with a somewhat prolonged lecture (III, 988–1050) on Troilus's "fantasie" (III, 1032) and "illusioun" (III, 1041) that jealously signifies love. Her truth for "ay" (III, 1000) shall be proven—"what al this is to seyne / Shal wel be told" (III, 1003–4). She proposes to endure trial by ordeal or "oth" (III, 1046) or sortilege or whatever and (if found guilty) death: "What myght I more don or seye?" (III, 1050). And then, after a few persuasive tears, Criseyde "held hire pees; nought a word spak she more" (III, 1057). In response to Criseyde's self-defense, Chaucer himself sounds somewhat hopeful (III, 1059) about such a happy turn of events as "men sen alday, and reden ek in stories" (III, 1063). Troilus, however, "when he hire wordes herde" (III, 1065), is initially nonplused. "What myghte he seyn" (III, 1081)—a normal enough reaction. "But al was hust" (III, 1094) by his physical collapse. The passionate excessiveness of Troilus's heartbreak at this crisis has proven to be such a central interpretive crux for future readers precisely because there are so few textual indicators of Chaucer's original rehearsal tone at this critical moment; the thematic significance of such incomprehensible sincerity remains uncertain for modern readers, therefore. Once too intense Troilus has been "revoked" (III, 1118) to life, Chaucer and Pandarus can both sound playfully skeptical again (for example, III, 1135–37, 1146–47). Less willingly, Troilus, when asked by Criseyde to explain the "sygne" (III, 1152) that (wrongly) motivated his (fraudulent) jealousy, must continue to "feyne ... Noot I nought what, al deere ynough a rysshe / As he that nedes most a cause fisshe" (III, 1158–62). Apparently unsatisfied by his cover story, Criseyde

BOOK III, PILLOW TALK

poses a purely hypothetical question: "al were it so, / What harm" (III, 1163–64) if she let her glance wander "syn I non yvel mene?" (III, 1164). Troilus's counter-arguments in defense of his "contrefete" suspicions are "naught worth a beene" (III, 1167). Perhaps, he needs a good spanking (III, 1168–69).

As if reciting the Pater Noster by rote, Troilus asks Criseyde's forgiveness for his trespasses "if that tho wordes that I seyde / Be any wrong" (III, 1174–75), and she quickly grants Cupid's absolution: "misericorde!" Just in case, she translates her meaning: "That is to seyn" (III, 1177–78). Troilus firmly resolves to sin no more. Criseyde, in turn, asks forgiveness of Troilus "that mente" after all "nothing but wel" (III, 1185–86). Pandarus provides a quick tuck-in "with a ful good entente" (III, 1188).

And Chaucer becomes quite carried away by it all. He asks a rhetorical question: "What myghte or may the sely larke seye, / Whan that the sperhauk hath it in his foot?" (III, 1191–92). But to whom does this analogy apply? To physically taken Criseyde (III, 1187)? To infatuated Troilus? To both? And to whom is the question posed? Chaucer too seems somewhat taken aback by his task in hand: "I kan namore"; furthermore, he has no idea how others will take it:

> ... but of this ilke tweye—
> To whom this tale sucre be or soot—
> Though that I tarie a yer, somtyme I moot,
> After myn auctour, tellen hire gladnesse,
> As wel as I have told hire hevynesse. (III, 1193–97)

And then Criseyde "felte hire thus itake" (III, 1198).[11]

Troilus strains "in armes" to force Criseyde to yield—at least

---

11. Interpretation of the word *raptus* has become one of the most controversial tonal issues in Chaucer studies. See Kathryn Gravdal's *Ravishing Maidens: Writing Rape in*

BOOK III, PILLOW TALK

that is what Troilus is quoted to have "seyde" (III,1205–8). Captured Criseyde triumphs in surrender by disclosing that yielding had been her intent all along or "ywis, I were now nought heere!" (III, 1211). Chaucer interrupts to state his present position about postponed passion: "O, sooth is seyd ... as men may ofte se ... I mene it here" (III, 1212–17).[12] Chaucer promises "and now" (III, 1219) and "now" (3, 1221) and "now" (III, 1223) that prolonged denial, like foreplay, only enhances eventual bliss (III, 1220). Chaucer encourages "every womman ... To werken thus, if it comth to the neede" (III, 1224–25), a blatant sales pitch that might have made even the most obliging lady in Chaucer's audience laugh.

Having targeted himself for some comic relief, Chaucer focuses again on the "feste" of Troilus and Criseyde that "it joye was to sene" (III, 1228). Like a jittery nightingale who sings only when "siker" (III, 1237), Criseyde opens her heart to speak her "entente" (III, 1239). However, as Louise Fradenburg sees, "the narrator ... does not tell us what that 'entente' is," and so "Chaucer draws attention to the inaudibility at the core of this most voluble poem."[13] Apropos of the near-death simile for Troilus (III, 1240–45), Chaucer's anaphora ("And right as ... And ... And ... And") requires an almost drowning loss of breath before the reciter can inhale.

Medieval French Literature and Law (Philadelphia: University of Pennsylvania Press, 1991); Christopher Cannon's "Raptus in the Chaumpiegne Release and a Newly Discovered Document Concerning the Life of Geoffrey Chaucer," *Speculum* 68 (1993): 79–94, and "Chaucer and Rape: Uncertainty's Certainties," *Studies in the Age of Chaucer* 22 (2000): 67–92; my own "The Rapes of Chaucer," *The Chaucer Yearbook* 5 (1998): 1–17; and Corinne J. Saunders's *Rape and Ravishment in the Literature of Medieval England* (Cambridge: D.S. Brewer, 2001).

12. Barry Windeatt omits Stephen Barney's comma after "O," so the exclamation "O, sooth is seyd" reads "O sooth"—that is, "one truth is said." Barney's "here" suggests "here and now," whereas Windeatt's "here as" means "in this case."

13. L. O. Aranye Fradenburg, *Sacrifice Your Love: Psychoanalysis, Historicism, Chaucer* (Minneapolis: University of Minnesota Press, 2002), 229.

BOOK III, PILLOW TALK

Chaucer wishes (for everyone's sake): "With worse hap lat us nevere mete!" (III, 1246), and lets us all enjoy glimpse of naked Criseyde (III, 1247–50). Chaucer's wistfulness makes the sight sound more nostalgic than pornographic.[14] Troilus hardly knows what to do with all this verisimilitude (III, 1253); so he recites a rather clumsy ballade, "than seyde he thus" (III, 1254–74). Starting with a hodgepodge of apostrophes to "Venus mene I " (III, 1257), Troilus's prayer becomes an epithalamion, but only Troilus has read any mention of marriage into the preceding dialogue.[15] He poetizes until he "kan namore" (III, 1273) and "therwithal" kisses Criseyde, "of which certein she felt no disese" (III, 1275–76).

Grandiloquent Troilus carries on—"and thus seyde he"(III, 1277)—a syntactically choppy and theologically flavored (III, 1282, 1284, 1286, 1290) paean to Criseyde that apparently requires some deciphering: "As thus I mene" (III, 1291). Troilus vows, "For certes ... / This dar I seye," he will be true, diligent, and discreet whether "present or in absence" (III, 1300).Criseyde tries to preempt any further verbiage with one word:

But lat us falle awey fro this matere,
For it suffiseth, this that is seyd is heere,
And at o word, withouten repentaunce,
Welcome. (III, 1306–9)[16]

---

14. Windeatt remarks, "The description of love-making is much more explicit in physical detail than Fil 31–32, yet is free of the titillation and archness in Fil" (*Troilus* [1984], 311, n. 1247–53).

15. Troilus may, like Troilo, be thinking of "*another* Venus ... a heavenly Venus who presides over matrimony and the getting of children" as proposed by Robert Hollander in *Boccaccio's Two Venuses* (New York: Columbia University Press, 1977), 5.

16. Barney rejects a suggestion made by James A. Devereux, S.J., that Criseyde's phrasing echoes the "levation prayers" ("A Note on *Troilus and Criseyde*, Book III, Line 1309," *Philological Quarterly* 44 [1965]: 550–52), but Chaucer's quasi-liturgical recital (comparable to his possible chanting of the proem) could achieve such a tone, or parody thereof.

Their ensuing bliss transcends Chaucer's ability to rehearse: "Were impossible to my wit to seye / But juggeth ye that han ben at the feste / ... I kan namoore" (III, 1311–14); the experience itself "is so heigh al ne kan I telle!" (III, 1323), though this mere mention of such inexpressible rapture might catapult the imaginations of some of "ye" beyond articulation.

Chaucer must instead apologize for the shortcomings of his efforts. He has translated only the heart of his superior source, and "yow" who speak the language of love better should revise at will:

> But sooth is, though I kan nat tellen al,
> As kan myn auctour, of his excellence,
> Yet have I seyd, and God toforn, and shal
> In every thyng, al holly his sentence;
> And if that ich, at Loves reverence,
> Have any word in eched for the beste,
> Doth therwithal right as youreselven leste.
>
> For myne wordes, heere and every part,
> I speke hem alle under correccioun
> Of yow that felyng han in loves art,
> And putte it al in youre discrecioun
> To encresse or maken dymynucioun
> Of my langage, and that I yow biseche.
> But now to purpos of my rather speche. (III, 1323–37)

Long before sending his "in-eched" revision to Gower and Strode for still further correction (V, 1856–59), Chaucer-the-reciter here begs more experienced listeners to fine-tune the feeling of his work in progress.

Back in bed, a new doubt troubles the post-coital couple, "lo, this was hir mooste feere" that their love may be merely a fiction,

BOOK III, PILLOW TALK

"that al this thyng but nyce dremes were," an anxiety that motivates more dialogue "for which ful ofte ech of hem seyde" (III, 1341–43) and more love-play to show "that it be soth" (III, 1348). Troilus tries to read the expression in Criseyde's "eyen clere" (III, 1353): "Though there be mercy writen in youre cheere, / God woot, the text ful harde is, soth, to fynde" (III, 1356–57), whereas Troilus's own sighs more clearly "shewed" his true "affeccioun within" (III, 1363). Chaucer sounds a bit dismissive of the rest of the lovers' small talk: "Soone after this they spake of sondry thynges, / As fel to purpos of this aventure" (III, 1366–67). They exchange ambiguously significant rings, and Criseyde pins a heart-shaped ruby set in a gold and azure brooch upon Troilus's shirt, a gift that sparks the court performer to celebrate largesse (or castigate miserliness) "as I shal yow rede" (III, 1383).[17]

Chaucer recovers his composure enough to restart the suspended story "that I yow seye" (III, 1394). He recaps Troilus's and Criseyde's impressions of the plot so far:

Tho gonne they to speken and to pleye,
And ek rehercen how, and whan, and where
Thei knewe hem first. (III, 1396–98)

---

17. The exchange is made "in pleyinge" (III, 1368), and Chaucer cannot read the inscriptions. This scene is not to be read in il *Filostrato*, though Wimsatt compares it to il *Filocolo* IV, 121, 1ff. Wimsatt questions Henry Ansgar Kelly's reading of the scene as a recognizable albeit clandestine engagement (*Chaucer and His French Contemporaries*, 317 n. 1368). However, Karl Wentersdorf's "Some Observations on the Concept of Clandestine Marriage in *Troilus and Criseyde*," *The Chaucer Review* 15 (1980): 101–26, and Frederik Pedersen's "Did the Medieval Laity Know the Canon Law Rules on Marriage? Some Evidence from Fourteenth-Century York." *Mediaeval Studies* 56 (1994): 111–52, also defend the legitimacy of this interpretation of the relationship as marriage. The ambiguity itself seems recollective of Virgil's treatment of the cave-coupling of Aeneas and Dido—"coniugium vocat" (*Aeneid* IV, 172). C. S. Lewis felt that "the loves of Troilus and Criseyde are so nobly conceived that they are divided only by the thinnest partition from the lawful loves of Dorigen and her husband. It seems almost an accident that the third book celebrates adultery instead of marriage" (*The Allegory of Love* [Oxford: Oxford University Press, 1936], 197).

BOOK III, PILLOW TALK

Distressing episodes "when that hem fel to speke" (III, 1401) are erased "with kissyng al that tale sholde breke" (III, 1403). Their confabulation must end with the rising of the sun, to describe which Chaucer sounds a bit Dantean, astrologic, geomantic, and so pedantic but obliquely positive—"to hym that koude it knowe" (III, 1419). Troilus and Criseyde complain, as Chaucer's aubade must do as *an aubade*. They fill their first night's last minutes together with an exchange of verses (III, 1422–1518)—rather than sex.[18] Criseyde's lyrics embrace those of Troilus. Chaucer announces the recital of each embedded poem, and each announcement suggests some level of impersonation: "to Troilus thus seyde" (III, 1421); "and seyde in this manere" (III, 1449); "Therwith ful soore he syghte, and thus he seyde" (III, 1471); "To that Criseyde answerede right anon, / And with a sik she seyde" (III, 1492–93).

First, Criseyde regrets the night's anticipated departure: "O blake night, as folk in bokes rede" (III, 1429). Criseyde would keep her hemisphere forever in the dark. Troilus tops Criseyde's frustration by cursing the envious, spying, murderous, thieving, meretricious daylight—"Go sell it hem that smale selys grave" (III, 1462). Criseyde's departure will break his heart "a-two"(III, 1475)—like a broken seal—because he dreads he has not yet made a deep enough impression "iset" (III, 1488) in Criseyde's heart. Criseyde then rivals Troilus's habitual hyperbole; she could not, not even under torture, not even if she wanted to, "torne out" the imprint of Troilus from her imagination: "Ye ben so depe inwith myn herte grave" (III, 1499–1500). His brain should not admit any such "fantasie" (III, 1504), and could not "and that ye me wolde han as faste in mynde / As I have yow" (III, 1506–7).

18. Windeatt remarks, "Although Ch. omits the lovers' renewing fiery passion at dawn (Fil 42/3,8), he much expands the lamenting speeches of T and C at parting" (Troilus [1984], 321, n. 1422ff).

BOOK III, PILLOW TALK

So, "withouten more speche," Criseyde says most simply: "Beth to me trewe, or ellis were it routhe / For I am thyn, by God and by my trouthe" (III, 1511–12). Criseyde then says—though some might say, incredibly—"Thus seyde I nevere er this, ne shal to mo" (III, 1514). Troilus must say farewell "and with such vois as though his herte bledde" (III, 1524). Criseyde's final sorrow can only be silent (III, 1527), and Troilus feels the same "soth to seyne" (III, 1530).

Failing to sleep, Troilus's imagination reconstructs every detail of Criseyde's real presence and the real emotional effect her presence causes:

> And in his thought gan up and doun to wynde
> Hire wordes alle, and every countenaunce,
> And fermely impressen in his mynde
> The leeste point that to him was pleasaunce;
> And verraylich of thilke remembraunce
> Desir al newe. (III, 1541–46)

Criseyde's heart "right in the same wyse" (III, 1548–49) contains her dear heart (III, 1553).

When Pandarus comes to Criseyde still in bed, she acts outraged: "for al youre wordes white. / O, whoso seeth yow knoweth yow ful lite" (III, 1567–68). Chaucer has apparently embarrassed himself by describing the uncle groping his niece as she hides under the sheets and so refuses to uncover other causes for their play: "But of this thing right to the effect to go ... Pandarus hath fully his entente" (III, 1580–82).

"Now torne we ayeyne" to a far more serious Pandarus being summoned "pryvely" (III, 1583–85) by Troilus. Pandarus attends promptly, "nought ones seyde he nay" (III, 1587). Troilus falls to his knees yet again with "dar I seye" (III, 1608) extreme gratitude.

BOOK III, PILLOW TALK

Pandarus "ful sobrely hym herde / Tyl al was seyd, and than he thus answerede" (III, 1616–17). Pandarus acts modest and must be tactful: "tak now nat a-grief / That I shal seyn" (III, 1621–22). Troilus really should "bridle alwey wel thi speche and thi desir" (III, 1635–36). Pandarus flatters "wis ynough" (III, 1629) Troilus, but Troilus mostly misses the point. Troilus has indeed been transfigured by his first sexual experience. He has been transformed from mere auditor into an insatiable rehearser: "This is o word for al: this Troilus / Was nevere ful to speke of this matere, / ... This tale ay was span-newe to bygynne" (III, 1660–65).

Troilus and Criseyde are soon reunited, "and lat se now if that he kan be merie!" (III, 1673). Chaucer does not bother to repeat the same script: "As it was erst, which nedeth nought devyse. / But pleynly to th' effect right for to go" (III, 1676–77). Though Troilus's performance does improve with each encore of opening night, Chaucer bows out: "Nought nedeth it to yow, syn they be met, / To axe at me ... this nedeth nought enquere" (III, 1682–84). Troilus and Criseyde achieve "as muche joie as herte may comprehende" (III, 1687), and Chaucer can say no more: "This is no litel thyng for to seye; / This passeth every wit for to devyse" (III, 1688–89).

What truly remains untranscribable is complete and perpetual felicity: "This joie may nought writen be with inke" (III, 1693). More mundane, real, temporary reunions "but nedes" require other sad departures "whan hire speche don was" (III, 1709–10). For some period of time, "a world of folk, as com hym wel of kynde, / The fresshest and the beste he koude fynde" (III, 1721–22)—like Chaucer's audience—party. Among them, Troilus "demed" himself happiest in love; from the margins, Chaucer can only "gesse" (III, 1727) how that feels or what that means. Then Troilus sings for real if Chaucer can.

BOOK III, PILLOW TALK

Troilus becomes a trend-setter: "And over al this, so wel koude he devyse ... that every lovere thoughte / That al was wel, what so he seyde or wroughte" (III, 1796–99). As a paradigm of Ricardian courtly taste, Troilus's benign demeanor could not be more appealing, and Chaucer tries to join the celebration of Love "yheried be his grace!" *in propria persona* as much as he can (III, 1804).

Chaucer closes this recital installment as he began, praising the court of Venus. This last hymn is also a recessional "syn that you wol wende" and since "I kan namore" (III, 1812) and since "thorugh yow have I seyd fully in my song / Th'effect" (III, 1814–15). Chaucer regrets if his intention to please may have intermittently caused "som disese ... as to myn auctour listeth to devise" (III, 1817). Chaucer's comment "my thridde bok now ende ich in this wise" (III, 1818) may be the notation of a writing translator but need not be recited as such. Chaucer would leave his listeners with an indelible illusion of "lust" and "quiete" (III, 1819): Troilus being with Criseyde. Book IV, however, begins "but al to litel, welaway the whyle" (IV, 1).

5

BOOK IV, CONJUNCTIONS

BOOK IV of *Troilus and Criseyde* starts with "But." If Chaucer ever did read this proem aloud, his very first word would have sounded rather startling. But this particular "But"—indeed, this entire proem—looks very bookish, perhaps a studied allusion to Book IV of Virgil's *Aeneid*, perhaps an addition composed during revision.[1] Most of the fourth book itself is just talk. As its narrator, Chaucer does little more than conjoin the text's direct quotations. As reciter, however, Chaucer finds all the tonal features of his script's conversations immediately relevant: the longing for presence, the lamenting of absence, the anxieties about transmission, the anticipation of reception, and the frequent disconnect between intention and perception. But first the proem focuses on Chaucer's isolated self-consciousness as an author.

Chaucer seems to retreat into his atelier, where he anticipates

---

1. Aeneas has finished reciting Book III; Virgil proceeds to narrate "At" how his hero's report of the burning of Troy has now ignited Dido's fatal fever. Chaucer later echoes the far more familiar first line of Virgil's epic (V, 1766) in order to renounce reiterating epic battle scenes.

BOOK IV, CONJUNCTIONS

the process of inscribing his own response to this "matere" (IV, 17): "And now my penne, allas, with which I write, / Quaketh for drede of that I moste endite ... hennesforth" (IV, 13–17). The flow of Chaucer's heart's blood will be recorded (IV, 12) by ink. By foretelling a yet-to-be-written ending, Chaucer predicts its "fyne" (I, 26; cf. V, 1828–32), indelibly recorded long ago "as writen folk," a reading of which Chaucer now has "in mynde" (IV, 18). Fearing that his future readers will respond differently and refute his own response with false opinions of false Criseyde, Chaucer expresses no sympathy for such unsympathetic critics:

Allas, that they sholde evere cause fynde
To speke hire harm! And if they on hire lye,
Iwis, hemself sholde han the vilanye. (IV, 19–21)

The last stanza of Chaucer's proem starts with a dark invocation of the Furies, who complain forever (IV, 23). Feeling much the same, Chaucer braces to inscribe "this ilke ferthe book" (IV, 26).[2]

Returning to his act of recital "as I have seyd er this" (IV, 29), Chaucer must relate that, after some indeterminate delay between intent and action (IV, 36), Hector misled the folk "soth for to telle" (IV, 47). The Greeks request "a tyme of trewe" (IV, 57–58).[3] News of a prisoner exchange is broadcast "in every strete, / ... and

---

2. Although Troilus survives till the end of Book V, Chaucer anticipates the worst with a zeugma: "the losse of lyf and love yfeere / Of Troilus be fully shewed heere" (IV, 27–28). *Here* here may refer to the entire manuscript which he is preparing for circulation.

3. Boccaccio, more logically, had had the routed Trojans ask for a truce. Chaucer changes Boccaccio's account to agree with Benoît and Guido. Barney suggests the possibility that "one of Chaucer's drafts agreed with Boccaccio and was revised later" (Riverside, 1045, nn. 57–58).

Chaucer reports the Trojan dread with a tonally contradictory conjunction of rhymes: "Troie/joie" (IV, 55, 56). The phrasing "tyme of trewe" (II, 58) can also be played to sound paradoxical because this truce calls for Criseyde's untruth; see MED s.v. "treu(e, n.(1) Also trewe [etc.]" def.1(a) "A pledge to cease hostilities" and def. 8 "Belief, trust, faith, confidence; also, overconfidence."

BOOK IV, CONJUNCTIONS

everywhere, / And with the firste it com to Calkas ere" (IV, 61–63). Chaucer reintroduces the "gret devyn" (I, 66) who presents himself "in my propre persone, / To teche" (IV, 83–84) the noisy Greek "consistorie" (IV, 65) what to do. Calkas knows how to take the floor:

> And sette hym there as he was wont to doone;
> And with a chaunged face hem bad a boone,
> ... to don that reverence,
> To stynte noyse and yeve hym audience. (IV, 67–70)

Chaucer's exclamation "for love of God" adopts Calkas's tone of voice even before he quotes directly "thus: 'Lo ... I am Calkas'" (IV, 71–73). Although Calkas recalls his expertise in predictions (IV, 114–15), it is mostly the prophet's oratorical skills that Chaucer most admires and displays.

Calkas regrets his prior silence: "For by that cause I say no tyme er now.... But now or nevere" (IV, 99–100). He denies having had any profit motives when he left Troy, as he now appeals to the Greeks for a "bounte" (IV, 109). If Chaucer's voice begs the analogy, Pandarus's petition can sound like the reciter's own quête—at least to his more astute and so amused listeners. Chaucer himself especially appreciates Calkas's *pronuntiatio* and kinesics:

> Tellyng his tale alwey, this olde greye,
> Humble in his speche, and in his lokyng eke,
> The salte teris from his eyen tweye
> Ful faste ronnen down by either cheke. (IV, 127–30)

The sad father's request is granted, and Chaucer asks his audience to share Calkas's joy, using a rhetorical question: "But who was glad ynough but Calkas tho?" (IV, 134). Ambassadors are sent, and their "cause itold" (IV, 141) to Priam's court, but Chaucer does not recount the specifics of the following Trojan "parlement ... Of which th'effect rehercen yow I shal" (IV, 143–44). Troilus himself fails to speak though he "was present in the place" (IV, 148); even though he almost died "with tho wordes ... / But natheles he no word to it seyde" (IV, 151–52). As he waits for what the lords "wolde seye" (IV, 156) aloud, Troilus presides silently over his internal debate between Love and Reason before making his secret love "iblowe" (IV, 167). He decides to "telle his lady first what that they mente" (IV, 172) and then obey Criseyde's wishes when "she hadde seyd hym hire entente" (IV, 173).

It is Hector who speaks up, but even he is overruled by the "noyse of peple" (IV, 183) who speak in unison: "thus sygge we, / That al oure vois is" (IV, 194–95). Chaucer responds to the *vox populi* with sarcasm: "O nyce world, lo, thy discrecioun" (IV, 206).[4] Chaucer makes their vulgar "cloude of errour" most clear, "and lo, here ensample as yerne" (IV, 200–201). To authorize his scorn, Chaucer speaks to absent Juvenal, whose "sentence" is affirmed in recital by such purely present interjections as "lord" (IV, 197), "lo" (IV, 201), and "allas" (IV, 205).

Nevertheless, the appearance of a consensus has been achieved regarding Criseyde: "thus seyden here and howne" (IV, 210).[5] Her exchange "delibered was by parlement ... And it pronounced by the president." Hector has no veto: "and fynaly, what wight that it withseyde, / It was for nought." Chaucer himself seems to surrender to due process; "it moste ben and sholde, / For substaunce of the parlement it wolde" (IV, 211–17).[6] Mute Troilus must exit from

---

4. Barney hears a possibly "satiric reference to the popular phrase 'vox populi vox Dei'" (*Riverside*, 1045, n. 183).

5. Even if this odd phrasing means merely "master and members" (*Riverside*, 1045, n. 210), it sounds contemptuous here, perhaps even ridiculous if confused with the confusion caused by a hare and hounds.

6. The text is curiously silent about King Priam's consent (until 350 lines later and even then only obliquely). Many readers follow Carleton Brown's reading of Chaucer's

BOOK IV, CONJUNCTIONS

the current proceedings "withouten wordes mo" (IV, 219) except to excuse himself once or twice "as he seyde" with a story of hasty fatigue (IV, 223).

Mute Troilus becomes wintry (IV, 225) at the "chaungynge of Criseyde" (IV, 231); "lik a ded ymage" (IV, 235), Troilus momentarily "his speche hym refte; unnethes myghte he seye" (IV, 249) until Chaucer revives his suicidal voice: "as I shal yow devyse" (IV, 238), "that I yow devyse. / Than seyde he thus" (IV, 259–60). Troilus soon catches enough breath to complain for eleven stanzas, until he passes out (IV, 260–336). Each stanza of Troilus's "pleyntes new" (IV, 339) sounds like a discrete sigh (IV, 337).

Pandarus, "which that in the parlement / Hadde herd what every lord and burgeys seyde, / And how ful graunted was by oon assent" (IV, 344–46), is initially rendered speechless too: "wel neigh wood out of his wit to breyde, / So that for wo he nyste what he mente" (IV, 348–49)—that is, understood his own intentions. When he rejoins Troilus in the dark (IV, 354), he approaches the bed "as stille as ston, / ... So confus that he nyste what to seye" (IV, 354–56). Chaucer too can say little more than that they could say nothing: "And specheles thus ben thise ilke tweye, / That neither myghte o word for sorwe seye" (IV, 370–71). Chaucer thus not only narrates the characters' interplay of ambivalent intentions and ambiguous perceptions, he demonstrates in his denied recital their tone of choked frustration and thereby participates with his audience in a parallel tonal experience of the unspoken.

---

line "As breme as blase of strawe iset on fire" (IV, 184) as an oblique reference to Jack Straw and the Rising of 1381 ("Another Contemporary Allusion in Chaucer's *Troilus*," *Modern Language Notes* 26 [1911]: 208–11). John McCall has proposed an alternative parallel between the Parliament of 1386 and Chaucer's scene ("The Parliament of 1386 and Chaucer's Trojan Parliament," *JEGP* 58 [1959]: 276–88). John Ganim sees "no reason why Chaucer may not have conflated into this image two expressions of group action, politically very different, but both hostile to his political position, indeed, to his position in general" (*Theatricality*, 111).

BOOK IV, CONJUNCTIONS

For Chaucer to resuscitate the dialogue, Troilus must recover consciousness and emit an almost bestial "rore" and "sorwful noise" (IV, 373–74) before asking "thus" if Pandarus has heard the news at parliament (IV, 377). The simple, true answer is "yis" (IV, 380). "That I have herd, and woot al how it is" (IV, 382), and Pandarus cannot simply rewrite parliament's decree—"As wisly were it fals as it is trewe" (IV, 381). Pandarus tries instead to alter Troilus's reaction: "But telle me this" (IV, 393). Troilus needs to revise his love "as writ Zanzis" (IV, 414) in a memorable saying (though the author's identity has been lost). Chaucer explicitly absolves Pandarus of being so sincerely cavalier: "Thise wordes seyde he for the nones alle, / ... He roughte nought what unthrift that he seyde" (IV, 428–31). Troilus allegedly perceives neither the content nor the intent of Pandarus's saying; he "took litel heede of all that evere he mente—/ Oon ere it herde, at tother out it wente" (IV, 433–34). Nevertheless, Troilus can repeat and will reject every point of Pandarus's argument: "what so thow seye" (IV, 442), "ther thow seist" (IV, 449), "so hold thi pees; thow sleest me with thi speche" (IV, 455), "thow biddest me" (IV, 456). Troilus mimics (and so can Chaucer) Pandarus's "unthrift": "As he that ... seith right thus:" (IV, 464–65); "Thow hast made an argument for fyn, ... Whi gabbestow, that seydest unto me" (IV, 477, 481); "O, where hastow ben hid so longe in muwe, / That kanst so wel and formely arguwe?" (IV, 496–97). Chaucer's body language could easily put some English on Troilus's question "kanstow playen raket, to and fro" (IV, 460). But Troilus then reverts from sarcasm to despair "withouten wordes mo" (IV, 500) and welcomes Death now that the "quyete" (IV, 505) of his life is over: "Com now, syn I so ofte after the calle ... soth for to seyne ... ofte ycleped ... O deth" (IV, 502–9).[7]

7. See Sebastian Sobecki regarding the highly problematic representation of "legitimate suicide" ("'And to the Herte She Hireselven Smot': The Loveris Maladye and

BOOK IV, CONJUNCTIONS

Pandarus is struck dumb again, and downcast he "gan holde his tunge stille" (IV, 521). Chaucer too can cast down his eyes (IV, 522) and pause before reporting Pandarus's shocking next gambit: "'Yet shal I somwhat more unto hym seye' / And seyde ... 'Go ravysshe here!'" (IV, 525–30). Pandarus and Troilus (and Chaucer) then debate the semantics of *rape* quite politely (IV, 540). Troilus asks for "audience" first and then will listen in turn to his friend's "sentence" (IV, 545–46). Troilus explains "whi this thing is laft, thow shalt wel here" (IV, 544). Criseyde's "eschaunge" has been "enseled" by parliament, and Priam will not repeal this "lettere" (IV, 559–60). Given that this text is irrevocable, Troilus's silence avoids any "disclaundre" to Criseyde's name (IV, 562–64). Pandarus argues that the very ephemerality of *Fama* offers a solution to Troilus's dilemma. Talk exhausts itself (IV, 584–88). Furthermore, Criseyde might misinterpret Troilus's respect as indifference. Pandarus is most certain of "o thyng I dar the swere" (IV, 610): if Criseyde does not oblige, "thanne is she fals" (IV, 616)—a dramatically ironic prediction (unintended by Pandarus, disclosed later by the plot, meant to be heard now by the reciter).

Pandarus's blunt talk does stimulate Troilus; he "gan with tho wordes quyken" (IV, 631). Troilus first wants to make the semantics of *voluntary rape* perfectly clear: "it is nat myn entente, / At shorte wordes" (IV, 635–36) to force Criseyde. Pandarus assures him, "Whi, so mene I" (IV, 638). But Pandarus proposes the problematic possibility that Criseyde might welcome some rough love: "But telle me thanne ... That nost nat that she wol ben yvele appayed / To ravysshe hire, syn thow hast nought ben there, / But if that Jove told it in thyn ere" (IV, 639–44).

---

the Legitimate Suicides of Chaucer's and Gower's Exemplary Lovers," *Mediaevalia* 25 [2004]: 107–21). I fear that the solitary reader (of Spenser or Goethe or Salinger, for example) is far more in danger from the tonal contagion of experiencing such suicidal impulses than Chaucer's listening audience.

BOOK IV, CONJUNCTIONS

Having seduced Troilus's "assente" (IV, 632), Pandarus sets to "werke" (IV, 651) again; he is again fully, though now falsely, confident in his directorial control: "I shal shape it so" (IV, 652). Pandarus promises that the actual presence of Criseyde will clarify everything:

> Come speken with thi lady pryvely,
> And by hire wordes ek, and by hire cheere,
> Thou shalt ful sone aperceyve and wel here
> Al hire entente, and in this cas the beste.
> ... for in this point I reste. (IV, 654–58)

Pandarus thus rests his case and departs. Meanwhile, rumors run to Criseyde:

> The swifte Fame, which that false thynges
> Egal reporteth the thynges trewe,
> Was thorughout Troie yfled with preste wynges
> Fro man to man, and made this tale al newe. (IV, 659–62)

Each retelling is novel.

Criseyde seems to lose her proper name as her tale is passed "fro man to man"; their concern is primarily not with "Calkas doghter" but with what happened "at parlement, withouten wordes more" (IV, 662–64). Criseyde herself was not present at this parliament; one presumes that Chaucer's audience presumed that women were not permitted to be present. When Criseyde "hadde herd" this "tale anon-right" (IV, 666–67), Chaucer's syntax becomes as confused as she: it seems when Criseyde heard what her father "roughte" she agreed "right nought" and cursed it and him (IV, 667–70). Such grammar expresses primarily the reciter's distress. Chaucer shares only this brief glimpse of Criseyde's silent distress before obtuse guests invade her privacy.

A "route" (IV, 682) of chatty women come to console Criseyde:

"And with hire tales, deere ynough a myte, / ... They sette hem down and seyde as I shall telle" (IV, 684–86). This parlor scene (drawn from il *Filostrato*, iv, sts. 78–85) represents the tonal (that is, unwelcome so comic) antithesis of Criseyde's sophisticated and sisterly "compaignie" in Book II (86). Three unidentified and so stereotypically girly voices try to say all the right things. For now, at present, Criseyde listens no better than Troilus does with Pandarus: "Thos wordes and tho wommanysshe thynges, / She herde hem right as though she thennes were" (IV, 694–95). In other words, physical proximity does not achieve real presence (that is, attention); conversely, absence does not deny intimacy:

> For God it woot, hire herte on othir thynge is,
> Although the body sat among hem there,
> Hire advertence is alwey elleswhere,
> For Troilus ful faste hire soule soughte;
> Withouten word, on hym alwey she thoughte. (IV, 696–700)

Criseyde's silent communion with the idea of Troilus obliterates any good intentions of "thise wommen, that thus wenden hire to plese, / Aboute naught gonne all hire tales spende. / Swych vanyte ..." (IV, 702–3). Indeed, such "compaignie" wearies Criseyde almost unto death (IV, 706–7). And "thilke fooles sittynge hire aboute" (IV, 715) completely misread the "signes" (IV, 710) of her tears. They mean to entertain "and with hire tales wenden hire disporten" (IV, 724), though their attempted therapy only intensifies Criseyde's pain (IV, 726–28).

Criseyde sobs for eight stanzas: "And thus she wroughte, as I shal yow devyse" (IV, 735), "and thus she spak" (IV, 742). Now and then, however, Chaucer must interrupt to provide an annotation, as if his audience needs to know Criseyde's mother's name (IV, 762). So, too, Chaucer provides "ful ofte a by-word here I

BOOK IV, CONJUNCTIONS

seye" (IV, 769). Chaucer's recital tone can duplicate Criseyde's emotion or stand aloof or both intermittently, a performed vacillation that shows Chaucer's own anguish too.

Questioning only herself, Criseyde asks how she could possibly survive physical separation from Troilus. As an alternative to suicide, she will costume herself again as a widow or nun whose "ordre" keeps silence. Her "observance evere, in youre absence" demands morbid sorrow, complaint, and abstinence (IV, 778–84) rather than the *regula* of blessed poverty, chastity, and obedience. Out of tune with her tone, Chaucer plays with his own puns: "Eternaly, for they shal nevere *twynne*; / For though in erthe *ytwynned* be we *tweyne*" (IV, 787–88); Criseyde and Troilus shall be "yfeere" like Orpheus and Eurydice "his feere" (IV, 790–91).[8] Criseyde addresses her final apostrophes to an absent Troilus (IV, 778, 792, 795). She hopes her absence (or death) will allow him to "foryete this sorwe and tene / And me also" (IV, 796–97). Having been "chaunged," Criseyde's present concern, "soothly for to seye" (IV, 797), is only for Troilus's anticipated response.

Chaucer confesses that Criseyde's complaint can be neither repeated nor transcribed adequately: "How myghte it evere yred ben or ysonge[?]" (IV, 799). Chaucer modestly calls upon his audience to imagine her unspeakable grief because his actual quotation now would only diminish its tonal impact:

> I not; but, as for me, my litel tonge,
> If I discryven wolde hire hevynesse,
> It sholde make hire sorwe seme lesse
> Than that it was, and childisshly deface
> Hire heigh compleyente, and therfore ich it pace. (IV, 801–5)

---

8. The rhyme is weak and so is the analogy because "Orpheus ... lost hire, and was deed" (*Boece* III m.12, 5). Barney sees an analogy between Criseyde's allusion and the

BOOK IV, CONJUNCTIONS

Pandarus, whom Troilus has sent "as ye han herd devyse" (IV, 807), arrives "in a ful secree wise, ... to telle al hoolly his message" (IV, 810–12).

At first, Criseyde tries to hide the spectacle of herself as the "verray signal of martire / Of deth" (IV, 818–19) from Pandarus's view (IV, 820–21). Pandarus can hardly abide Criseyde's "aspre pleynte," which Chaucer has added to sound "thus she seyde" (IV, 827) a thousand times worse.[9] Criseyde is unsure of her reaction to Pandarus's immediate presence: "Wher shal I seye to yow welcom or no" (IV, 831). She sees herself as an allegorical abstraction (IV, 841), but Pandarus addresses her with atypical familiarity, "thow, my suster" (IV, 848), as if to recall her from suicidal distraction: "what thynkestow to do?" (IV, 849). Pandarus would prevent Criseyde's anticipated deed with a rehearsal of Troilus's words:

Leef al this werk, and tak now heede to
That I shal seyn: and herkne of good entente
This which by me thi Trolius the sente. (IV, 852–53)

Criseyde cannot imagine what speech Pandarus could repeat on Troilus's behalf that would not only intensify her own pain: "what wordes may ye brynge? / What wol my deere herte seyn to me" (IV, 857–58). Chaucer faces the same tonal challenge facing Pandarus—to move beyond this moment of despair, "But natheles, as he beste myghte, he seyde" (IV, 874). Chaucer has Pandarus move quickly: "I trowe ye han herd al how" (IV, 876), "short and pleyn, th' effect of my message" (IV, 890), "no long prologe as now entende" (IV, 893). It seems to Pandarus (IV, 887) that Troilus, who

---

"joint damnation of Paolo and Francesca (Inf. 5)" (*Riverside*, 1048, nn. 785–87). In the *Inferno* 4, 132, Orpheus is named among the company of philosophers, but there is no mention of Eurydice among the other righteous heathens in Limbo.

9. "Instead of Pandaro, Ch has Criseyde speak first, in an added complaint" (Windeatt, *Troilus* [1984], 399, nn. 827–47).

BOOK IV, CONJUNCTIONS

similarly suffers "that may non erthly mannes tonge seye" (IV, 881), wants to discuss the matter with Criseyde in person and "ye may answere hym sende" (IV, 894). However, Pandarus warns Criseyde to "lef this wo er Troilus be here!" (IV, 896).

This account of Troilus's grief only doubles Criseyde's sorrow (IV, 903). Although it will be harder still for her to see directly his sorrow (IV, 905–6), she consents to welcome Troilus to her death bed (IV, 909–10), and—"Thise wordes seyd"—she collapses "gruf" (IV, 911–12). Pandarus again warns, "forthi yet I seye: / So lef this sorwe" (IV, 924–25), because its effect on Troilus would be fatal. Rather, Criseyde must control the tone of their next meeting, "I mene thus" (IV, 932). Since "wommen ben wise in short avysement" (IV, 936), Criseyde does promise that "I shal don al my myght to restryene / From wepyng in his sighte" (IV, 940–41) but fails (IV, 1128–41).

Troilus, "shortly, al the sothe for to seye" (IV, 953), has reverted to lugubrious philosophizing—"right thus ... his argument alway" (IV, 956). Troilus lectures only himself—the most familiar "thee" (IV, 1030, 1035, 1037, 1038, 1040, 1043)—about a prolonged squabble among "grete clerkes many oon" (IV, 968, 972). Troilus recapitulates what some men "seyn" (*say*) in texts (IV, 970, 974, 997, 999, 1006) about what God has "seyn" (*seen*) from on high (IV, 962, 998), concluding "wherfore I sey" in this fixed text "we han no fre chois, as thise clerkes rede" (IV, 978–80).[10]

---

10. The most obvious textual misrepresentation of Chaucer's source in Troilus's soliloquy is his omission of Lady Philosophy's correction (*Cons.* V. Pr. 4) of the dreamer's bout of fatalism (*Cons.* V. Pr. 3). Troilus argues by analogy: "For if ther sitte a man yond *on a see*" (IV, 1023), he sits of necessity. Chaucer here freely provides a "moeble," an imagined chair for the hypothetical man to sit upon, a seemingly trivial detail which is not mentioned in *Boece* V, pr. 3, 54. Chaucer may have added this "see" simply because he was confronting the predestined necessity of providing a rhyme for "be" (IV, 1025). Troilus "certeynly" (IV, 960) repeats Boethius's example of a man sitting (*Cons.* Bk. V. Pr. 3, 54–82) but makes many more frequent references to someone sitting (IV, 1034, 1038, 1039, 1043). During recital, Chaucer's seemingly superfluous reference to this "see" can indicate "in shewynge" (IV, 1016) the familiar occupant of a real chair.

BOOK IV, CONJUNCTIONS

As author, Chaucer intrudes only once, "Thanne seyde he thus" (IV, 1079). As reciter, however, Chaucer's voice can constantly redirect his soliloquy's direct self-address to individual members of "oure" (IV, 1059) audience, acknowledging "thyn Opynyoun" (IV, 1025) as opposed to what "thow mayst seyn" (IV, 1037). "Disputyng with hymself in this matere" (IV, 1084), Troilus imagines a somewhat impatient audience: "As thus—now herkne, for I wol nat tarie" (IV, 1029); "yet sey I more herto" (IV, 1072)—a narrative fiction that serves Chaucer's recital reality. The primary tonal effect of Chaucer's impersonation of Troilus's philosophical circumvolutions "and further over now ayeynward yit" (IV, 1027) is confused delay—a recital experience of frustration as well as grief.[11]

Pandarus catches at least the conclusion of Chaucer's monopolylogue, "and seyde as ye may here" (IV, 1085). He asks for special attention—"tak hede of that I shal seye" (IV, 1107). Since Pandarus has just "with hire yspoke and longe ybe" (IV, 1108), he claims a privileged insight into Criseyde's "privete ... if I shal right arede" (IV, 1111–12). His male intuition is optimistic: "Myn herte seyth, 'Certeyn, she shal not wende'" (IV, 1118). Troilus assents: "Thow seist right wel" (IV, 1122). And Pandarus amplifies what Troilus wants to hear, "And what hym liste, he seyde unto it more" (IV, 1123).

The final meeting between Troilus and Criseyde "and how they wroughte" requires that their unutterable grief be reported; "I shal yow tellen soone" (IV, 1127). The intensity of their tears chokes off dialogue, however: "Soth is ... neyther of hem other myghte grete, ... ne myghte o word out brynge, / As I seyde erst" (IV, 1128–34). Eventually, Criseyde can speak, but only "with bro-

---

11. Barney notes that Root described this verse as "'probably the least poetical line that Chaucer ever wrote.' Cf. PardT VI. 648" (Riverside, 1048., n. 1027).

BOOK IV, CONJUNCTIONS

ken vois, al hoors forshright" (IV, 1147); and, after only one and a half lines, she again "loste speche" (IV, 1151). Repeating exactly "thise ilke wordes seyde" (IV, 1048), Chaucer gives a special emphasis to "mercy" (IV, 1149). And "right with the word" (IV, 1153), Criseyde collapses.

Troilus does not try to revive Criseyde. Instead, he wrings his hands and weeps "and seyd that was to seye" (IV, 1171) and prays for her soul and dresses her corpse. Chaucer reports that Troilus spoke "with sorweful vois" about the dearly departed. Chaucer does not repeat his long dirge (IV, 1168–70) except to say that "his song ful ofte is 'weylaway!'" (IV, 1166). Troilus is certain Criseyde is dead on the basis of empirical evidence and finds his voice again—"Than seyde he thus, fulfild of heigh desdayn" (IV, 1191). He plans to play Pyramus (who unfortunately misinterpreted appearances). After delivering his haughty, hasty swan song (IV, 1192–1210), Troilus comes to the point of puncturing himself, "but" (IV, 1212) Criseyde "as God wolde" recovers in the nick of time.[12]

Only Criseyde's serendipitous sigh—"Than if I nadde spoken, as grace was" (IV, 1233)—prevents Troilus's premature tragedy. Chaucer must make her sound in some measure moved, astonished, equally dedicated to suicide and semiconscious until she changes the conversation: "But hoo, for we han right ynough of this" (IV, 1242). Instead, Criseyde calls Troilus to bed, "and there lat us speken of oure wo" (IV, 1244). After allowing a stanza of face-to-face private grief, "at the laste" Chaucer quotes "thise ilke wordes seyde" (IV, 1252–53), first by Criseyde to line 1414 and

---

12. Until this moment, Criseyde's physical collapse seems as intense and honest as had Troilus's heart attack in Book III. Her limbs and lips are cold (IV, 1158, 1161, 1171). She shows no "signe of lif" (IV, 1164), "specheles she lay"(IV, 1167), apparently "withouten sentement," and yet, in retrospect, some readers still suspect Criseyde's hypocrisy, an invisible (if not inaudible) tone refuting the "pregnant argument" of Troilus's immediate perception "For aught he woot" (IV, 1177–79).

then by Troilus till line 1687, with minimal (textually recorded) interruptions or indications of his own take on their dialogue. Criseyde's first speech requires a remarkable change of voice, however; rather than more woe "quod she" (IV, 1254), Criseyde renounces any further display of "folie" (IV, 1257). For one thing, Chaucer has her stereotype her own gender's tonal fickleness: "I am a womman, as ful wel ye woot, / And as I am avysed sodeynly, / So wol I telle yow, whil it is hoot" (IV, 1261–63).

Criseyde states her private plan but curiously shares Chaucer's self-consciousness as a public speaker:

> For which I wol nat make long sermoun—
> For tyme ylost may nought recovered be—
> But I wol gon to my conclusioun, ...
> If I speke aught ayeyns youre hertes reste; ...
> For trewely, I speke it for the beste,
>
> Makyng alwey a protestacioun
> That now thise wordes which that I shal seye
> Nis but to shewen yow my mocioun ...
> And taketh it non other wise, I preye. (IV, 1282–93)

Criseyde claims she remains completely subordinate to Troilus's "comaunde, / That wol I don, for that is no demaunde" (IV, 1294–95). But her recommendations are meant to sound irrefutable:

> "Now herkneth this" (IV, 1296)
> "The soth is this" (IV, 1303)
> "And thenk right thus" (IV, 1317)
> "Ye knowe ek" (IV, 1331)
> "Have here another wey, if it so be / That al this thyng ne may yow nat suffise" (IV, 1366–67)
> "And how I mene, I shal it yow devyse" (IV, 1379)

BOOK IV, CONJUNCTIONS

Criseyde's plan is simple: she will go and then return. To be true, she must lie. Criseyde's proposition takes so long to quote because she tries to anticipate every contingency and counter-argument. By repeating her every prolepsis, Chaucer attempts to demonstrate her innocence in his court. But, with malice aforethought, his listeners and readers alike find Criseyde's desire to take her "moeble" (IV, 1380) dubious at best. Criseyde's relentless rhetoric eventually wears down Troilus's resistance—"herkeneth how, if that ye wol assente" (IV, 1372). But Criseyde's decreasingly woeful strategizing increasingly fuels suspicion: Troilus's and the reader's and, in recital perhaps most evidently, Chaucer's own.

For better or worse, Criseyde denies the synonymity of *proximity* and *presence*. She argues, abstractly, that there exists no real difference between being separated a little or a lot: "I se that ofttyme, there as we ben now, ... / oure counseyl for to hide, / Ye speke nat with me, nor I with yow" (IV, 1324–26). Criseyde suspects that Troilus expects that her father will be able to persuade her to stay among the Greeks. Criseyde predicts "another way, if it so be" (IV, 1366), and plans her own *pronuntiatio* and body language for the performance needed to effect her release: "And I right now have founden al the gise" (IV, 1370), "shal I take, and seye" (IV, 1381), "Thus shal I seyn (IV, 1388), "I shal ek shewen hym" (IV, 1390). She will delude and so elude Calkas: "So what for o thyng or for other ... / I shal hym so enchaunten with my sawes / ... That, as me lyst, I shal wel make an ende" (IV, 1394–1400).[13] "And yf" (IV, 1401) Calkas divines her deception (IV, 1401–2), Criseyde can deny his certainty "in certayn ... For goddes speken in amphibologies, / And for o soth they tellen twenty lyes" (IV,

---

[13]. Though there are several other footnotes, Criseyde's idiomatic reference to "thre hawes" (IV, 1398) may mean nothing other more than she plans to laugh at her father's divination: "haw, haw, haw."

131

1402–7). Criseyde champions skepticism. Both she and Chaucer, "I suppose," must play the atheist, "thus shal I seyn," (IV, 1408–9) to deceive Calkas (and debunk Troilus's fatalism, at the same time disorienting Chaucer's audience). Only cowardice makes man "amys the goddes text to glose" (IV, 1410).[14] Chaucer has Criseyde win Troilus's consent without convincing him of anything. Calkas will be a different story.

The concurrent doubts that Chaucer can convey to his audience while re-enacting Criseyde's certainty is explicitly voiced by his following renunciation of any such doubt:

> And treweliche, as written wel I fynde
> That al this thyng was seyd of good entente,
> And that hire herte trewe was and kynde
> Towardes hym, and spak right as she mente, . . .
> And was in purpos evere to be trewe:
> Thus writen they that of hire werkes knewe. (IV, 1415–21)

Chaucer is probably (and perhaps patently) truly lying about what he has found written well; his sympathy for Criseyde is notably at odds with his sources' antagonism, and his recital may have sounded conspicuously nervous, desperate.

Meanwhile, Troilus has been listening as attentively as a puppy to all of Criseyde's wagging argument: "with herte and erys spradde, / Herde al this thyng devysen to and fro" (IV, 1422–23). In general, Troilus thinks he thought the same: "And verrayliche him semed that he hadde / The selve wit" (IV, 1424–25). Troilus has

---

14. Since Criseyde swears quite conventionally, "Or ellis se ich nevere Joves face" (IV, 1337), it seems unlikely that her quotation (of Petronius, Statius, Lucretius, et al., but not of Boccaccio in this instance) would sound like a sincere affirmation of Epicurean skepticism regarding the existence of gods, or God. Such atheism, as V. A. Kolve explains, was normally perceived as a lack of reason, "God-Denying Fools and the Medieval 'Religion of Love.'" *Studies in the Age of Chaucer* 19 (1997): 3–59.

some intuitive misgivings, "But fynaly, he gan his herte wreste / To trusten hire, and took it for the beste" (IV, 1427–28). For most of one whole stanza, "the grete furie" of Troilus's "penaunce" is silenced by hope. The two lovers harmonize "as the briddes" in spring "deliten in hire song . . . / Right so the wordes that they spake yfeere / Delited hem" (IV, 1429–35).

"But natheles" (IV, 1436), after their brief "amorouse daunce" (IV, 1431), Chaucer allows Troilus to respond for about half the time he had allotted Criseyde. Chaucer could accentuate this shift in point of view simply by moving from one part of his playing area to another—from siding with the flowers, as it were, to assuming the tonal perspective of his fellow leaves. As Troilus begins "and seyde hire" (IV, 1440), Chaucer can turn about and speak at the women (or some one woman) of his audience.

Troilus's reply provides some skeletal indications of his intended tone—"as I have told yow yore" (IV, 1497), "doth somwhat as that I shal yow seye" (IV, 1502), "I mene thus" (IV, 1506), "thus mene I" (IV, 1511)—all of which can be fleshed out by recital. Troilus's most recurrent, indeed quite redundant, argument is that he must die without Criseyde (IV, 1446, 1477, 1498). He balks at her plan, "for trewely" Troilus has little real faith that Criseyde can control their future: "Tho sleghtes yit that I have herd you stere / Ful shaply ben to faylen alle yfeere" (IV, 1451–52). Countering with his own sayings (IV, 1453–58), Troilus warns Criseyde that, by virtue of being woman (IV, 1462), she will fail in any duel of "sleighte" with her father, who "kan the craft" (IV, 1458–61, 1496). She will not "feyne aright" (IV, 1463); her confidence that she can turn her father, his having once "lost so foule his name, / . . . nys but a fantasie" (IV, 1467–70). Troilus worries that Calkas is the better hermeneut: "Ye shal ek sen, youre fader shal yow glose / . . . as he kan wel preche" (IV, 1471–72). She

BOOK IV, CONJUNCTIONS

may be raped by rhetoric: "That ravysshen he shal yow with his speche, / Or do yow don by force as he shal teche" (IV, 1474–75), "and thus he shal yow with his wordes fere" (IV, 1483). Troilus means well—"for as in myn entente, / This is the beste"—but (or therefore) gives Criseyde an escape clause: "if that ye wole assente" (IV, 1525–26).

Criseyde first answers with a very imitable sigh that dismisses Troilus's "unthrifty weyes newe" (IV, 1530), and the debate is substantially over. Criseyde binds herself with a formal oath: "I swere" (IV, 1542). Chaucer's actual performance of this *performative* makes its subsequent violation much more vivid: "Ber witnesse of this word that seyd is here" (IV, 1550). Criseyde's hyperbolic protestations force Chaucer to suppress his narrative anticipations—"If I be fals! Now trowe me if yow leste" (IV, 1547).

Criseyde continues to talk, reasonably it seems (cf. IV, 1583), against Troilus's effeminate scheme, "but that ye speke" (IV, 1555). Her primary concern is that others will misread Troilus's motive for fleeing as lust (which may be considered correct by some people in the audience):

What trowe ye the peple ek al aboute
Wolde of it seye? It is ful light t'arede.
They wolden seye, and swere it out of doute,
That love ne drof yow...
But lust voluptuous. (IV, 1569–73)

Such "filthe" would spot her "honeste" (IV, 1576–78) as well, prescribing that "my name sholde I nevere ayenward wynne" (IV, 1581).

Criseyde concludes with proverbs that "men seyn" (IV, 1584), including one of Chaucer's favorite phrases (IV, 1586). Yet, Troilus still sounds rather reluctant to accept either the necessity or

BOOK IV, CONJUNCTIONS

the virtue of her plan: "And now, so this be soth ... / Syn that I se that nede it mot be thus. / But ... if it be may ... Myn herte seyth." (IV, 1597–1603). Such doubt slays Criseyde; she says: "I se wel now that ye mytrusten me, / For by youre wordes it is wel yseene" (IV, 1606–7). Her tonal truth is a logical tautology: "Mistrust me nought thus causeles, for routhe, / Syn to be trewe I have yow plight my trouthe" (IV, 1609–10). Criseyde asks Troilus to control his imagination and "drif out the fantasies yow withinne, / And trusteth me ... / Or here my trouthe" (IV, 1615–17), because she "kan ymaginen a wey" (IV, 1626).

Although Criseyde is clearly Troilus's idol, she pretends to "pray" to him for permission to depart (IV, 1632–33, 1639). Criseyde's final, most effective, and most tonally elusive strategy is simply to appropriate Troilus's apprehension as her own: "whil I am absent, no plesaunce / Of oother do me fro youre remembraunce" (IV, 1642–43). Criseyde imagines an alternative universe in which it is Troilus who would be shamed "if that ye were untrewe" (IV, 1647). His infidelity would be unspeakable because she "alle trouthe in yow entende" (IV, 1649). Troilus calls God to witness, only "to whom ther nys no cause ywrye" (IV, 1654), and "it shal be founde at preve" (IV, 1659) by the rest of Chaucer's recital.

Criseyde's final promise seems an imperfect echo of Troilus's vow: "I was youre, and shal *while I may dure*. / And this may *lengthe of yeres* naught fordo" (IV, 1680–81). It is difficult to say how her somewhat qualified expressions "as long as I may last" and "length of years" should be read. But some tone must be supposed by the reader; in good faith, why not some approximation of the one presumably imposed by Chaucer during recital?

Book IV concludes with Chaucer questioning faith in trust. Criseyde's eulogy to the truth of Troilus, including his disdain of

BOOK IV, CONJUNCTIONS

"every thyng that souned into badde" (IV, 1676), serves Chaucer as a sort of peroration. Chaucer says it is now pointless to ask whether Troilus was sad: "this holde I no demaunde" (IV, 1694). Instead, and in counterpoint to 1 Corinthians 2:9–10, Chaucer imagines the ineffable hellishness of Troilus's perfect woe: "For mannes hed ymagynen ne kan, / N'entendement considere, ne tonge telle" (IV, 1695–97). At the end of this book, Troilus's "soule" (IV, 1700) departs only metaphorically. Ultimately speechless, Troilus leaves, and perhaps at this same recital moment silent Chaucer exits too.

Book Five begins with the entrance of Destiny.

6

BOOK V, DECEPTIONS AND RECEPTIONS

THOUGH Book V lacks a proem, Chaucer's final installment of *Troilus and Criseyde* starts formally and ominously enough. The poet acknowledges that Jove has commissioned the Parcae "to don execucioun" (V, 4) of the rest of his plot. A very purple periphrasis states the simple fact that three years have passed (V, 8–11) since Troilus first sighted Criseyde. It is certain that Criseyde will depart tomorrow (V, 14). Throughout the rest of Book V, however, Chaucer's high style often entertains a circumlocution that seems primarily dedicated to obscuring the exact timing of Criseyde's inevitable infidelity.

Chaucer's final act of recital readily divides into three main scenes: Troilus's initial longing for Criseyde to return (V, 1–686); Criseyde's simultaneous acceptance of inevitable change (V, 687–1099); and Troilus's fatal despair (V, 1100–1764). The rest is epilogue (V, 1765–1869). Barry Windeatt observes that "as the text progresses and the book grows larger, the sense of a performance gives way somewhat to the processes of composition."[1] Book V voices

---

1. Barry Windeatt, *Troilus and Criseyde*, Oxford Guides to Chaucer (Oxford: Clarendon Press, 1992), 17.

BOOK V, DECEPTIONS

Chaucer's most writerly consciousness and may indeed represent his most revised (hence longest) installment of *Troilus and Criseyde*. In the end, Troilus's and Chaucer's own struggle to comprehend the final absence of Criseyde offers a maddening analogy for the frustration of every reader who tries to comprehend the tonal intentions of this text's author in absentia.

Criseyde "nyste what was best to rede" (V, 18); Troilus too waits "withouten reed or loore" (V, 22). Diomede, however, is already "ful redy" (V, 15) to undertake his appointed role. Since Troilus has "heretofore" thought Criseyde the "sothfast" source of "lust or joies," now likewise melancholy Chaucer addresses Troilus directly: "For shaltow nevere sen hire eft in Troie!" (V, 28). But Troilus is not listening. "Soth is" (V, 29), manliness requires Troilus to maintain a shaky silence though he torments himself with unspoken verbosity: "And seyde to hymself this ilke sawe: / 'Allas,' ..." etc. (V, 38–49).[2] Chaucer thoroughly sympathizes with such self-censorship; Troilus avoids making a scene, "and ellis, certeyn, as I seyde yore, / He hadde it don, withouten wordes more" (V, 55–56).

Troilus puts on a fairly good show (V, 64, 74–75), though he lowers his mask for a momentary memento: "ful softe and sleighly gan hire seye" (V, 83). Diomede rightly reads the subtext of Troilus's pale silence (V, 86–87) because he "koude more than the crede / In swich a craft" (V, 89–90). With Criseyde in tow, Diomede himself has a rather carefree attitude about speaking aloud.

---

2. The author of *The Laste Epistle of Creseyd to Troyalus* (ca. 1600) questions this reading of Troilus's inaction when Criseyde explicitly asks:

Howe could thy knightly harte consent,
Or eyes abyde the sight,
To see me under Diomedes guarde
From Troy to Greikes so stray? (ll. 111–14)

See Anne McKim, ed., *The Laste Epistle of Creseyd to Troyalus* (Kalamazoo, Mich.: Medieval Institute Publications, 1970).

BOOK V, DECEPTIONS

He assumes that, at the very least, conversation with Criseyde will kill some time: "for somwhat shal I seye, / For at the werste it may yet shorte oure weye" (V, 95–96; cf. *CT* I, 791). Diomede has "herd seyd" (V, 97) that self-interest is wisdom, "but natheles, this thoughte he wel ynough" (V, 99) that the rhetoric of successful seduction depends primarily on timing and tone: "Certeynlich I am aboute nought, / If that I speke of love or make it tough" (V, 100–101). Diomede recognizes the merits of misdirection: "but I shal fynde a meene / That she naught wite as yet shal what I mene" (V, 105). Chaucer's listeners are invited to grant a certain grudging respect.

The fall of Criseyde begins with mere chitchat: "Whan tyme was, gan fallen forth in speche / Of this and that" (V, 107–8). Diomede swears (V, 113, 127) and prays (V, 117) and repeatedly assures her that "we Grekis" can be as true as Trojans (V, 118, 123–25, 141). Although recital can make Diomede seem completely smarmy, Chaucer's stated intent to excuse Criseyde is such that he makes attractive Diomede sound rather persuasive.[3] Chaucer suppresses, therefore, any mention of Diomede's prior marriage. Chaucer allows Diomede to state an initial offer that sounds mostly friendly, altruistic, indeed brotherly, and "ek thus" (V, 120) most plausible. Chaucer tests the tonal limits of gullibility, however, when Diomede claims (as Troilus had incredibly but truly confessed): "Thus seyde I nevere er now to womman born, ... I loved never womman here-biforn" (V, 155–57).

Diomede explains that his present dialogue with Criseyde must sound so guarded because Chaucer has not yet granted them an entirely private scene: "And nere it that we ben so neigh

---

3. Chaucer's contemporaries need not have had an entirely negative predisposition toward Diomede, and Alexandra Hennessey Olsen, for one, defends Diomede's reputation in "In Defense of Diomede: 'Moral Gower' and *Troilus and Criseyde*," *Geardagum* 8 (1987): 1–12.

BOOK V, DECEPTIONS

the tente / Of Calcas, which that sen us bothe may, / I wolde of this yow telle al myn entente— / But this enseled til anothir day" (V, 148–51). Instead, Diomede manipulates Criseyde's body language: "Yeve me youre hond" (V, 152). Like Troilus (like Chaucer), Diomede presents himself as a self-effacing lyric poet—"Al kan I naught to yow ... / Compleyne aright, for I am yet to leere" (V, 160–61). He justifies his obviously sudden attraction (V, 164–65) on the basis of Criseyde's hearsay inspiration. All the while that Diomede plays the novice lover (falsely like Troilus), heartbroken Criseyde seems to remain (truly like Troilus) completely distracted:

> Criseyde unto that purpos lite answerde,
> As she that was with sorwe oppressed so
> That, in effect, she naught his tales herde
> But here and ther, now here a word or two.
> Hire thoughte hire sorwful herte brast a-two. (V, 176–80)

Only some indication of Chaucer's corresponding attitude as rehearser of this exchange can distinguish the integrity of Criseyde's distraction from the fraud of Diomede's flattery.

Whereas Criseyde had been most scrupulous about the semantics of her first concession to Troilus, she now consents to accept Diomede with what seems an almost absent-minded oath: "And tristen hym she wolde, and wel she myghte, / As seyde she ..." (V, 188–89). Criseyde then dismounts, greets her happy father with what may not be a lie, and keeps silent (V, 193–94) as Chaucer returns to talk of Troilus (V, 196).

Troilus also dismounts and refuses to speak with others, though not so mildly as Criseyde: "Ne non to hym dar speke a word for drede" (V, 203). Only when alone he "yaf an issue large" and loud (V, 205). Chaucer's paraphrase somewhat assuages the

BOOK V, DECEPTIONS

intensity of Troilus's cursing, or suggests the worst that can be imagined rather than recited. Troilus blames all except Criseyde (V, 205–10). Troilus's rage decreases enough to be quoted directly and so sounds self-wallowing: "And to hymself right thus he spak, and seyde" (V, 217). Chaucer's recital must share the tenor of Troilus's owl-like possessiveness:

> *Who* seth yow now...
> *Who* sit right now or stant in youre presence?
> *Who* kan conforten now...
> ... *whom* yeve ye audience?
> *Who* speketh for me right now in myn absence? (V, 233–36; my italics)

Chaucer will ask these very same questions of his book in hand once released from his own recital control. Such authorial jealousy is erotic, fantastic, and real.

Troilus has nightmares that prove the actual physical effects of mere imagination, "that wonder to here his fantasie" (V, 261), which Troilus tries to dismiss as "folie" (V, 263) but fails "eft" (V, 265). Chaucer as book-writer then explicitly challenges each reader, "every man" (V, 266), to imagine more than the text can contain:

> Thow, redere, maist thiself ful wel devyne
> That swich a wo my wit kan nat diffyne
> On ydel for to write it sholde I swynke,
> Whan that my wit is wery it to thynke. (V, 270–73)

This unique direct address to "thou, reader" in *Troilus and Criseyde* may be Chaucer's homage to Dante; it may be a post-recital revision; the text now speaks to his foreseen though unseen audience who hopefully can *divine* its intended tone in good faith.

BOOK V, DECEPTIONS

Failing—no doubt for good reasons—to keep his promise "although he on his hed it hadde sworn" (V, 283; cf. V, 354–57), tardy Pandarus needs no gloss to read that Troilus will recite his grief:

> For in his herte he koude wel devyne
> That Troilus al nyght for sorwe wook;
> And that he wolde telle hym of hys pyne,
> This knew he wel ynoughe, withoute book. (V, 288–91)

Troilus scripts the "feste and pleyes palestral" (V, 304) of his own very theatrical funeral (cf. CT I, 2912ff.). He imagines that "a vessell that men clepeth an urne" (V, 311) holding the ashes of his heart will be bequeathed to Criseyde so that she can "kepe it for a remembraunce" (V, 315)—like a book. But Troilus's definition of "urn" seems gratuitous, and Chaucer's end-rhyme sounds strained; both details are both trivial and disruptive—the (deliberate) tonal falterings of a poet-translator overstretched by direct quotation of Troilus's excessive anguish.

Troilus reads all signs as fatal (V, 316–20). Again a bookish Chaucer seems to step on his character's lines by providing a tangential, mood-breaking detail; Chaucer uses a quite artsy end-rhyme "Escaphilo" (V, 319) to remind us of the owl's name and then has Pandarus remind Troilus "as I have told the yore" (V, 324) that his causeless sorrow is "folye" (V, 325). But the art of persuasion (including distraction) has its limits:

> But whoso wil nought trowen reed ne loore,
> I kan nat sen in hym no remedie,
> But lat hym worthen with his fantasie. (V, 327–29)

"But" (V, 330), in fact, most of the rest of Book V presents just such an exercise in futility.

Attempting to change Troilus's immutable folly, Pandarus

offers three arguments: 1) that the separation of lovers is a common experience, 2) that dreams are illusory, and 3) that pleasant pastimes will shorten their wait. The patience that Pandarus recommends may be read as true fortitude (as in the Book of Ecclesiastes) or as jaded sophistication: "So shuldestow endure, and laten slide / The tyme" (V, 351). Like Criseyde before, Pandarus preaches skepticism. He debunks the preternatural import of dreams: "A straw for alle swevenes signifiaunce!" (V, 362). He opposes what "leches seyn" to what "prestes ... tellen" (V, 365–70)—authority vs. authority:

> Who woot in soth thus what thei signifie?
> Ek oother seyn ...
> And other seyn, as they in bokes fynde. (V, 371–75)

Pandarus rejects all "swich ordure" (V, 385) outright, he says. And such indeterminacy should liberate Troilus from obligatory penance: "Unto thiself that al this thow foryyve; / And ris now up withowten more speche" (V, 387–88). Such self-forgiveness mandates that Troilus "foryete or oppresse" (V, 398) his own imagination, however.

It is Pandarus's enthusiasm rather than his logic—his tone, not his theme—that gets Troilus out of bed: "lat us speke of lusty lif" (V, 393). Pandarus anticipates what "folk wol seyn" if Troilus fails to rise in three days' time: in Troy, they will imagine that he only pretends to be sick "for cowardise" (V, 412); in New Troy, they will recognize that this son of Cupid does not prefigure Christ.

In his own defense, Troilus appeals to different "folk" (including presumably the true lovers in Chaucer's audience) who have shared his experience. Nevertheless, Troilus consents "of fyne force" (V, 421) to do as Pandarus says and attend the "pleye" (V, 429, 431) at Sarpedon's, "so longe of this they speken up and down" (V, 432). Chaucer has heard tell "as seyden bothe the mooste and ek the leeste" (V, 440) that Sarpedon's festivities transcend comprehension; this extravagant, indeed Pauline, praise—"That tonge telle or herte may recorde ... was nevere iseye with ië" (V, 445–48)—is qualified by "er tho," which (given the right intonation) challenges the present party, including "ladys ek so fair a compaignie" (V, 447), to surpass.

But Troilus's response proves antithetical to Pandarus's intention. The memory of Criseyde distorts his perception of the performances of all other ladies: "It was his sorwe upon hem for to sen, / Or for to here on instrumentes pleye" (V, 458–59). Chaucer's use of negative expressions reinforces the negativism of Troilus's disposition: "Nor ther nas houre ... Whan he was there as no wight myghte hym heere, / That he ne seyde" (V, 463–65). When Troilus welcomes Criseyde herself to the party (V, 467), Chaucer steps away from this deluded vocative to make a comment that sounds both sympathetic and sarcastic: "But weylawey, al this nat but a maze. / Fortune his howve entended bet to glaze!" (V, 468–69). Troilus retreats from courtly pastimes to his solitary reading of Criseyde: "The lettres ek ... he wolde allone rede" and re-read a hundred times "refiguryng hire shap" (V, 470–74).

After four days, Pandarus can keep Troilus from leaving only by recalling his promise: "Syn that we seyden" (V, 491). None of Chaucer's time-killing recital serves much narrative purpose except to create some analogous experience of the frustration caused by Criseyde's delay. Finally, after the full week, Troilus may depart, and he sings (V, 504), expecting Criseyde to have already returned—a happy hope that Pandarus immediately contradicts with suppressed sarcasm: "And to hymself ful softeliche he seyde" (V, 506). Pandarus feigns optimism: "But natheles, he japed thus, and pleyde, / And swor, ywys" (V, 509–10). Chaucer's voice must empathize with

BOOK V, DECEPTIONS

the integrity of both Troilus's naive self-deception and Pandarus's more jaundiced but well-meaning fraud—and so sounds torn.

To discover if Criseyde is at home, Troilus must invent another cover story, "and therwithal, his meyne for to blende, / A cause he fond" (V, 526–27). Troilus almost reveals himself when he grows pale at the wintry sight of Criseyde's empty palace, but "withouten word, he forthby gan to pace ... / That no wight of his contenance espide" (V, 537–39). With only Pandarus as his audience, Troilus recites a poem to an empty house: "seide he thus" (V, 540). Without Criseyde (or her moebles), this "hous of houses whilom best ihight" is a "desolat" site and a "disconsolat" sight (V, 540–42). Troilus hesitates to kiss Criseyde's closed doors in view of "this route" (V, 552), and Chaucer escapes further direct impersonation of this abject lament (with what might be a rather ironic autocitation; cf. "Against Women Unconstant," 15).

Troilus can perceive present stimuli only as images of the past: "And every thyng com hym to remembraunce" (V, 562); "Lo, yonder saugh ich last ... That in my soule yet me thynketh ich here / The blisful sown" (V, 565–80). Troilus views everything as "whilom" (V, 564). Perhaps Chaucer's most ironically self-referential gesture in Book V occurs when an increasingly solipsistic Troilus "thoughte he thus: / ... 'Whan I the proces have in my memorie / ... Men myght a book make of it, lik a storie'" (V, 582–85). Troilus too has read the *Thebaid* and sincerely prays that Cupid will be less cruel than Juno, a prayer that Chaucer voices in vain. Troilus restages past scenes with Criseyde (V, 603–14) and drafts future scripts for himself to play: "And of hymself ymagened he ofte" (V, 617), "Another tyme ymaginen he wolde" (V, 624). Chaucer has Troilus envision himself as an occasion for confabulation: "and that men seyden softe, / 'What may it be? Who kan the sothe gesse[?]'" (V, 619–20). And yet all this fantasy kills only a day or

BOOK V, DECEPTIONS

two (V, 628). The voice of Chaucer recalls the real performance at hand "as ye have herd" (V, 629).

Troilus likes to show his vacillation between hope and dread in lyrics (V, 631); he wants to reveal himself and so "made a song of wordes but a fewe" (V, 633). Chaucer sounds less than certain about the success of Troilus's poem: "as he best myghte ... Somwhat" (V, 632–34) and recites only one stanza: "With softe vois ... as ye may heere" (V, 636–37) to "absent" (V, 637) Criseyde. After what may have been Chaucer's singing of "this song whan he thus songen hadde" (V, 645), Troilus is reduced to inarticulate exhalations: "He fil ayeyn into his sikes olde" (V, 646). In performance, Chaucer must share the pain of these sighs though moved by authorial rather than amorous frustration. Troilus talks to the moon; Chaucer is on display.

Walking the walls, Troilus "on the Grekis oost he wolde se; / And to hymself right thus he wolde talke" (V, 667–68) about mere air. Troilus listens to "this wynd" (V, 673) blowing from the Greek camp and hears "my ladys depe sikes soore" (V, 675). Logic enthralled by desire proves what it will; so Troilus can confirm his fantasy with a peculiar exercise in empiricism: "I preve it thus: for in noon other place / Of al this town, save onliche in this space, / Fele I no wynd that sowneth so lik peyne" (V, 676–78). Troilus translates his sense of mere wind into a melancholic line of alliteration, assonance, and aspiration: "It seyth, 'Allas! Whi twynned be we tweyne?'" (V, 679). Present (though unnoticed till now) Pandarus has remained "ay bisyde " (V, 682) self-absorbed Troilus. Pandarus would "bisily" talk Troilus into hoping (V, 683–86), but Chaucer has already conceded that this effort is merely a waste of air.

"Upon the other syde" (V, 687), Criseyde is sighing as expected: "For which ful ofte a day 'Allas,' she seyde" (V, 689). At first, Criseyde also feels a morbid despair (V, 690–91). Yet, she far more readily (and quickly) adapts to her present reality. She wonders if Troilus will misinterpret her delay: "in his herte deme / That I am fals, and so it may wel seme" (V, 697–98). Talking only to herself, Criseyde regrets the plausibility of this suspicion and thus anticipates the consensus opinion of Chaucer's contemporaries: "Thus shal ich have unthonk on every side" (V, 699). Like Troilus, Criseyde too is profoundly affected by constructs of her own imagination: "in hireself she wente ay purtraynge / Of Troilus ... thus she sette hire woful herte afire / Thorugh remembraunce of that she gan desire" (V, 716–21). In particular, she recalls "al his goodly wordes recordynge" (V, 718). Chaucer challenges his audience not to be moved to tears if they could actually hear her: "In al this world ther nys so cruel herte / That hire hadde herd compleynen" (V, 722–23). But, for a while, Chaucer supplants the intense tone of Criseyde's own voice with mere paraphrase: "And this was yet the werste of al hire peyne: / Ther was no wight to whom she dorste hire pleyne" (V, 727–28). She cried a lot, so much so that Chaucer remarks, "Hire nedede no teris for to borwe!" (V, 726), which seems an emotionally inadequate nonce rhyme.

When Criseyde does speak on her own behalf, she seems to be trying to convince primarily herself that she will keep her word. Criseyde concedes too late (V, 741, 743) the validity of Troilus's doubts (V, 736–37) and will regret her improvidence, "But future tyme ... Koude I nat sen" (V, 748–49). Chaucer has Criseyde keep talking to herself (V, 731, 734) though "to late is now to speke of that matere" (V, 743). Criseyde still thinks she plans to escape "bityde what bityde" (V, 750) despite "wikked tonges janglerie" (V, 755). She (or Chaucer) sounds especially insistent on this point: "For whoso wol of every word take hede, / Or reulen hym by every wightes wit, / Ne shal he nevere thryven." (V, 757–59). Having defined her own philosophic terms, Criseyde intends to escape "withouten any wordes mo ... as for conclusioun" (V, 764–65). But Chaucer now explicitly belies her sincere (because privately spoken) purpose:

> But God it wot, er fully monthes two,
> She was ful fer fro that entencioun! ...
> For she wol take a purpos for t'abide. (V, 766–70)

Criseyde unties herself from the past (V, 769) only to be netted by Diomede (V, 775). She will be kept.

Returning to Diomede "of whom yow telle I gan" (V, 771), Chaucer reports that this Greek too has been talking to himself—"withinne hymself ay arguynge" (V, 772), though he hardly sounds tortured by self-doubt. He is concerned only about maximum rhetorical efficiency: "How he may best, with shortest taryinge" (V, 774) seduce Criseyde. Chaucer can repeat what Diomede "seyde he to hymself" (V, 785)—the "sleghte and al that evere he kan" (V, 773)—with a grudging admiration. Diomede utters a brutally clear-headed and so utterly unromantic assessment of the present situation. Diomede has learned his lessons about context from texts: "For wise folk in bookes it expresse, / 'Men shal nat wowe a wight in hevynesse'" (V, 790–91). Diomede's lust sounds more competitive (V, 792). Perhaps deepening his own voice a bit, Chaucer repeats "as bokes us declare" that Diomede had a "sterne vois ... / And som men seyn he was of tonge large" (V, 799–804). This trivial though provocative factoid about Diomede's tongue may report a physical oddity, or it may be a figure of speech meaning only that "rakel"-tongued Diomede (cf. CT 9, 339) is a braggart who devalues the substance of words: "I shal namore lesen but my speche" (V, 798).[4]

---

4. Cf. Chaucer's "litel tonge" (IV, 801). In *The Laste Epistle of Creseyd to Troyalus*, it is noted that Diomede also has "sleated lipps" (McKim, l. 123).

BOOK V, DECEPTIONS

Chaucer now provides snapshots of the love triangle. He brackets our first objective glimpse of Criseyde (V, 806–26) with miniature evaluations of Diomede and Troilus. The preceding description of Diomede ends with a recollection of his attractive patrimony. The following description of Troilus celebrates his "paregal" endurance as "certeynly in storye it is yfounde" (V, 827–40). In between, the "mene" (V, 806) Criseyde is seen, if not objectively, then rather more matter-of-factly than before. Chaucer, having drawn unnecessarily specific attention "in aught I kan espien" (V, 814) to Criseyde's unibrow, overcompensates: "But for to speken ... / Lo, trewely, they writen that hire syen / That Paradis stook formed in hire yën" (V, 815–17).[5] Criseyde appears sober, simple, wise "withal," "goodly of hire speche in general" (V, 822), but rather average. Chaucer's *descriptio* encourages a varied though limited range of audience responses to Criseyde's attractiveness. Troilus's infatuation may no longer seem compelling, but Diomede's interest does seem likely.

Troilus and Diomede may be read as antipodal exemplars of male desire—and, as such, both are simple. In between, Criseyde is ambiguous. Chaucer can comprehend his masculine stereotypes, but the feminine mystique eludes his personal grasp. Diomede's mood seems obvious to Chaucer when he "feyned" (V, 846) his visit to Calkas's tent: "But what he mente, I shal yow tellen soone" (V, 847). Chaucer plays Diomede precisely as a faux-Troilus.[6] And yet Criseyde falls for his line. It is the recital tone of

---

5. Conjoined eyebrows may seem attractive in other cultural contexts, but here and now Chaucer explicitly reports this detail as a "lak" (V, 813–14). Over-reading might see Criseyde's flaw as a metonymy for defective vision while Diomede's tongue suggests imperfect speech—or not.

6. Jennifer Summit remarks that "if Pandarus earlier expresses the opinion that women are entirely interchangeable, the text suggests that Troilus and Diomede are no less interchangeable. They are described in virtually the same terms" ("*Troilus and Criseyde*," 235).

such throwaway expressions as "but for to tellen forth" (V, 841), "at shorte wordes for to telle" (V, 848), and "of which som shal ye heere" (V, 854) that indicates Chaucer's response to this turn of events—his contempt for (and envy of) Diomede's rhetorical success.

Diomede and Criseyde chat over wine "of this and that yfeere" like "frendes" (V, 853–54). Diomede offers a descending (V, 859) or increasingly narrow choice of topics for their conversation. He asks (and so seems to care about) Criseyde's opinion regarding the siege (V, 858), then her reaction to the strangeness of new Greek customs, and then—most on target—her father's plans for her surprisingly postponed remarriage. So far, Criseyde still holds to Troilus, at least "as ferforth as she konnyng hadde or myght" (V, 866). Chaucer somewhat dubiously doubts that Criseyde truly perceives Diomede's motives as yet; she "answerde hym tho; but as of his entente, / It semed nat she wiste what he mente" (V, 868); this text's tone correlates directly to every reader's assumed intonation of the author's recital of *it seemed not*. "But natheles" (V, 869) Diomede remains silently confident that he can refashion Criseyde's mood "aright" (V, 871). Diomede says out loud "kan I nat seyn" (V, 876) what is the cause of Criseyde's sad *Daunger*. He does, however, accurately deduce that Criseyde is still beguiled by "som Troian" (V, 877), only to have her renounce such a futile love. His main gambit is to convince Criseyde that Troy is truly doomed: "as who seyth, alle and some" (V, 883). Diomede denies there has been any doublespeak in her father's prophecy, and Criseyde will see this truth directly: "Ye shal wel knowen that I naught ne lie, / And al this thyng right sen it with youre yë" (V, 900–901). Diomede wants Criseyde to exchange her "bittre hope" for "good cheere" (V, 913) and then acts the blushing lover: "And with that word he gan to waxen red, / And in his speche a litel wight he quok, /... And ... And ... And ... And ... / As gentil man as any wight in Troie" (V, 925–31). Diomede even pretends to rival Troilus as a virgin lover (V, 940) and ostensibly requests only that Criseyde grant him audience tomorrow.

Criseyde's slightest concession, like the trivial bite of an arbitrary apple, seems fatal to many readers even though Chaucer slithers around this instant when Criseyde first yields:

> What sholde I telle his wordes that he seyde?
> He spak inough for o day at the meeste.
> It preveth wel; he spak so that Criseyde
> Graunted on the morwe, at his requeste,
> For to speken with hym at the leeste—
> So that he nolde speke of swich matere.
> And thus to hym she seyde, as ye may here. (V, 946–52)

Only the presumed intonation given by Chaucer to his report that Criseyde agreed "to speak with Diomede *at the least*" defines the tonal implications of this first concession. C. David Benson feels "our distance from Criseyde is especially pronounced during her betrayal of Troilus in book V."[7]

Chaucer desperately wants to maintain that Diomede has not yet erased (V, 954) Criseyde's true love of Troilus. He quotes her "strangely" (V, 955). She grants the doom of Troy (V, 961–62), the worthiness of Greeks in general, and the suitability of Diomede in particular (V, 972–73). Then she balks: "'But as to speke of love, ywis,' she seyde" (V, 974) ... nothing about Troilus. Instead, Criseyde, portraying herself as a born-again widow, like Dido (V, 977–78), speaks in *ambages*. Criseyde acknowledges Diomede's (rich) pedigree: "I have wel herd it tellen"—from Diomede himself (V, 980; cf. 935). But Criseyde renounces the most obvious

---

7. C. David Benson, *Chaucer's Troilus*, 109.

BOOK V, DECEPTIONS

motive for this conversation: "Ek, God woot, love and I ben fer ysonder!" (V, 983). "Love" here can be read two ways at once: she is not interested in loving (*daunger*); she is distant from Troilus (verbal irony). Criseyde claims to hear Diomede's devotion as scorn, which he hears as a conventional trope. Criseyde insists she is now "disposed" (V, 984) to be in mourning till death, but "what I shal after don I kan nat seye" (V, 986). "After" can mean "forever after" or "tomorrow" or anything in between. Criseyde demurs that she "trewelich" does not wish to play "as yet" (V, 987). Diomede takes this adverb as a promise.

Criseyde says seeing is believing and, pending clarification, does promise something:

> Herafter, whan ye wonnen han the town,
> Peraventure so it happen may
> That whan I se that nevere yit I say
> Than wol I werke that I nevere wroughte!
> This word to yow ynough suffisen oughte. (V, 990–94)

Criseyde's word does seem sufficient for Diomede to understand as he pleases, and Criseyde does welcome Diomede's future conversation: "To-morwe ek wol I speken with yow fayn" (V, 995). She tries to conclude today's exchange with a hypothetical promise, "thus muche I sey yow here" (V, 998): if she would ever love any Greek, it should be Diomede "by my trouthe!" (V, 1001). Chaucer quotes what she says she will not say: "I say nat therfore that I wol ... N'y say nat nay; but in conclusioun, / I mene wel" (V, 1002–4). She sighs and (sadly/coyly) casts down her eyes, and Diomede, "in effect, and shortly for to seye" (V, 1009), takes advantage of Criseyde's doubt or duplicity, and "after this, the sothe for to seyn" (V, 1012), takes her glove, though Chaucer hesitates to admit that Criseyde freely gave Diomede this first trophy. De-

BOOK V, DECEPTIONS

fending already fallen Criseyde from his audience's complete contempt requires Chaucer to sound as crestfallen (or self-loathing) by his own submission to the text's necessity.

In bed alone, Criseyde reinvents herself:

> Retornyng in hire soule ay up and down
> The wordes of this sodeyn Diomede,
> ... and thus bygan to brede
> The cause whi, the sothe for to telle,
> That she took fully purpos for to dwelle. (V, 1023-29)

Finding a proper tone for this "sothe for to telle" is Chaucer's primary crisis. He sounds strangely reticent as he recites the next seventy lines. Chaucer's expression "and gostly for to speke" (V, 1030) can modify either Diomede's persuasiveness or his own embarrassment. He anticipates some impatient skepticism: "And shortly, lest that ye my tale breke, / ... the sothe for to seyne" (V, 1032-35). Criseyde is "refte" (V, 1036) of her prior pain, and Chaucer's stated intentions have been taken over by the imperatives of history: "And after this, the storie telleth us" (V, 1037); "I fynde ek in stories elleswhere" (V, 1044); "But trewely, the storie telleth us" (V, 1051). His sources make Chaucer report that Criseyde gave significant presents to Diomede, but he refuses to repeat the worst possible interpretation of this fact: "Men seyn—I not—that she yaf hym hire herte" (V, 1050); yet, even Chaucer as her last friend in the room regrets Criseyde's re-gifting of Troilus's brooch: "and that was litel nede" (V, 1040). Eventually, Chaucer must simply admit that, though Criseyde grieved, "she falsed Troilus" (V, 1053).

Chaucer lets Criseyde exit with a prolonged soliloquy (V, 1054-85) in which "she seyde" what amounts to Chaucer's reading of all the interpretations of her story that precede *Troilus and Criseyde*:

BOOK V, DECEPTIONS

> Allas, of me, unto the worldes ende,
> Shal neyther ben ywriten nor ysonge
> No good word, for thise bokes wol me shende.
> O, rolled shal I ben on many a tonge!
> Thorughout the world my belle shal be ronge!
> And wommen moost wol haten me of alle. (V, 1058–63)

What specifically "thei wol seyn" (V, 1065) will vary according to their various appraisals of her dishonor "in as muche as in me is" (V, 1065). Chaucer lets Criseyde try to mitigate her hardly unique case in vain: "Al be I nat the first that dide amys, / What helpeth that to don my blame awey?" (V, 1067–68). Criseyde thus provides Chaucer's audience with their main talking point.

Criseyde firmly resolves henceforth to remain "algate" true to Diomede (V, 1071). She does not think herself a runaway; rather, she sees her separation from Troilus as a mutual parting—"thus departen ye and I" (V, 1074). She promises only "my good word" of him; she vows to hate Troilus never even if she should live forever (V, 1080–81)—a doubly strange or strained promise. Criseyde's isolation seems to validate the emotional integrity of her confession (V, 1078)—she truly feels forced to be false. Whereas "best" (V, 1077) Troilus stays perfectly immutable in love, Criseyde accepts the truth of an Epicurean dictum that "al shal passe" (V, 1085). Chaucer gives her a weak, perhaps emotionally drained rhyme to say farewell, "And giltless, I woot wel, I yow leve. / . . . and thus take I my leve" (V, 1084–85). Criseyde means Troilus is guiltless, but Chaucer's syntax lets the adjective "giltless" audibly cling to "I."

Many readers find Chaucer's anxiety at this point much more convincing than Criseyde's regret. Chaucer highlights an apparent lacuna in his sources: "But trewely, how longe it was bytwene / That she forsok hym for this Diomede, / Ther is non auc-

BOOK V, DECEPTIONS

tour telleth it, I wene" (V, 1086–88). Chaucer challenges "every man now" to collate all texts; "he shal no terme fynden, out of drede" (V, 1089–90). Chaucer would discuss Criseyde's relative innocence in measured terms: "For though that he bigan to wowe hire soone, / Er he hire wan, yet was ther more to doone" (V, 1091–92). Even though the expression "refte ... of ... peyne" (V, 1036) may be interpreted to mean "had sex"—"as I byfore have told" (V, 1100)—Chaucer refuses to recite that Criseyde accepted Diomede by the eleventh day after her departure from Troy, and his pace camouflages any impression of her too hasty capitulation.

In between the misogynist tradition of his sources and the anticipated, concordantly hostile confabulation of his audience, Chaucer dissents:

> Ne me ne list this sely womman chyde
> Forther than the storye wol devyse.
> Hire name, allas, is publysshed so wide
> That for hire gilt it oughte ynough suffise.
> And if I myghte excuse hire any wise,
> For she so sory was for hire untrouthe,
> I wis, I wolde excuse hire yet for routhe. (V, 1093–99)

Anticipating an open-and-shut sentence against Criseyde, Chaucer appeals for mercy rather than justice; such a plea may be termed "Christian" or "feminine," but it also sounds self-consciously futile. Chaucer's soft sympathy echoes the pitiable desperation of Criseyde's immediately preceding soliloquy, "and that to late is now for me to rewe" (V, 1070).[8]

A new dawn comes with the "fressh entente" of chirpy Ciris.[9]

---

8. In *The Laste Epistle of Creseyd to Troyalus*, Criseyde imagines that, had she remained faithful, "then should no poet have the cause / Faire Creyseydes treuthe to blame" (McKim, ll. 25–26).

9. The subtext of allusions is much darker. Scylla had been transformed into the

BOOK V, DECEPTIONS

Sleepless, fevered Troilus sends for Pandarus "to loke if they kan sen aught of Criseyde" (V, 1113); their play quickly enough turns into embarrassing make-believe: "they seyden it was she—/Til that thei koude knowen hym aright... And thus byjaped stonden for to stare/Aboute naught" (V, 1116–20).

Troilus fabricates an excuse for Criseyde; he speculates she must dine with her father. Pandarus approves—"It may wel be, certeyn" (V, 1128)—but only to recommend that they dine too "withoute more speche" (V, 1131). When Pandarus and Troilus return to keep watch, however, Chaucer can no longer hold his tongue: "but longe may they seche/Er that they fynde that they after cape./Fortune hem bothe thenketh to jape!" (V, 1132–34). Chaucer himself seems especially disturbed now by Troilus's presumptuous obtuseness. Troilus pretends to know too much: "By God, I woot hire menyng now... Now douteles, this lady kan hire good;/I woot she meneth..." (V, 1147–50). Since he thinks he knows what Criseyde "thenketh," Troilus tells Pandarus what to "thynk" (V, 1154–55). Chaucer makes Troilus's passionate "trouthe" (V, 1158) appear (al)most ludicrous when he misinterprets the sight of "a fare-carte" (V, 1162) as Criseyde. Pandarus is already much more clear-sighted. But Troilus's blind optimism (masking unspeakable doubt) lets him translate even such a complete error into a good omen:

---

painted bunting (*Passerina Ciris*) to escape her father, King Nisus, who is transformed into an osprey (Ovid's *Metamorphoses* viii 1–151). In the *Legend of Good Women*, Chaucer proposes a rather whitewashed analogy between the traitor Scylla (LGW 1902–21) and Ariadne, in that each woman chose the love of a foreign conqueror over obedience to her father the king. Though Boccaccio notes that some would excuse Scylla's crime (*Teseida* VI, st. 50), Suzanne C. Hagedorn reads her *exemplum* as "one of the main points of the *Thebaid* and the *Teseida*—that uncontrolled desire for a person or thing, like Scylla's for Minos, can result in the fall of a city" (*Abandoned Women: Rewriting the Classics in Dante, Boccaccio, and Chaucer* [Ann Arbor: University of Michigan Press, 2004], 81).

BOOK V, DECEPTIONS

"Allas, thow seyst right soth," quod Troilus.
"But, hardily, it is naught al for nought
That in myn herte I now rejoysse thus;
It is ayeyns som good I have a thought." (V, 1163–66)

Inexplicably "not I nat how" (V, 1167), Troilus cherishes the comfort of his fiction "dar I seye" (V, 1168).

Pandarus laughs slightly but speaks the cruel truth both "sobreliche" and sarcastically only to himself (V, 1172–75). Increasingly sad and absurd Troilus next "gladed hym in this" (V, 1184)—that he miscalculated, "and seyde, 'I understonde have al amys'" (V, 1186). He grants Criseyde a large margin of error, "but al for nought, his hope alwey hym blente" (V, 1195). He comes to comprehend only that he does not comprehend: "He nyste what he juggen of it myghte" (V, 1203). He becomes an inscrutable cripple who "nolde his cause pleyne" (V, 1230). Troilus is fading into silence till disease grants him a telling dream (V, 1238–42) which makes him cry out to Pandarus: "now know I crop and roote ... Criseyde, hath me bytrayed" (V, 1245–47). Even though this dream-vision "yshewed it ful right" (V, 1251), Chaucer still lets Troilus refuse to see Boccaccio's interpretation as a proper response to the dream: "whereas Troilo disassociates himself from Criseida ... Chaucer repudiates Troilo's repudiation of his beloved."[10]

Instead, Chaucer has Troilus translate his individual fear of betrayal into a universal crisis of faith: "Who shal now trowe on any othes mo? / God wot, I wende ... / That every word was gospel that ye seyde!" (V, 1263–65). By apposition, Troilus's apostrophes equate "O trust, O feyth! O depe asseuraunce!" (V, 1259)

---

10. David Wallace, "Troilus and the Filostrato: Chaucer as Translator of Boccaccio," in Shoaf, ed., "Subgit to alle Poesye," 257–67, 265.

BOOK V, DECEPTIONS

with "O lady bright, Criseyde" (V, 1264). Only gullibility (or good faith) made her lies so plausible (V, 1266–67). Faced by the danger of such suicidal despair, Pandarus lies for good effect: "Lat be this thought; thow kanst no dremes rede" (V, 1281). Unsurprised by the truth, Pandarus now tries to talk Troilus out of his true dream's true interpretation. Pandarus reiterates his categorical skepticism: "Have I nat seyd er this, / That dremes many a maner man bigile? / And whi? For folk expounded hem amys" (V, 1276–78). Pandarus then illustrates that the surest way to subvert an overly confident reader's sure because valid response is to fabricate an alternative, somewhat plausible interpretation: "It may be so that it may signifie / ... Thus sholdestow thi drem aright expounde!" (V, 1283–88).

Troilus is all too willing to revise his own suspicions if he knew how, and Pandarus approves this self-denial: "Now seystow wisly" (V, 1291). He recommends that competent Troilus write (V, 1292–93) to absent Criseyde because Pandarus apparently believes that letter writing can and should approximate the candor of person-to-person conversation—"tanquam cum amiculo in angulo sussures," as Erasmus would say. Pandarus has confidence that Troilus's letter will serve: "To know a soth of that thow art in doute" (V, 1295)—a confidence in written communication many dismiss as "blind faith."

Pandarus anticipates only two possible responses by Criseyde. Either she will fail to answer at all: "And se now whi: for this I dar wel seyn, / That if so is that she untrewe be, / I kan nat trowen that she wol write ayeyn" (V, 1296–98). Or she will state clearly an honest excuse: "And if she write, thow shalt ful sone yse / ... or ellis in som clause, / ... she wol assigne a cause" (V, 1299–1302). Troilus's ignorance of absent Criseyde's intent has been exacerbated by their mutual negligence: "Thow hast nat writen hire syn that

BOOK V, DECEPTIONS

she wente, / Nor she to the" (V, 1303–4). Pandarus suggests that, upon receiving Criseyde's reply, Troilus may even come to accept her unwelcome point of view:

> ... and this I dorste laye,
> Ther may swich cause ben in hire entente
> That hardily thow wolt thiselven saye
> That hire abod the best is for yow twaye. (V, 1305–7)

Writing will both reveal the true facts and achieve the desired effect: "Now writ hire thanne, and thow shalt feele sone / A soth of al" (V, 1308–9).

In lieu of direct contact, the reader and writer must trust the page: "Ther is namore to done" (V, 1309). The paper in hand records the voice of Troilus's doubt and desire: "He wrot right thus, and seyde as ye may here" (V, 1316). Troilus sits quickly (V, 1312) and muses "to and fro / How he may best descryven hire his wo" (V, 1313–14). He then writes at length (V, 1317–1421)—relatively speaking. As a text embedded in Book V, the "litera Troili" is formatted with its Latin title and French signature to represent the physical pages delivered to Criseyde—"this lettre to byholde" (V, 1341) which "forth was sent" (V, 1422). But, read aloud, Troilus's composition sounds pathetic as he struggles with the task of writing itself. His first stanza sounds especially bad, its diction clichéd, its syntax tortured, its meter halting, its phrasing strained (for example, "part of elleswhere servyse") or stilted ("that tonge telle") or conceited ("as ofte as matere occupieth place")—all compositional failures by Troilus for the sake of Chaucer's recital success.[11]

Troilus would simply and sincerely translate the intentions of

---

11. Troilus's "matere" seems to suggest the terminology of hylomorphism; cf. the "matere" of Criseyde's letter (V, 1372).

BOOK V, DECEPTIONS

his "dredful herte trewe" (V, 1331) to the page, in order to achieve the "redresse" of Criseyde's real presence, her "comyng hom ayeyn" (V, 1380–81). Yet, Troilus doubts the efficacy of his art even as "I write ... as I dar or kan endite" (V, 1331–34). Troilus wishes his tears which deface the page "wolden speke, if that they koude" (V, 1337) to Criseyde face-to-face. He beseeches her clear eyes to behold the foul papers that she holds (V, 1338–39).[12] Troilus feels especially entitled to write his complaint now because of what Criseyde "seyden, soth to seyne" (V, 1349)—two months ago (V, 1351). Troilus wants his writing to provoke her clear response (as Pandarus promised): "Yow write ich ... desiryng evere moore / To knowen fully, if youre wille it weere " (V, 1355–57).

But the absent author must worry if his distant reader still cares: "And if yow liketh knowen of the fare / Of me" (V, 1366). The evidence of Troilus's own hand makes manifest the obvious to Criseyde: "At wrytyng of this lettre I was on-lyve" (V, 1369)—that is, the author and his intent really exist although his spirit abides only to receive her (hopefully concordant) response: "Upon the sighte of matere of youre sonde" (V, 1372). Since Troilus can now neither see Criseyde herself nor foresee her anticipated reply, his cupidinous eyes have forfeited the power of immediate perception: "Myn eyen two, in veyn with which I se" (V, 1373). Love-blind Troilus asks invisible Criseyde: "if yow list namore upon me se, ... hereupon ye wolden write me" so he "may make an ende" (V, 1388–93) and die, or "with youre lettre ye me recomforte ... with youre lettre of hope ... Now writeth, swete, and lat me thus nat pleyne" (V, 1395–99). Troilus will recover as soon "as I yow se" (V, 1385), even though "when ye next upon me se" (V, 1402) Criseyde

---

12. Cf. Chaucer's complaint that reading the story of Tereus makes his eyes bloodshot (LGW 2239–40).

BOOK V, DECEPTIONS

will not be able to recognize Troilus.[13] Troilus ends with a showy but explicitly inadequate farewell. Troilus knows he cannot fully express himself on paper: "I say namore, al have I for to seye / To yow wel more than I telle may" (V, 1408–9).

In pronounced contrast to his verbatim repetition of the entire "litera Troili," Chaucer all but obliterates Criseyde's reply letter. Its paraphrase sounds quite jejune:

> hire answere in effect was this:
> ... she wroot ayeyn, and seyde ...
> And fynaly she wroot and seyde hym thenne,
> She wolde come, ye, but she nyste whenne. (V, 1423–28)

She reportedly composed "ful pitously" (V, 1424), but the recital tone of "ywis" and "ye" suggest that Chaucer is less than sure—indeed, authorial *pronuntiatio* can here invert the intended effect of the words in print, signaling uncertainty rather than confidence. Chaucer notes that "in hire lettre" Criseyde wrote wonderful endearments, but he will now repeat none of it. On the contrary, getting a little ahead of himself, Chaucer says that Troilus "fond" all her promises "but botmeles bihestes" (V, 1431)—because it is Chaucer himself who *now* feels moved to say so, not Troilus. It *is* Chaucer who needs to blow off some frustration now: "But Troilus, thow maist now, est or west, / Pipe in an ivy lef, if that the lest!" (V, 1432–33). As Criseyde went, "thus goth the world, God shilde us fro meschaunce" (V, 1434); this "us" refers to the author himself, his present audience, his future readers, and "every wight that meneth trouthe avaunce" (V, 1435).

---

13. "Criseyde" in line 1404 is not a vocative, as if Troilus imagines *she* (rather than *you*) fails to recognize himself though face-to-face. Robert Henryson provides a mirror image of this failure-to-recognize scene in his *Testament of Cresseid*, where it is Criseyde who "was in sic plye he knew hir nocht" (501). See Robert L. Kindrick, ed., *The Poems of Robert Henryson* (Kalamazoo, Mich.: Medieval Institute Publications, 1997).

BOOK V, DECEPTIONS

The increasingly sad and mad imagination of Troilus loiters "ay" (V, 1441) on the idea of Criseyde's absence. Chaucer reminds his less attentive listeners about the dream "of which I told have ek byforn," a presentiment that has never left Troilus and "may nevere outen of his remembraunce" (V, 1443–44). Troilus had correctly interpreted this dream's meaning until dissuaded by Pandarus. Troilus remembers again the divine "purveyaunce" (V, 1446) revealed to him, "the signifiaunce / Of hire untrouthe" (V, 1447–48). So he seeks interpretation of his recollection by an expert reader who can "right thus his drem expounde" (V, 1456).

The Cassandra episode in Book V may seem quite bloated on first (silent) reading, perhaps a scene intended simply to enhance the illusion of narrative time passing. Cassandra is required to explicate the truth of Troilus's dream-vision. Though Troilus feels he truly wants to be relieved of doubt (V, 1453), Cassandra knows that no one really wants to hear what she has to say. So "she gan first smyle" (V, 1457). Cassandra talks like a bookman: "If thow a soth of this desirest knowe, / Thow most a fewe of olde stories heere" (V, 1458–59), "as men in bokes fynde" (V, 1463), "as olde bokes tellen us" (V, 1478), "or ellis olde bookes lye" (V, 1481). She sounds, in other words, like the rehearser of *Troilus and Criseyde*.

Cassandra promises Troilus that "withinne a throwe, / Thow wel this boor shalt knowe" (V, 1461–62). But she requires seven stanzas to explain why this dream image "bitokneth" (V, 1513) Diomede's coat of arms—a digression within Chaucer's digression. Cassandra's explanation of the boar's significance may sound boring or bored, pedantic or sympathetic, or some combination thereof. But there is nothing truly sibylline about her interpretation; it is merely learned.

For three stanzas, Chaucer quotes Cassandra directly, ending with her avoidance of yet another digression: "... wol I yow

BOOK V, DECEPTIONS

naught telle, / For al to longe it were for to dwelle" (V, 1483–84). And then Chaucer does his best to hurry up her prolixity:

> "She tolde ek ... er she stente" (V, 1485)
> "This tolde she by proces, al by lengthe" (V, 1491)
> "She tolde ek how" (V, 1492)
> "She tolde ek alle ... by herte" (V, 1494)
> "And how ..." (V, 1495)
> "And of ..." (V, 1497)
> "And of ... al she gan hym telle" (V, 1498)
> "And how ..." (V, 1500)
> "How ..." (V, 1501)
> "And how ..." (V, 1502)
> "And also how ..." (V, 1504)
> "She gan ek telle hym how" (V, 1506)
> "And how ... she tolde ek tho" (V, 1510)
> "... and thus she spak and tolde" (V, 1512)

Chaucer's recital sounds increasingly impatient to finish the cursed seer's synopsis, a tragically comic tone that many fifteenth-century readers simply failed to hear; instead, scribal insertions of a Latin argument to Statius's *Thebaid* only pads further Cassandra's frustrating postponement of the relevant insight. Cassandra's conspicuously abbreviated but still conspicuously long précis of a story that "so descendeth down from gestes olde" (V, 1511) finally explains how Diomede himself "down descended is" (V, 1514). Cassandra avoids naming Troilus's "lady, wherso she be, ywis" (V, 1516), but she concludes with brutal clarity "for out of doute / This Diomede is inne, and thou art oute" (V, 1518–19).

Of course, Troilus suspected this worst possible reading of his dream. He rages at smiling Cassandra mainly because she has spoken the truth out loud. Confronted by her compelling ar-

BOOK V, DECEPTIONS

gument, Troilus has only one option—absolute contradiction: "Thow seyst nat soth" (V, 1520). His only rebuttal is *ad feminam* (V, 1521–26). Troilus takes Cassandra's libel as a categorical "lye" about all ladies (V, 1524). She might as well slander Alceste, who stayed true, or " men lye . . . as us the bokes telle" (V, 1528, 1533).[14] But, in truth, Cassandra has not lied, nor have men's books falsely reported that Criseyde was untrue. Illogically but not surprisingly, the Cassandra interlude does have a therapeutic effect on Troilus, "as though al hool hym hadde ymad a leche" (V, 1537). His "angre of hire speche" at least gets him out of bed to "enquere and seche / A sooth of this" (V, 1535–39).

The time of truce having ended—"the fyn of the parodie . . . wonder blyve" (V, 1548–49)—Hector dies "unwar" (V, 1559).[15] Chaucer is moved by mutability—"allas!" (V, 1554)—and asks all knights present to join his lament though he cannot express the sorrow of Troy "as olde bokes tellen us, / . . . swich wo that tonge it may nat telle" (V, 1562–63). His recital must refocus on sad Troilus, who henceforth "may nat contrefete" (V, 1578; cf. II, 1532) and who writes "yet ofte tyme al newe" (V, 1583). Whereas Chaucer had previously read aloud the entire "litera Troili" and

---

14. This stanza (V, 1527–33) seems superfluous. It is frequently read as a set-up for the Prologue to the *Legend of Good Women*; cf. V, 1777–78. Alternatively, these textual "anticipations" may be a product of revision, added after Chaucer had been commissioned (or condemned for slander) to compose a palinode to *Troilus and Criseyde*.

15. "Travesty" seems an inappropriate—that is, too early and too dark—reading of "parodie" in this context. Barney considers it a corruption of "period" (*Riverside*, 1055, n. 1548), and it is glossed as "duracioun" in MSS H1, H4, and Cp, a usage Lydgate adopts (see *OED* s.v. "parody . n1. obs."). Chaucer's (mis)pronunciation of "period" provides an exact rhyme for the curious verb "unbodye" (which suggests the metempsychosis of Hector's soul). See *MED* s.v. "parodi(e n." which cites V, 1548, as the first usage, a "Distorted form of OF *periode* or ML *periodus*; possibly influenced by Gr. *parodeia* or *parados*." Though it seems unlikely that Chaucer would have known the Greek terminology first hand, "parodos" designated a pathway for the chorus entering and exiting the orchestra (also the songs performed in transit)—a meaning which does suit both this narrative and recital context.

then only briefly paraphrased Criseyde's reply, he now reverses his method of presenting their respective compositions. Chaucer simply reports that persistent Troilus wrote several times "ful pitously"; Chaucer adds, "he lefte it nought for slouthe" (V, 1584), a comment that seems curiously irrelevant (except perhaps to alleviate the fatigue of an emotionally overworked translator). Chaucer then reads aloud the last "litera Criseydis" in full (V, 1590–1631), a text which displays the "straunge" (V, 1632) act of writing as a masquerade. Criseyde's *ars dictaminis* hides all but the act of hiding itself.

Although John McKinnell rightly reads Criseyde's composition as a fundamental betrayal of "the idea of a letter as storage of the *spoken* word," Chaucer prefaces his recital of it with a statement of his own belief in her compassion as a writer—"for routhe—/ I take it so"—which he will faithfully read aloud: "and seyde as ye may here" (V, 1587–89).[16] Criseyde has clearly seen the signs of authorial grief in Troilus's letters, both the ink and tears:

Youre lettres ful, the papir al ypleynted, ...
I have ek seyn with teris al depeynted
Youre lettre. (V, 1599–1600)

Criseyde (plausibly) conceals the real reason for her continued reticence: "But whi, lest that this lettre founden were, / No mencioun ne make I now, for feere" (V, 1601–3). She challenges Troilus's (more plausible) pessimism regarding her failure to write back or return: "It semeth nat ye take it for the beste. / Nor other thyng nys in youre remembraunce, / As thynketh me." (V, 1606–8). Criseyde's "routhe" voices itself as criticism of Troilus's lust, and

---

16. John McKinnell, "Letters as a Type of the Formal Level in *Troilus and Criseyde*," in Salu, *Essays*, 73–89; "The effect is to distance us from any involvement with her.... This distancing is also inherent in the use of the letter form itself" (ibid., 88).

BOOK V, DECEPTIONS

she blames "wikked speche" (V, 1610) for his doubts. She has heard gossip about Troilus too, but she can still "with dissymelyng amende" (V, 1613). She cannot "gesse" (V, 1616) that Troilus means anything but truth and gentility "but now no force" (V, 1616); Chaucer cannot not make Criseyde sound too aloof as she writes only briefly and only means no harm (V, 1625) to a *friend*. Criseyde's text draws attention to its own tonal inadequacy: "I dar nat, ther I am, wel lettres make, / Ne nevere yet ne koude I wel endite" (V, 1627–28). She claims size does not matter: "Ek gret effect men write in place lite; / Th'entente is al, and nat the lettres space" (V, 1629–30). But Troilus reads the nonperformance of her reply both sorrowfully and correctly "whan he it saugh" (V, 1633).

Troilus sighs, and "but fynaly" Chaucer expresses his distrust as a painfully grudging litotes: "he ful ne trowen myghte / That she ne wolde hym holden that she hyghte" (V, 1635–36). Troilus's "wille" still resists, and "but natheles" Chaucer has Troilus yield to a truism: "men seyen that at the laste, / For any thyng, men shal the soothe se" (V, 1637–40). Empathy for Troilus makes Chaucer understate Criseyde's fault: "that she / Nas nought so kynde as that hire oughte be" (V, 1642–43). And so "fynaly" Troilus consents to the consensus regarding Criseyde's untruth "now out of doute" (V, 1644).

Chaucer then presents the physical evidence, "as seith the storie" (V, 1651), "as telleth Lollius" (V, 1653), that corroborates Troilus's "suspecioun" (V, 1647): the *cote-armure* of Diomede. Troilus gives the happy prize of Deiphebus a very close reading (V, 1656–57) till he discovers its saddest detail, Criseyde's brooch. Troilus's gift has clearly lost its intended significance "in remembraunce" (V, 1663). And Chaucer sounds finally sure that Troilus has lost any vestige of doubt: "now ful wel he wiste" (V, 1665). Troilus tells Pandarus "word and ende" (V, 1669) until he cries for death "withouten wordes moore" (V, 1672). But "than spak he thus" (V, 1674). He asks questions that Criseyde cannot hear. He anticipates and regrets the downfall of her name. He theorizes that she intended to hurt him by re-gifting his/her/Diomede's/Deiphebus's brooch: "for despit, and ek for that ye mente / Al outrely to shewen youre entente" (V, 1693–94). Although Troilus neither can nor may "unloven" her (V, 1696–98), he assumes that Criseyde has cast his image "clene out of youre mynde" (V, 1695) because only such willful amnesia could totally kill her sympathetic response to his intended tone.

Troilus prays for vengeance "to fortheren trouthe" (V, 1707) and concedes, *pace* Pandarus and his own blind hope, that nightmares do come true: "Now maistow sen thiself, if that the liste / ... and by my drem it is now sene" (V, 1711–15). He seeks death "certeynly, withouten moore speeche" (V, 1716), and, after one last apostrophe to "trewely, Criseyde, swete may" (V, 1720) who done him wrong, is done. As for Pandarus "that al thise thynges herde" (V, 1723) , the saying *qui tacit consentit* proves true: "And wiste wel he seyde a soth of this, / He nought a word ayeyn to hym answerde" (V, 1724–25). Both ashamed of his niece and "sory of his frendes sorwe" (V, 1726), it is Pandarus's stupefaction that seems to interest Chaucer most. Pandarus stands "astoned ... stille as ston; a word ne kowde he seye" (V, 1728–29) until "at the laste thus he spak, and seyde: / ... 'What sholde I seyen?'"(V, 1730–32). When Pandarus does declare all too clearly that he hates Criseyde "ywys" and "evermore" for "this tresoun now" (V, 1731–38), he makes Chaucer voice the first *brotherly* (or misogynist) response to *Troilus and Criseyde*.

Chaucer also permits Pandarus, before departing from the text, to speak in his own self-defense. Like Criseyde, he only intended well: "I did al that the leste" (V, 1736). He would revise the resolution if he could: "Right fayn I wolde amende it, wiste I how" (V, 1741). Pandarus exits with a prayer that Criseyde drop dead: "And fro this world, almyghty God I preye / Delivere hire soon! I kan no more seye" (V, 1742–43). Chaucer can vent but does not endorse this male response.

Since the story is effectively over, however, Chaucer now states its *moralitas*—with insufficient enthusiasm for the didactic moment:

> Swich is this world, whoso it kan byholde;
> In ech estat is litel hertes reste.
> God leve us for to take it for the beste! (V, 1748–50)

Chaucer has a good deal more to say. He confesses his own text's omissions—"As men may in thise olde bokes rede" (V, 1753). He refuses, however, to satisfy any manly desire for a decisive duel between Diomede and Troilus, "Fortune it naught ne wolde" (V, 1763), though "I fynde" (V, 1758) they had several chances. Chaucer maintains he could have been an epic poet had he wished, but that was not his authorial intent:

> And if I hadde ytaken for to write
> The armes of this ilke worthi man,
> Than wolde ich of his batailles endite;
> But for that I to writen first bigan
> Of his love, I have seyd as I kan—
> His worthi dedes, whoso list hem heere,
> Rede Dares, he kan telle hem alle ifeere—. (V, 1765–71)

This singular imperative "rede" apparently anticipates a solitary, silent reading, but even here *reading* must attempt to hear what *Dares tells*.

For what he has done, rather than for what he has failed to

do, Chaucer also apologizes to "every lady bright of hewe, / And every gentil womman, what she be"—this distinction (if any) may be between those ladies whom he sees before him and those who will see some copy of his poem (V, 1772–73). He begs them all together "be not wroth with me" (V, 1775), but he cannot deny the potential offensiveness of his rehearsal. He likewise invites all women to read other texts for confirmation of his own recital's truth: "Ye may hire gilt in other bokes se" (V, 1776). Chaucer suggests to a familiar court of "yow" ladies that they assign him another commission, something to be written about true and good women: "And gladlier I wol write, yif yow leste" (V, 1777). Chaucer offers now, in propria persona, a sisterly reading: women are not to blame—"N'y say nat this ... And this commeveth me / To speke, and in effect yow alle I preye" to distrust men "and herkneth what I seye!" (V, 1779–85; cf. LGW 2561).[17] Chaucer recovers his storyline: "But yet to purpos of my rather speech ... as I bigan yow for to seye" (V, 1799–1800).[18] But, in between these apparent recital remarks, Chaucer sends forth his "litel bok" (V, 1786) to some unknown promised land where, God willing, the poet himself may make comedy someday (V, 1787–88). Chaucer writes like a worried parent warning his abandoned child to remain humble in the land of dead authors.

Chaucer recognizes that his tongue is inherently vulnerable to multiple acts of misrepresentation. Dialectical variation and an absence of a standard orthography both threaten the text's integrity: "And for ther is so gret diversite / In Englissh and in writyng

---

17. Clare Regan Kinney ("Who Made This Song?") reads Chaucer's Marian devotion—the final note of Troilus and Criseyde—as giving a voice to women; in this not yet pious moment, Chaucer's sisterly tone may be less than sincere.

18. William Kamowski has suggested, however—against the manuscript evidence—that four stanzas may be moved on the assumption of revision ("A Suggestion for Emending the Epilogue of Troilus and Criseyde," The Chaucer Review 21 [1987]: 406–18).

BOOK V, DECEPTIONS

of oure tonge" (V, 1793–94). Transcription errors and pronunciation differences both result in misreadings: "So prey I God that non myswrite the, / Ne the mysmetre for defaute of tonge" (V, 1795–96). Chaucer prays that the intent of his distant brainchild survive both silent reading and subsequent prelection: "And red wherso thow be, or elles songe, / That thow be understonde, God I biseche!" (V, 1797–98). God has become Chaucer's only guarantor of the reader's comprehension and empathy.

Chaucer returns to telling "yow" (V, 1800) his scrap of an epilogue. Chaucer may sound initially neo-Pelagian as Troilus ascends "ful blisfully" (V, 1808), but the pagan lover's soul is only momentarily aloft, "shortly for to telle" (V, 1826). Chaucer's text completely obfuscates the final disposition of Troilus's soul; his ghost (like the voice of Book V's author) seems ultimately "lost in space."[19] From an ephemeral glimpse of "pleyn felicite / That is in hevene above" (V, 1818–19), Troilus laughs at his mourners below who include his fellow Trojans and Chaucer and his present listeners and future readers. Troilus's last performative is a curse damning "al oure werk that foloweth so" (V, 1823) blind, mundane love.[20]

Chaucer echoes this *contemptus mundi* as the *finit* (V, 1828–32) of Troilus's text "as I have told" (V, 1834). But Chaucer's voice continues; for two stanzas, he calls "O yonge, fresshe folkes" (V, 1835) home to a True Lover who "nyl falsen no wight, dar I seye" (V, 1845). Chaucer's own Christianity becomes increasingly loud (V, 1860, 1868). Both rhetorical scorn and charitable

---

19. Allen J. Frantzen, *Troilus and Criseyde: The Poem and the Frame* (New York: Twayne, 1993), 132.
20. Sheila Delany reads the conclusion of *Troilus and Criseyde* as "a devastating attack on La Vita Nuova, on the conviction that human love can lead to divine love" ("Techniques of Alienation in Troilus and Criseyde," in Shoaf, ed., "*Subgit to alle Poesye*," 29–46, 46).

pity may inform the intent of his anaphora (V, 1828–32, 1849–55) renouncing the allure of all idolatrous "travaille" (V, 1852). This speech-act culminates in Chaucer's performance of a line that, by metonymy, can serve as the translator's dedication of a presentation copy: "Lo here, the forme of olde clerkis speche / In poetrie, if ye hire bokes seche" (V, 1854–55).[21]

Chaucer's entrusts his final copy to Gower and Strode as solitary first readers "to the ... and to the" (V, 1857). The author's text asks his fellow authors to act as benign and zealous editors: "this book I directe / ... ther nede is, to correcte" (V, 1857–58).[22] And then it all ends with Chaucer's voice preserved in a perpetual prayer: "evere I preye, ... right thus I speke and seye" (V, 1861–62). Chaucer addresses his Audience "eterne on lyve" (V, 1863) Who condescends to be called "Thow" (V, 1863).

The rhapsodic intent of Chaucer's last seven lines defies explication; yet, the author is merely joining a choir of devotion.[23] Incomprehensible in English or Italian or any tongue, God remains the Unwritten Writer, Who alone is "Uncircumscript, and al maist circumscrive" (V, 1865). St. Augustine, another old clerk, had once surprised himself with the realization that such prayers do not simply talk at God. The dialogue of true prayer requires listening for insight: "You called me; you cried aloud to me; you broke my barrier of deafness. You shone upon me; your radiance envel-

---

21. Wondering just how inclusive Chaucer's "Lo" might be, E. Talbot Donaldson supposed that "it refers to the poem as a whole.... If this is so, then the form of *olde clerkes speeche* is being damned as well as *payens cursed olde rites*—by parataxis, at least. Yet it is not.... The form of old clerk's speech in poetry ... is significant, for it is poetry." (*Speaking of Chaucer* [New York: Norton, 1970], 99).

22. A. C. Spearing sees Chaucer's envoy (V, 1786–96) as an underlining of the whole text's "written status. He imagines it being read aloud, certainly, but read from a text from which the poet is absent" (*Textual Subjectivity*, 12).

23. Chaucer translates Dante (*Paradiso* xiv 28–30) verbatim with "word-perfect, beautiful English" (Wetherbee, *Chaucer and the Poets*, 242).

BOOK V, DECEPTIONS

oped me; you put my blindness to flight."[24] Human words quickly pass away, however.[25] Therefore, Chaucer prays that the Incarnate Word defend "Us ... everichon" (V, 1866–67)—author and audience and readers alike. *Troilus and Criseyde* ends with Chaucer wooing Mary, trusting only in Christ as our true *amis*.

24. Augustine, *Confessions*, X 27 (R. S. Pine-Coffin, 232). Jeffrey J. Cohen has remarked that "few of us would dare second guess Augustine, especially because whenever something new arrives in critical theory, it so often turns out that the African bishop was there long before" (*Medieval Identity Machines* [Minneapolis: University of Minnesota Press, 2003], 2).

25. Karla Taylor says that "Chaucer affirms the comprehensive supremacy of the Word, but he does not include his own poetry in this affirmation" (*Chaucer Reads*, 200).

7

FINISHING TOUCHES

IN THE beginning was Geoffrey Chaucer.
Troilus and Criseyde was not transcribed ex nihilo.
If, then, Chaucer did recite some version of *Troilus and Criseyde*, it seems likely that his script-in-hand would indeed have been written in his own hand, perhaps a scribble readable only by himself, perhaps defaced with marginal self-prompts. Modern readers desire a much fairer, more finished "best text"—some editorial approximation of the final draft that Adam Scriveyn failed to copy with sufficient care and that Chaucer felt obliged to correct.[1] Whenever Chaucer finally let go of this alpha-revision of his recital rendition for others to read, his "double sorwe of Troilus to tellen" started to become ISBN: 0-395-29031-7. The achievement of such a definitive edition of *Troilus and Criseyde* customarily preempts any further critical inquiry into its transmission history. Once the witnesses to the text have been professionally transcribed, collated, punctuated, regularized, and so on, the manu-

---

1. As discussed in chapter 1, Jackson J. Campbell proposed that "the ancestor of the manuscript of which CF ["The Cecil Fragment"] formed a part was derived from Chaucer's 'foul papers' at some intermediate stage in the successive derivations" ("A New Troilus Fragment," 307).

scripts are returned to the vault as priceless relics but surpassed versions. Few now read facsimiles of Chaucer's poem for fun, though that was each manuscript's original function. Almost every scribe who copied *Troilus and Criseyde* aspired to produce a best reading—and, to some extent, in various ways failed to reproduce a reliable record of its authorial recital.[2]

Every manuscript pretends to present Chaucer's authorial intent, but each was made in anticipation of its own context of interpretation. In A. S. G. Edwards's words, "Manuscript transmission manifests the possibility of multiple, variant responses to the text, responses capable of reconstituting it in markedly different forms," whereas "the early print editors of Chaucer began a tradition of recontextualizing his poems that has continued to the present."[3] Each scribe anticipated and so regulated a particular reading of *Troilus and Criseyde*. Barry Windeatt sees Chaucer's manuscripts as running commentaries:

> With varying levels of attainment, the scribes—as the near-contemporaries of Ch—can offer us the earliest line-by-line literary criticism of Ch's poetry.... Scribal transcribing is a form of writing which constitutes an "active reading," an active reading which involves judgement-through-variation on the difficulties and peculiarities of what it encounters. In the age of print an author speaks directly to each reader through his multiply-reproduced text, whereas each manuscript offers a text already "read."[4]

---

2. There are several piecemeal transcriptions of *Troilus and Criseyde*, appropriations or adaptions of select lines from Chaucer's poem copied for other purposes, not fragments of lost manuscripts. In CUL MSS Ff 1. 6 (the "Findern Manuscript") and Trinity (Cambridge) MS R 4, three stanzas are excerpted from Chaucer's poem (III, 302–22) and used in a lyric called "The Tongue." A more complicated harvesting of Chaucer's lines, recombined to present a "new" poem, may be found in MS Rawlinson C. 813, and at least three such patchwork poems are included in BL MS Add. 17492 ("The Devonshire Manuscript").

3. Edwards, "Chaucer from Manuscript to print," retrieved from http://o-search.proquest.com.library.uark.edu/docview/205366701?accountid=8361.

4. Windeatt, ed., *Geoffrey Chaucer, Troilus* (1984), 26. This active reading manifests

Although Seth Lerer has characterized these fifteenth-century scribes as "those apparently least qualified" to discern Chaucer's authorial intent,[5] he would "restore a critical authority to the early manuscripts of Chaucer's poetry" and so liberate modern readers from their subjugation to editors who have been "privileged as those apparently most qualified to transmit the poet to his readers."[6] It may seem paradoxical to so malign the scribes as readers and then to totemize each manuscript as a reading opportunity. But this interpretive gesture establishes the modern reader's only critical advantage: a self-consciousness regarding each text's historicized context of reception.

Whereas the normal editorial goal is to scrutinize the textual witnesses for the sake of gleaning a best reading, the project of this chapter is to glance at these same evidentiary texts as hostile witnesses to the poem's prior (and too soon forgotten) authorial recital. To the extent that the extant manuscripts of *Troilus and Criseyde* do preserve the content of Chaucer's unrevised composition, they still provide valid internal evidence for its authorial recital. Sometimes scribes tried to entextualize Chaucer's voice; more often, scribal reproductions tacitly superimpose surrogate tonal signals for reading Chaucer's poem in quite different reception contexts, including both prelection and silent reading. Antici-

---

itself especially as a "tendency for scribes to gloss their text in cases of what strikes them as strange or awkward diction," as well as instances of Chaucer's more figurative language (28). Montague Rhodes James, *A Descriptive Catalogue of the Manuscripts in the Library of Corpus Christi College* [Cambridge], vol. 1. CUP, 1912. MS. 61 [item 61], 126–27. Margaret Jennings, C.S.J., considers the effects of scribal bias upon transcription ("To Pryke or to Prye: Scribal Delights in the Troilus, Book III," in *Chaucer in the Eighties*, ed. Julian N. Wasserman and Robert J. Blanch, 121–33 [Syracuse, N.Y.: Syracuse University Press, 1986]); in general, "to Troilus, they seem generally favorable and supportive; to Pandarus, just the opposite; with Criseyde they vacillate between defensiveness and neutrality" (130).

5. Lerer, *Chaucer and His Readers*, 3.
6. Ibid., 6.

pated contexts of reading are also differentiated by class, gender, time, place, and ultimately by each reader's individual perspective. I want, therefore, to consider to what extent the physical appearance of each of the extant primary textual witnesses to *Troilus and Criseyde* provides some indication of a particular reading (or misreading) of Chaucer's recital intentions.

Unlike the mass marketing of machined books, the construction of each manuscript assumes a far more familiar exchange between its scribe and his readership. For A. S. G. Edwards, "The most immediate consequence of the shift to a print culture is, of course, a loss of particularity."[7] Although a careful script may look quite standardized at first, the individual style of every scribe maintains a recognizable uniqueness. Each copy is originally and intimately *owned* by its scribe. And reading such a text, as A. C. Spearing appreciates, offers a tactile as well as an aural and/or visual experience: "Unlike the textuality of the electronic age, that of the age of manuscript is not disembodied or immaterial ... for parchment, *boc-felle*, is bodily in origin and is itself produced by bodily labour"—preserving a more convincing sense of the real presence or the "I" of the scribe.[8] Unless one assumes an infinite regression, this contact extends back to the hand of Chaucer.

Leonard Koff writes that Chaucer's early readers did feel, therefore—rightly or wrongly—that they could faithfully reiterate the text's proto-performance:

Private performance in Chaucer's day repeated at home what was in fact public performance. It implied that the private performer—we can call him a reader, though we mean something special by that term—was

---

7. Edwards adds, "The markets for printed books in England were largely speculative, commercially-driven ones aimed at a generalized public rather than an individual private audience, as would be the case with the audience for manuscript texts" ("Chaucer from Manuscript to Print," Pro-Quest Document ID 9156451).

8. Spearing, *Textual Subjectivity*, 14.

participating, and was continuing to participate (consciously, through the sound of his own voice), in a public act of storytelling that constituted for him the civilized life of the community.[9]

Printed editions of *Troilus and Criseyde* can also serve this same performance function only if so read—as in the classroom. Modern print editions of Chaucer actually do provide a panorama of reading possibilities—one of which remains authorial recital. It is the individual reader who is responsible for denying the resurrection of Chaucer's voice, not the prima facie appearance of the book.

Every publication—be it recited, chirographic, printed, or electronic—is, by definition, a show, a designed rendition of authorial intent. I would like, therefore, to consider how the appearance of each significant copy of *Troilus and Criseyde* reinterpreted yet again Chaucer's own revision of his performance script. Claire Donovan, describing the much earlier but still analogous production of *Books of Hours*, explains the interpretive import of a manuscript's entire *mise-en-page* as the stage for its intended reading:

The layout of a book, its size and format, the appearance and feel of the binding and the ease with which it opens and can be read, the arrangement of words on the page (the length of the lines, the height of individual letters, the spacing between letters, the occurrence and size of decorated initials, line fillers, and border decoration), the occurrence and design of programs of illustration: all these add to the appreciation, and to the understanding and use, of any manuscript.... They also reflect the requirements of the person for whom the book was made.[10]

---

9. Koff, *Art of Storytelling*, 21.
10. Claire Donovan, "The Mise-en-Page of Early Books of Hours in England," in *Medieval Book Production: Assessing the Evidence*, Proceedings of the Second Conference of the Seminar in the History of the Book to 1500, Oxford, July 1988, ed. L. L. Brownrigg, 147–61 (Los Altos, Calif.: Anderson-Lovelace, 1990), 149.

The quality of any one scribal hand itself—without regard to the accuracy of transcription—offers some physical evidence of each manuscript's intended market and use.

Several, indeed a disproportionate number, of the extant copies of *Troilus and Criseyde* seem high-end or trophy texts—deluxe copies meant to be admired as possessions rather than casually read. Others seem quite utilitarian. Since the extant manuscripts are very rare and largely arbitrary survivals, it seems ridiculous to deduce a normative early reading of Chaucer's composition from such scant records.[11] My point instead is to suggest that "normative" reading is a modern misnomer for late medieval *confabulatio*. The variety of textual prompts provided even by this restricted body of early modern evidence indicates an enduring diversity of scribal expectations for mutually viable readings of *Troilus and Criseyde*—including an imagined (because remembered) reenactment of its authorial recital.

Corpus Christi College, Cambridge, MS 61 provides a best text for most recent editions of *Troilus and Criseyde*, including those of Robinson, Donaldson, Baugh, Windeatt, and Barney. This manuscript dates from perhaps the very beginning of the fifteenth century, some twenty years after Chaucer's putative recital in the mid-1380s.[12] Cambridge MS 61 presents a rather large standalone copy of *Troilus and Criseyde*. Two very similar hands working in close collaboration, perhaps working simultaneously, copied five stanzas per page with clear (if not always rigorous) book divisions—a format that is maintained in all but four of the six-

---

11. M. C. Seymour guesses that "nine of every ten copies made have been lost" ("The Manuscripts of Chaucer's *Troilus*," 108).

12. It could not have been produced later than 1456 when John Shirley handled it. It is arguably "contemporary with the earliest datable manuscript of this text, the Campsall [Morgan] manuscript ... which must be assigned to date between 1399 and 1413 " (Parkes and Salter, *Corpus Facsimile*, 2).

teen manuscripts. William Hodapp sees this layout as itself highly conducive to prelection: "Considering that in the fifteenth century ... someone would read the text aloud to a group of listeners, it is not surprising that the manuscripts in general reflect concerns for legibility and clear division in the presentation of the text."[13] However, an exceptionally luxurious program of illustrations was planned for the Corpus manuscript,[14] and the handwriting itself is quite splendid—enhancing the pleasure of simply viewing this text as an art object in its own right.[15] The scribes highlighted proper names and titles with the frequent use of *litterae notabiliores* yet also made unusually frequent use of abbreviations.[16] As a result, the page looks beautiful but requires a somewhat expert reader of these scribal conventions to be read aloud. Although it must be conceded—again and again—that the evidentiary significance of this manuscript's frontispiece is quite suspect, the illustrator's intent was clearly to make the text itself an aristocratic showpiece by representing Chaucer at the center of a royal circle. If its decoration had been finished, this staging of Chaucer's text would indeed have seemed the textual equivalent of a reliquary. The Corpus Christi manuscript is also only one of two manuscripts in which the original scribes name Chaucer as the author of *Troilus and Criseyde*. It enshrines the poet.

In the St. John's College, Cambridge, MS L.1, *Troilus and Criseyde* (fols.1r–119v) "was originally conceived and executed as

---

13. William F. Hodapp, "The Visual Presentation of Chaucer's *Troilus and Criseyde* in Three Fifteenth-Century Manuscripts," *Manuscripta* 38 (1994): 237–52, 249.

14. It was probably commissioned either by an aristocratic (though not inexhaustibly wealthy) patron or by "an entrepreneur ... as a speculative venture.... It would seem either some mishap befell the patron, or the speculation did not payoff" (Parkes and Salter, *Corpus Facsimile*, 11).

15. The choice of such a display script makes the Corpus manuscript "almost twice as expensive as books copied in other scripts" (ibid., 13).

16. Ibid., 7.

a copy of a single work."[17] The page size of this vellum manuscript presents a durable, somewhat smaller, more modest (and so perhaps more portable) staging of the poem than the Corpus or Morgan manuscripts. The main hand is that of a late-fifteenth-century scribe using Anglicana Formata with some influence of Secretary.[18] Proem and book divisions are clearly marked by four-line flourished initials; yet, "while accentuating the division of the work into books, the scheme of decoration also stresses the individual stanza by the unusually extended alternating blue and red paraph marks placed to the left of each stanza; these complement the layout of the manuscript page."[19] Some subsequent reader's (or readers') crude markings in the margins of folios 1r through 24v seem intended to enhance the scribe's original designation of each stanza as such. Squiggled, block, or triangular lines bracket each stanza. The reading purpose of these superfluous and sloppy markings—such as re-reading, copying, or memorization—now seems far less obvious and significant than the defacement of the precious text. But an apparently solitary reader with pen in hand clearly felt entitled by present ownership to track the page while reading.

The original scribe made free use of abbreviations.[20] This feature, easing the travail of the professional scribe at the inconvenience of all less expert lectors, seems a step away from vocalizing the text by the silent reader, though a public recital by a scribe-reciter would presumably decompress the text. This manuscript also contains, however, a rather extensive complement of mar-

17. Richard Beadle and Jeremy Griffiths, St. John's College, Cambridge, Manuscript L.1, A Facsimile (Norman, Okla.: Pilgrim, 1983), xix.
18. "By the beginning of the fifteenth century it [Anglicana Formata] was favored by many scribes for the transmission of vernacular texts" (ibid., xxiii).
19. Ibid., xxi.
20. Ibid., xxv.

ginal non-decorative elements and annotations.[21] These later additions seem most probably intended to assist solitary reading. A much later italic hand additionally provides simple, literal glosses in the margins adjacent to the Middle English verse lines—as if reading the poem had become a school assignment, a task that intermittently required such editorial assistance. Both the main scribe and second hand took some care to correct the transcription proper, so there was a clear priority given to correct reading rather than to the artifact's unsullied display.[22] The copied text itself is perceived as a correctable entity subject to ongoing revision. And it seems safe enough to say that its anticipated users wanted an accurate, straightforward, and affordable copy of the poem that they intended to read (perhaps on loan) rather than to keep as a trophy text on display.

Except in such broad terms, it is difficult to describe the anticipated readership of this transcription's original staging of *Troilus and Criseyde* because "nothing precise is known about the origins of the St. John's Manuscript."[23] The donor remains unidentified.[24] With no evidence other than the text's ambiguous paleography, Richard Beadle and Jeremy Griffiths suggest that this copy of *Troilus and Criseyde* was probably produced during "the second quarter of the fifteenth century."[25] But R. K Root observed that the orthog-

---

21. "The manuscript provides some clues to the evolution of the practice of glossing the poem" (ibid., xxiii). The five-stanza-per-page layout often causes crowding for the insertion of annotations (ibid., xxi). For descriptive analyses of such marginalia and scribal annotations, see Barry A. Windeatt, "The Scribes as Chaucer's Early Critics," *Studies in the Age of Chaucer* 1 (1979): 119–41; Ardis Butterfield, "Mise-en-page in the Troilus Manuscripts: Chaucer and French Manuscript Culture," *Huntington Library Quarterly* 58 (1996): 49–80; and Julia Boffey, "Annotation in Some Manuscripts of Troilus and Criseyde," *English Manuscript Studies, 1100–1700* 5 (1995): 1–17.
22. Beadle and Griffiths, *St. John's Facsimile*, xxv–xxvii.
23. Ibid., xxix.
24. M. R. James, *A Descriptive Catalogue*, xiii. MS L. 1 is item 235 described on page 274.
25. Beadle and Griffiths, *St. John's Facsimile*, xx.

raphy of the St. John's manuscript seems similar to that of the Corpus Christi manuscript.[26] Beadle and Griffiths, therefore, tentatively propose that the St. John's manuscript may likewise have circulated in London, perhaps in the circle of John Shirley during the first quarter of the fifteenth century, a society of urbane "new men."[27] This manuscript makes *Troilus and Criseyde* available as a more utilitarian tool for either group recital or solitary reading; its target audience, however, is clearly no longer dominated by the ladies who may have attended Chaucer's recital.

A few brief and thematically complementary lyrics were added at various times in the later fifteenth and sixteenth centuries to the St. John's manuscript of *Troilus and Criseyde*. The most significant re-invention of this manuscript's reading context was the addition of Henryson's *Testament of Cresseid* (copied from Speght's 1602 edition of Chaucer's *Works*) as an apparent sequel to Chaucer's narrative. The additional text (fols. 121v–128v) is in a conspicuously different hand and format. But both scribes neglect to identify (and so differentiate) their respective authors. And there is no consistent distinction maintained between the names "Criseyde" and "Cresseid," as in modern editions.[28] This conjunction

26. Robert Kilburn Root, *Troilus and Criseyde* (Princeton, N.J.: Princeton University Press, 1926), lxvii, lxxxv.

27. In *John Shirley: Book Production and the Noble Household in Fifteenth-Century England* (Aldershot: Ashgate, 1998), Margaret Connolly questions that John Shirley sought a broader, less aristocratic readership, as proposed by A. S. G. Edwards, "John Shirley and the Emulation of Courtly Culture," in *The Court and Cultural Diversity: Selected Papers from the Eighth Triennial Meeting of the International Courtly Literature Society, 1995*, ed. E. Mullaly and J. Thompson, 309–17 (Cambridge: D.S. Brewer, 1997). Connolly argues instead that Shirley's primary motive was more antiquarian than commercial; "there is plenty of evidence that Shirley lent out his books, and none at all that he sold them. His primary audience was that of the noble household of which he himself was a member.... What happened after his death is another matter" (Connolly, *John Shirley*, 195).

28. Henryson's text is obviously written by a different hand on a different quality of parchment. But this discontinuity of texts may not have seemed so apparent to late medieval and early modern readers who were accustomed to handling manuscripts pro-

of the *Troilus* and the *Testament* gives Chaucer's text a much more bourgeois, more male-oriented, and apparently more misogynist context for reading the composite story of Criseyde/Cresseid.[29]

Bodleian MS Arch. Selden B. 24 is a late-fifteenth- or early-sixteenth-century manuscript. Though it is difficult to affirm one specific occasion for its production with complete confidence, it is highly probable that Selden B. 24 was commissioned (ca. 1489) by Henry Sinclair, whose grandmother was sister to King James I of Scotland.[30] Its illustrations and general quality (by contemporary Scottish rather than French standards) indicate that it was designed to be an heirloom, though the choice of paper stock was too frugal (which is not to say "Scottish"). The Selden copy of *Troilus and Criseyde* was probably first made as a stand-alone text, though it is now presented as the head item of a *compilatio*. Not kept simply as a display copy, Selden B. 24 has been "extensively annotated in a variety of scripts."[31] There are book headings and marginal annotations that seem intended primarily to assist solitary perusal rather than public recital, although the former type of reading serves as rehearsal for the latter. Chaucer's dialect has been modestly asked to conform to Scottish ears.[32] The *Troilus* and

---

duced by multiple hands on parchment of varying quality. Both *Troilus and Criseyde* and the *Testament of Cresseid* are given much the same explicit: fol. 119v, "Explicit liber Troili & Criseid"; fol. 128v, "Explicit Lib. Troili & Creiseidos."

29. See, for example, Carolyn Ives and David Parkinson, "Scottish Chaucer, Misogynist Chaucer," in *Rewriting Chaucer: Culture, Authority and the Idea of the Authentic Text, 1400–1602*, ed. T. A. Prendergast and B. Kline, 186–202 (Columbus: Ohio State University Press, 1999). In "Henryson's 'ballet schort,'" *Studies in Scottish Literature* 32 (1999): 232–44, I have proposed that the *Testament* was initially composed for a quite different audience than Chaucer's *Troilus*—a female, religious readership comparable to that of the *Disce Mori*; see E. A., Jones, ed., *The "Exhortacion" from Disce Mori Edited from Oxford, Jesus College, MS 39*, Middle English Texts 36 (Heidelberg: Universitätsverlag Winter GmbH, 2006).

30. Julia Boffey and A. S. G. Edwards, *The Works of Geoffrey Chaucer and The Kingis Quair: A Facsimile of Bodleian Library, Oxford, MS Arch. Selden. B. 24*, introduction and an appendix by B. C. Barker-Benfield (Cambridge: D.S. Brewer, 1997), 19–20.

31. Ibid., 17.

32. According to Julia Boffey and A. S. G. Edwards, the Selden MS represents an

the majority of rhyme royal pieces in this manuscript generally have five stanzas per page with spacing between stanzas, though "the second scribe abandons the regular five stanzas per page format" to save paper, which does not severely diminish the legibility of his additions but does somewhat cheapen the look of the book as a whole.[33] The apparent purpose of this ongoing, familial, commissioned, and thematically programmed compilation was to record Chaucer as the "Da of Scottish Literature" too.[34]

The early-fifteenth-century Cambridge University Library MS Gg 4. 27(a) is a very impressive book qua book. It contains 488 folio-size leaves of parchment. Each page presents five stanzas as a norm with no spacing between stanzas. This very unsatisfactory transcription of *Troilus and Criseyde* (fol 14r–122v) is item 6 in the manuscript's *ordinatio*. It is preceded by a small collection of lyrics and followed by a likewise "mutilated copy of a composite text" of the *Canterbury Tales*.[35] Though it may represent only a haphazard attempt at chronological order, *Troilus and Criseyde* has been given priority of place in front of the *Tales*. There is, however, no suggestion that the *Legend* should be read next. Despite all its problems as a textual witness, the Gg presentation of *Troilus and Criseyde* was clearly part of a larger project intended from the start to answer a prospective owner's demand for a shelf-trophy, something

---

early stage of primarily orthographic assimilation, but the main scribe "had some interest in deliberately preserving the English flavor" ("Bodleian MS Arch. Selden B. 24 and the 'Scotticization' of Middle English Verse," in Prendergast and Kline, *Rewriting Chaucer*, 166–85, 182).

33. Boffey and Edwards, *Selden Facsimile*, 12. The second scribe occasionally tries to squeeze in a bit more than six stanzas per page.

34. "It seems that at least one impulse in the compilation of Selden was one that insisted on affirming a distinctively Scottish literary identity" (ibid., 21). For consideration of King James's authorial revision of the *Quair*, see my "Red-Lining and Blue-Penciling The Kingis Quair," *Studies in Philology* 108, no. 2 (Spring 2011): 189–214.

35. M. B. Parkes and Richard Beadle, *Poetical Works Geoffrey Chaucer, A Facsimile of Cambridge University Library MS GG. 4. 27*, with Introductions, 3 vols. (Cambridge: D.S. Brewer, 1979), vol. III, "Commentary," 2.

equivalent to *The Complete Works of Geoffrey Chaucer*. There seems to have been more attention paid to filling a handsome volume than to providing rigorously corrected transcriptions of what Chaucer meant to say.

Complementing the impressive size of this collection, the Gg manuscript originally had a remarkable number of illustrations, most of which have been excised. This harvesting offers rude evidence that this text came to be less valued as a depository of Chaucer's poetry than as a scrapbook of pretty pictures. But, in a real sense, much of Chaucer's voice had already been ripped out of this text. It seems that the scribe read a few lines of his exemplar and then wrote his text relying on short-term memory, transforming Chaucer's words into his own pronunciation, spelling, and phrasing preferences.[36] Entire stanzas are also sometimes omitted.[37] All in all, the scribe re-presents an East Anglian redaction of the *Troilus*, a copy perhaps intended to be read aloud (if at all) by an entirely new, less courtly or less urbane and so less attentive owner.

The Pierpont Morgan Library Manuscript M. 817 (formerly Campsall Hall, Doncaster) preserves the "earliest securely datable text" of *Troilus and Criseyde*. This excellent witness "belonged to, and may have been made for, Prince Hal in the decade be-

36. A curious example of the type of Gg's almost omnipresent alterations of "what-Chaucer-might-have-said" can be represented by its seemingly trivial substitution of "'Madame' quod Pandarus ..." as opposed to the preferred reading "Quod Pandarus 'Madame'" (T&C II, 85). Windeatt remarks that such "marked variableness of word-order within the lines ... is one of the most frequent differences between MSS. If a scribe copied by memorizing one line at a time, his allegiance to his copy would be strongest at the opening of the line and at the rhyme, with its own mnemonic effect" (Windeatt, ed., *Geoffrey Chaucer, Troilus* [1984], 32).

37. Stanza omissions seem eye-skips. For example, on fol. 90v the scribe skips Book IV lines 736–49; on fol 91v, he skips lines 806–33; and on fol. 93v, he skips fifteen stanzas, lines 952–1079 (the equivalent of about three pages of text). On fol. 112b he omits lines 713–19 of Book V, which seems a simple eye-skip from "And thus..." (713) to "And thus..." (720).

tween 1403 and 1413."³⁸ Yet, this copy looks hardly so grand as the Corpus or Gg manuscripts were meant to appear. The Morgan manuscript is a gathering of 120 folios of thin and surprisingly poor-quality vellum that has discolored. Perhaps, the text's slimness enhanced its portability. Nevertheless, this relatively modest book does preserve an exceptionally professional transcription of *Troilus and Criseyde* basically in a secretary hand that is "careful, elegant, highly individual, unusually formal and controlled, and astoundingly uniform from start to finish."³⁹

The layout of this manuscript is also "unusually careful."⁴⁰ Five stanzas are copied per page with a line space between each stanza (for a total of thirty-nine line spaces per page). The Morgan scribe omits glosses, showing "unusual restraint in presenting the poem with no editorial comment" that might distract attention from the primary text.⁴¹ Titles occupy a stanza's space, another feature that maintains the visual regularity of each page. This copy was probably produced in London and was originally intended to include only *Troilus and Criseyde*. There is little messing with the poem as received. "Punctuation is sparing but intelligent," and there are very few abbreviations.⁴² The Morgan manuscript aspires to present what every editor desires—a best copy of what Chaucer actually wrote. Perhaps, it was originally commissioned to be read aloud to the prince by a secretary or tutor, though it also serves the solitary, silent reader quite well. It lacks marginal paraphernalia, suggesting that there was little inclination to re-search this highly legible text for specific passages. As a reading tool, it seems primarily designed for the pleasure of

---

38. Jeanne Krochalis, The *Pierpont Morgan Library Manuscript M. 817, A Facsimile*, with Introduction (Norman, Okla.: Pilgrim, 1986), xvii.
39. Ibid., xix.
40. Ibid., xviii.
41. Ibid., xix.
42. Ibid., xviii.

FINISHING TOUCHES

someone wishing a reading of Chaucer's complete story in five installments, and no more.

Another excellent witness, Cosin MS V. ii. 13, presents a slightly smaller copy of *Troilus and Criseyde* on membrane of mediocre quality.[43] It is a composite of two main sections: (A) consists primarily of *Troilus and Criseyde* (item 3, fols. 4r–105v), and (B) consists of Thomas Hoccleve's "Epistle of Cupid" and the unique copy of the lyric NIMEV 2297. The *Troilus* again seems to have circulated as a stand-alone text prior to its inclusion in this manuscript. All thirty-nine lines of a typical page are used to transcribe the *Troilus*, with no spacing between stanzas.[44] Each stanza of the *Troilus* is clearly marked, however, by alternating red and blue paraphs, resulting in a visually clean and, as such, highly readable copy—a reading experience as readily enjoyed alone as aloud. The A-scribe quite comfortably divides stanzas across page breaks—for the sake of economy, perhaps deeming the five-stanza-per-page format (supposedly so conducive for reading aloud) unnecessary.

The formatting of the Cosin manuscript pays rather careful attention to marking book divisions within *Troilus and Criseyde*. Folio 6r is elaborately decorated with a red flourish of the initial three-line black "I" of "Incipit secundus liber" that covers three-fourths of the left margin plus a ten-line blue flourish of initial "I" in the first verse line ("In May ..." II, 50). This ornamentation effectively turns the entire left margin into a clear bookmark. Equivalent decoration marks the start of each following book as well, though after Books I and II there is no attempt to start each new book at

---

43. A. I. Doyle and A. J. Piper, "Description of Durham University MS Cosin V. ii. 13," in "Notes and Drafts of Descriptions of Medieval Manuscripts in Durham University Library," amended November 2003, http://www.dur.ac.uk/library/asc/theme/medmss/apviii13/.

44. The stanzas of the "Epistle of Cupid" are spaced by intervening blank lines in this manuscript.

the top of a new page, and a slight fatigue or indifference seems to set in for designating the later books. Scribe (A) also initiated a program of designating embedded texts by providing a number of side-notes.[45] As a result of these subheadings, *Troilus and Criseyde* itself looks a bit like a compilation, and the "Epistle of Cupid" does not appear to be appended as a simple patch-on. But the primary function of these scribal addenda seems to be to assist a (presumably solitary) re-reading of the text.

BL MS Additional 12044, like the majority of fifteenth-century stand-alone copies of *Troilus and Criseyde*, presents what might best be termed a very handy quarto-sized book designed to enhance the physical comfort of the solitary reading experience.[46] It allots five stanzas per page with spaces between each stanza, and it also provides alternating red/blue paraphs until fol. 65r; thenceforth, alternating red/blue initials are used to designate new stanzas. Book divisions are marked primarily by modestly decorated initials. This design program was not sustained, however; it seems to have been subsequently supplemented by a rather minimal notation of incipits and explicits. There are some corrections but minimal marginal markings. This copy provides little more than the "naked text" (cf. *Romaunt* 6555). This *Troilus and Criseyde* looks less classy—neither aristocratic nor ambitiously bourgeois. The text seems only a tool for the "common reader."

BL MS Harley 2280 is a complete transcription and not especially small,[47] but it seems a diminished thing: "A parchment Book reduced by the plough of a knavish Binder, from a folio to a 4to,

---

45. Additional side notes are provided "in the hand of William Browne" (Doyle and Piper, "Description").
46. *A Catalogue of Additions to the Manuscripts in the British Museum in the Years MDCCCXLI–MDCCCXLV* (London, 1850), 29.
47. "An old copy on vellum," *A Catalogue of the Harleain Manuscripts in the British Museum* (London, 1808), vol. III, 97.

containing, Geffrey Chaucers Poem of 'Troilus & Criseida,' in five Books."⁴⁸ Such rebinding seems more concerned with the book's shelf appearance than with its content's conservation. The scribe's elaborate ascenders have been severely cropped in the top margin. Each page presents six (rather than the more typical five) stanzas, and the handwriting is rather compressed. There are alternating red and blue paraphs marking the start of each stanza, and a space separates stanzas. The formatting very clearly indicates the divisions between books and sets off each proem from the book that it prefaces. There is no real concern to start proems or books at the tops of pages. A full stanza's space is used to mark the breaks between books. Less attention is drawn to signaling the beginning and end of each proem, as if the "reading proper" should focus on the plot rather than these lyric digressions.⁴⁹ Running footers (which serve only the transcription process) should be ignored.

But the scribe does provide significant marginalia of two types: there are some indications of subsections within each book—that is, embedded songs, letters, etc.; and there are also several marginal annotations in Latin. The data of each of these notes may seem somewhat minimal (or self-evident). The gesture of providing such notes speaks volumes, however, about the scribe's expectations regarding the education and reading habits of this manuscript's users. This type of note was surely never meant to be read aloud. Such elements of the manuscript apparently anticipate instead a proto-humanist readership, and so the text as a whole accommodates their more studied reading.

48. Ibid., vol. II, 641.
49. The transcription ends with five last stanzas on the recto of fol. 98 followed by an enlarged "Explicit liber Troili and Criseydis" and a cropped "Amen." This "amen" after the marked ending of the book has a different effect on the reader than its insertion immediately after the last line of Chaucer's prayer to the Trinity through Mary's intercession (as in *Riverside*); it reads more like the scribe's *punctus* than the prayer's formulaic closure.

The very trim BL MS Harley 3943 preserves *Troilus and Criseyde* as a stand-alone book with five stanzas per page and line-spaces between stanzas that begin with alternating red and blue initials. There are no incipits or explicits or labels of the proems as such. The use of initials to format the beginnings of the first four books is rather minimal and easy to overlook. On top of fol. 64v, an italic hand notes "4 stanzas omitted here," which should have been the "Canticus Troili" (III, 1744–71). Chaucer's preliminary remark "And thanne he wolde synge in this manere" (III, 1743) is reduced to nonsense by the jump to "In alle nedes for the townes werre" (III, 1772). However, silent reading is not so derailed by such an omission as public recital would be. Book V ends with three stanzas on fol. 116r followed by a peculiar explicit to fill the rest of the page. The scribe signs off with a "valete" that seems addressed to future readers (in the plural) rather than to the ghost of Troilus. There are no significant glosses. If BL MS Additional 12044 seems a naked text, this one looks like a rather skeletal effort—an adequate, economical copy for a quick read.

BL MS Harley 2392 presents only four stanzas per page; there are no paraphs, but there are spaces between stanzas.[50] There is no header or incipit on fol. 1r, but there is a three-line initial "T" in blue and red. More impressively, the entire first page of text is boxed and flourished with a red and blue decorative border. This design announces the start of the whole book as such but provides no indication of Book I as a discrete recital unit. Books II–IV apparently should have the same style of initials, but these books do not have comparably elaborate borders on their respective first pages; so these subunits (or reading installments) seem less significant as objects of interpretation (or confabulation) than

---

50. "A book in 4to. written partly upon Parchment, but mostly upon Paper." *A Catalogue of the Harleain Manuscripts in the British Museum*, vol. II, 682.

FINISHING TOUCHES

the whole. The same style of initialing is also used to introduce Book V—but with a bizarre miscalculation. On fol. 138r, an initial "E" (V, 1436) marks the start of a supposed proem; on fol. 140, an initial "F" starts the beginning of the book's narration at line V, 1541. The fifth book should have started on fol. 112v (as lightly noted in the left margin by a later hand). It seems as if this manuscript's demarcation of a last "book" was imposed for the sake of the whole text looking complete without actual recognition of its last installment's own integrity—almost as if formatted without re-reading.

In addition to emendations, the scribe provides rather frequent though brief Latin glosses in the right margins. Several are merely repetitions of the proper names given in the text itself; putting such notes in the right margin gives the reader a finding device rather than any real clarification of each corresponding line. The scribe also labels several embedded texts such as the letters of Criseyde (fols. 27r, 42r, 99r), the song of Antigone (fol. 35r), the *cantus* (fol. 83 r), testament (118r), and letter (fol. 136r) of Troilus, etc. Similar labels are provided to designate what appear to have been read as discrete scenes within Chaucer's narrative as well, including a peroration of Pandarus (fol. 26r at II, 316ff) and "verba" between Diomede and Criseyde (fol. 114v). Such notations help the solitary reader to take breaks, but they may also mark favorite passages for the sake of (dramatic, perhaps even memorized) °acquisition.

BL MS Harley 4912 consists of seventy-five folios with five stanzas per page with substantial margins; stanzas are not marked by paraphs, but there are clear spaces between them.[51] This textual witness ends at Book V, 686, but there is a footer in-

---

51. Ibid., vol. III, 219.

dicating its continuation with line V, 687 on the next folio. It is difficult to determine whether the missing copy has been lost or was never completed. Rather elaborate initials seem to have been intended to mark the start of each book, not the proems. There are some marginal indications of subsections within each book.

However, the most intriguing marginalia in this copy of *Troilus and Criseyde* are its intermittent designations of characters' names in what seems the same hand as that of the narrative text, though somewhat smaller and lighter. For example, on fol. 12v the scribe indicates: Troylus (at I, 820); Pandarus (at I, 829); Troylus (at I, 834); continuing on fol. 13r: Pandarus (at I, 841); Troylus (at I, 867); Pandarus (at I, 868); Troylus (at I, 872). A second flurry of names occurs starting on fol. 31v: Pandar (at II, 1093); fol. 31r: Cresseyde (at II, 1100); fol. 31v: Pandare (at II, 1142); fol. 31v: Criseyde (at X, 1163). These names are all placed in the right margins. The resulting copy looks almost like a modern play-book. The indicated dialogue can be divided among different readers. Or these designations of speakers by name can function as tonal prompts for a single reciter. Or, at the very least, these notations enhance a more histrionic silent reading in that they clearly indicate shifting from one character's point of view to another's and, thereby, call for each character's imagined *pronuntiatio*.

BL MS Harley 1239 is "an oblong Parchment-book" that preserves a quite different feel for its anticipated presentation of *Troilus and Criseyde*.[52] Perhaps, this holster-book format was chosen for portability or storage, or because it conformed to some shelving standard, or (most probably) simply because this format (often used for accounts) happened to be available. Its scribe usually squeezes nine stanzas on each tall-as-a-folio, narrow-as-an-octavo page. There is normally no spacing between stanzas

---

52. Ibid., vol. I, 618.

though some intermittent and seemingly random spaces are introduced beginning on fol. 22r. Stanzas are marked with alternating red and blue one-line initials, and each stanza is bracketed by a red line in the right margin. *Troilus and Criseyde* is the initial item (fols. 1–62), preceding selections from *The Canterbury Tales*: in order, "The Knight's Tale" (missing the first thirty-four lines), "The Man of Law's Prologue and Tale," "The Wife of Bath's Tale," "The Clerk's Tale," and a bowdlerized version of "The Franklin's Tale."[53] Although this copy of *Troilus and Criseyde* too may have circulated independently, its juxtaposition to "The Knight's Tale" in this compilation is an especially suggestive gesture.

Book I of the *Troilus* (and so of this manuscript as a whole) starts with an initial illuminated "T" containing a seven-line miniature that is severely damaged. It seems to show some scene (an exchange of gifts?) corresponding to the narrative, though it might be a dedicatory image. Except for the scribe's fancy ascenders, however, very little else in this utilitarian copy seems ornamental.[54] The sheer length of each page and the smallness of its lettering make this copy rather difficult to read. The reader cannot simply hold the text still and then scan entire pages; the small lettering must be held quite close, and so each page must be adjusted while reading. But the apparent shortcomings of this format pertain only to silent, solitary reading. The external appearance of this book is itself quite attractive, especially to an owner-listener who need not worry about the eye-strain of its prelector.

BL MS Arch. Selden Supra 56 has the size and feel of a com-

---

53. "It may seem therefore that the good Hermit of Grenewich who wrote this part of the Book, purposely omitted the Recital of the Conjurations & magical Ceremonies there mentioned" (*A Catalogue of the Harleain Manuscripts in the British Museum*, vol. I, 619).

54. The only other decoration (if so it may be called) is a doodle in the left margin of fol. 21v showing Cupid's name above a heart pierced by an arrow beside a quincunx of dots "∴" to the left of III, 99.

pletely functional, not too expensive book.[55] The text of *Troilus and Criseyde* is presented with adequate margins in a small but neat handwriting. The formatting provides a rather modest program of incipits, explicits, and annotations. But (like Gg and to a lesser extent like Selden B. 24) this manuscript revises Chaucer's dialect, a "contamination" that diminishes this copy's worth as a textual witness. Its scribe programmatically (rather than negligently) rewrites *Chaucer*. This scribe's translation (or modernization, as it were) makes the *Troilus* easier to read by anyone who shares the scribe's Northern dialect and who would therefore find "the original"—that is, Chaucer's own voice—increasingly difficult to understand while reading the text either silently or aloud.

BL MS Rawlinson Poet. 163 preserves what has become (rather than what was originally meant to be) an essentially stand-alone copy of *Troilus and Criseyde*.[56] This paper copy is very comfortably sized for the solitary reader. The scribe provides no paraphs, no spaces, and no special initials for the first line of each stanza; so, although there are regularly five stanzas per page, it is very difficult to see stanza divisions.[57] Short horizontal strokes in the same ink as the text are inserted above the top left start of lines beginning each stanza. There was very little concern to produce a

55. F. Madan and H. H. E. Craster, *Summary Catalogue of Western MSS. in the Bodleian Library*, Nos. 2354–3490 (Oxford: Clarendon Press, 1922), 636. Acquisition no. 3444.
56. There is a note by a later hand in the top margin of what is now fol. 1r that numbers it as folio 114. This copy of *Troilus and Criseyde* may at some time have been included as part of some *larger* gathering of texts—the only remnant of which is the enigmatic "To Rosemund," first published in print by W. W. Skeat (*Athenaeum*, 4 April, 1891).
57. F. Madan and H. H. E. Craster propose "Tregentil is probably the name of the scribe" rather than a recognition of *très gentil* Chaucer, *Summary Catalogue of Western MSS. in the Bodleian Library*, Nos. 8717–14671 (Oxford: Clarendon Press, 1922), 318. Acquisition no. 1465. Madan and Craster attempt to reproduce in print the layout of the explicit to *Troilus and Criseyde* on fol. 113v; "Here endith ..." is enclosed in brackets with (uncapitalized) "tregentyll" to left and "Chaucer" to right. At an angle below there is another (practice?) *signature* "tregentil" in what seems the same hand but different ink and slightly different display style. In the same ink as "To Rosemounde," what looks like its attribution to "tregentil————/—/————chaucer" follows on fol.114r (cf. *Riverside*, 649).

good-looking book, and its subsequent readers treated this copy with no special reverence. For example, its minimal indications of stanza breaks are occasionally supplemented by later attempts to connect the rhymes in the right margin. Who drew these lines is unknown, as is why; the execution seems very amateurish, perhaps the jottings of a would-be imitator or memorizer. There are quite frequent marginal notes, the majority of which seem to provide mini-"arguments" regarding the plot, such as one marking the commendation of Criseyde's beauty (fol. 2r) or "how" the feast of Palladion was held and Criseyde summoned (fol. 3r) or "how" Troilus played the comic (fol. 3v), and so forth, as well as more familiar though hardly complete designations of textual subsections like songs, testaments, and letters.

A marginal "Nota bene" to the left of Book IV, 940, on fol. 90r, alerts the reader to the fact that Criseyde will try to avoid crying. Such a note seems intended to report (or assist or control) the responses of a solitary reader. The addition of the ballade "To Rosemounde" may have been intended to serve as nothing more than page-filler. But, even if this unique copy of the lyric is read as a genuine appendage to the *Troilus*, it invites radically opposed perceptions of Chaucer's intended tone: it may celebrate a historical occasion (for example, the entry of Isabelle of Valois into London in 1396), or it may (as I think) provide some lighthearted relief. When read as just another item among "Chaucer's Short Poems," there is simply not enough deixis to discern with confidence the voice of "To Rosemounde"—except one's fundamental sense of Chaucer himself.

BL MS Digby 181 contains a very defective fifteenth-century copy of *Troilus and Criseyde*.[58] This manuscript seems to have been primarily planned as a collection of Lydgatian material gathered

---

58. John Brode, Jr., copying in Warwickshire, has been identified as the scribe of

together with a rather simple though not entirely consistent format. It does provide clear though somewhat ad hoc indications for the start and stop of each book of *Troilus and Criseyde*. The beginning of Book II in particular has a rather belt-and-suspenders look about it. This copy of the *Troilus* may, like so many others, have initially circulated alone prior to its inclusion (as an afterthought) at the end of this compilation.[59] The transcription itself breaks off mid-page at Book III, 532. Without the addition of this chunk of *Troilus and Criseyde*, the Digby manuscript looks tall enough and wide enough but perhaps not thick enough. There is no clear sign of loss or damage to explain the omission of over half of Chaucer's composition; more may have been simply unavailable.[60] A worst possible reading of this manuscript's content would be that its compiler was more interested in binding sufficient bulk for sale than in preserving Chaucer's complete book.

The Huntington Library MS HM 114 is "composed of three trade booklets produced around 1430, perhaps 'on spec' by a text-writer providing no-frills merchandise for a stationer, and later assembled in one volume for some down-market customer."[61] Its

---

fols. 1–53 of Digby 181 and Rylands 113 by D. W. Mosser, "A New Collation for Bodleian Digby MS. 181," *Papers of the Bibliographical Society of America* 82 (1988): 604–11, and "The Scribe of Chaucer Manuscripts Rylands 113 and Bodleian Digby 181," *Manuscripta* 34 (1990): 129–47.

59. Following stubs, fol. 54r seems darkened as if exposed as a front page for some period of time. But several other pages are darkened, and there is extensive water damage to this manuscript.

60. A. S. G. Edwards interprets this breaking off "in the middle of a verso page (fol. 93v) in the middle of Book 3" thus: "There is no indication that any more of the text ever existed in this copy. This would seem to suggest that the text of Troilus was only available to the scribe in a partial, fascicular form, and that he was ultimately unable to obtain any more of an exemplar" ("Manuscript and Text," in *A Guide to Editing Middle English*, ed. Vincent McCarren and Douglas Moffat, 159–68 [Ann Arbor: University of Michigan Press, 1998], 163).

61. John Bowers, "Two Professional Readers of Chaucer and Langland: Scribe D and the HM 114 Scribe," *Studies in the Age of Chaucer* 26 (2004): 113–46, 113. This manu-

FINISHING TOUCHES

325 pages are small; each page contains between thirty-two and thirty-six lines; all in all, it looks like an unimpressive book with a rather second-rate transcription.[62] The compilation is inclusive or eclectic or random; it presents a seemingly arbitrary gathering of vernacular texts that mixes prose and alliterative verse and rhyme royal pieces. The *Troilus* is followed immediately by the Lollard-like *Epistola Luciferi ad Cleros*. The scribe anticipates his potential market's broader but less affluent, less aristocratic taste, "the diverse interests of London readers around 1430 when the official literary tradition—the Chaucer tradition—had been established by his literary heirs Hoccleve and Lydgate but had not achieved the near exclusivity granted by Caxton at the end of the century."[63] The copyist appears to have been indifferent to each author's name, and he imposes his own dialect "colored by southeast Essex features."[64] Chaucer's courtly performance has again been largely overruled in this marketing of *Troilus and Criseyde* but not fully erased.

Three early print editions of *Troilus and Criseyde* are now also read as witnesses of lost manuscripts. William Caxton's standalone *Troilus* (ca. 1483) looks like a critical, so modern, so best edition. Like a medieval scribe, however, Caxton seems to have duplicated only one exemplar "with little or no collation of other MSS."[65] Caxton's *Troilus* may be read as a spin-off sale. Presum-

---

script was formerly identified as Phillips 8252, Cheltenham, misnumbered 8250 by Root and Robinson.

62. John Bowers perceives that "the HM 144 Scribe emerges as a less glamorous transitional figure. His contribution to the higher quality Harley 3943 manuscript of *Troilus* suggests that he made efforts, earlier in his career, to join the textwriters producing these more profitable Chaucer books for an upscale clientele. But the inferior quality of his performance in the Harley *Troilus* may have branded him unsuited to these more ambitious, classier-looking productions. So he remained a freelance copyist manufacturing vernacular works in relatively cheap, no-frills forms" (ibid., 113).

63. Ibid., 133.

64. Ibid., 132.

65. Windeatt, ed., *Geoffrey Chaucer, Troilus and Criseyde* [1984], 75. Only three copies

ably expecting greater sales, Caxton had published a fancier *Canterbury Tales* in 1476 and again in 1483. According to Caxton's market-driven reading, *Troilus and Criseyde* has already become Chaucer's second-best masterpiece. Wynkyn de Worde's edition (1517) mostly just reprints Caxton's edition,[66] but he adds three more final stanzas attributed to "The auctour" and thereby insists that readers clearly see Chaucer's anti-feminist intent.[67]

William Thynne's edition (1532) of Chaucer's collected works represents the culmination of a process of transmission that re-visioned Chaucer's recital as the reader's book. The title page—itself a significant requirement of fifteenth-century readers—advertises: "The Workes of Geffray Chaucer newly printed / with dyvers workes which were nevere in print before: As in the table more playnly doth appere. Cum privilegio."[68] Thynne's table of contents also seems an especially important prompt guiding the silent reader of the whole book.[69] Thynne regularizes the text a bit,

---

of Caxton's edition survive plus a fragment of eight leaves. Caxton's reliance on a single exemplar for his edition of *Troilus and Criseyde* may have been motivated by necessity—i.e., a lack of optional copies—rather than negligence. In contrast, as Alice Miskimin has observed, "Caxton's Preface to the second edition of his *Canterbury Tales* (1484) is clear proof... that comparisons were made between 'good' and 'bad' texts" (*Renaissance Chaucer*, 90).

66. Book I, 1–546 of de Worde's edition provides an independent textual witness. Richard Pynson's edition of the *Troilus* (1526)—likewise based on Caxton's edition with alterations—is not included by Barney as a textual authority (*Riverside*, 1161).

67. See C. David Benson and David Rollman, "Wynkyn de Worde and the Ending of Chaucer's *Troilus and Criseyde*," *Modern Philology* 78 (1981): 275–79.

68. Walter W. Skeat, *The Works of Geoffrey Chaucer and Others, Being a Reproduction in Facsimile of the First Collected Edition 1532 from the Copy in the British Museum with an Introduction* (London: [Oxford University Press, 1904]; A. Moring, H. Frowde, [1905]).

69. The table of contents (ibid., 6) only approximates modern editorial requirements; it designates the start of "The Knight's Tale" on "fo. Primo" and "The Miller's Tale" on "fo. xiiii."

Thynne provides folio numbering starting with fol xiii (p. 45), which contains the last seventy lines of "The Knight's Tale," its explicit, and the first seventeen lines of the Miller's "Prologue" labeled as such. "The Knight's Tale," being first, is easy enough to

but his double-column format elevates all of Chaucer's entertainments to the prestige they rightly deserve as the opus of a major author.[70] And his book's design introduces some very strong (albeit tacit) biases for reading *Troilus and Criseyde* in particular.

The *Canterbury Tales* as a unit is introduced by a title page (p. 9) with a woodcut illustrated border, a framing pseudo-frieze of cherubs, in the top center of which is a tonto portrait of the poet crowned with laurel, bracketed by two sphinxes. The framing decoration of this title page is duplicated for the *Romaunt* (p. 273), the *Troilus* (p. 357), but not for the *Testament of Criseyde* which follows starting mid-page (p. 457), without any attribution of the sequel to Robert Henryson. The following *Legend*'s title fills a blank following the last stanza and explicit of the *Testament* (on the second column of page 464 with the text of the "Prologue" starting page 465). Thynne thus invites the reader to appreciate these three pieces *seriatim*, as a cohesive subset of the author's corpus—as if together these three discrete texts comprised *The Matter of Troilus and Criseyde*.

It has become quite impossible to arrange all of these textual witnesses to *Troilus and Criseyde* in precise chronological order. And there are several inconsistencies regarding what is expected of Chaucer's readers—often within a single text. Nevertheless, there does seem to have been a fairly consistent shift in the perception of *Troilus and Criseyde* as a published artifact by the start of the sixteenth century. Chaucer has become *Chaucer*, the reader's property. This commonplace identification of a text by its author's name has become a dead metaphor, no longer truly anthropomor-

---

find since the *Tales* themselves have been given pride of place in Chaucer's canon, a now normative editorial and critical bias.

70. "Thynne rather injudiciously endeavoured to turn it into Southern English, doubtless in order to render it more acceptable to his readers" (ibid., xxxi).

phic, no longer requiring that we read that the text's living content as having been truly "person-shaped." Holding such a machined *Chaucer* in hand, we lose touch with Chaucer's personal intentions because we have persuaded ourselves to lose all confidence in written words as a means of listening to their maker's voice, and we tend thereby to translate the dynamic tone of Chaucer's intense doubts into our own static and smug themes of despair—with no final appeal to the Word.

8

POSTSCRIPT

> Well, well, I see
> I talk but idly, and you laugh at me.
> William Shakespeare,
> *Richard II* (III. iii. 170–71)

EX POST FACTO, the practical value of my attempt to read *Troilus and Criseyde* as if it were originally composed by Chaucer for his own recital speaks for itself—or not. The bulk of this book has been an exercise in expressive criticism. My responses to Chaucer's text are impressions (in Walter Pater's sense), perhaps at times only idiosyncratic intuitions.[1] My intent has been to suggest one legitimate account of some of Chaucer's tonal intentions. I do not wish to preclude alternative readings. Yet, refusing to be confined by the prescriptiveness of "self-referentiality," the reader can at least try to hear the author's ref-

---

1. Denis Donoghue affirms the legitimacy of a reader's perception of the *impression* of the author's voice "as a sign of personal presence" (*Practice of Reading*, 111). In terms of "medieval critical theory" (subsumed under epistemology), the legitimacy of such a reading could be defended by appeal to the *via analogica*.

erences to his own feelings while reading—these tonally expressive moments are not *écriture* or *fiction* but expository statements that, even if read again only as *phantasmata*, recall Chaucer's "I" in person. This type of reception-based analysis prioritizes the concurrent (so ephemeral) experience of reading itself (qua listening) as an interpretive focus. This (rather old-fashioned) type of reading puts Chaucer himself again in the way of every subsequent reading. More perdurable if not immutable statements of theme emerge therefrom only upon recollection and reflection. But interpretations should come filtered through the author's own emotionally charged expectations regarding his tonally affective presence. The poem so read becomes a playground for discussion, rather than an artsy homily.

I should be content if any other readers of *Troilus and Criseyde* share my perceptions of its author's tonal intentions. I do not believe this study offers "compelling proof" of Chaucer's own recital and subsequent revision of the extant text. I do believe that this historically plausible contention allows for an enriched perception of this one text's latent tonal features. I do not believe there is currently any better explanation of the text's voices. Consenting to the possible facticity of this notion that any Chaucerian text was initially composed for authorial recital and then revised for manuscript circulation has ramifications for a number of other current controversies regarding Chaucer's entire canon as well, including: competing conceptions of *why* his narrating "I" must now be read as such a complicated construct; uncertainty regarding the chronological order of several of his works; the editorial imposition of interpretive prompts, including punctuation; Chaucer's chronic failure to finish his compositions; and, I think most important, the author's contrasting anticipation of his reading absence while writing *The Canterbury Tales*.

POSTSCRIPT

A. C. Spearing clearly perceives the modern reader's problem of clearly perceiving Chaucer's "I" per se: "When we look closely at almost any narrative passage in Chaucer, we find not a single shaping subjectivity but the traces of many different centres of consciousness."[2] The simplest and so, I think, most plausible explanation for the observably self-conscious complexity and anxiety of Chaucer's narrative "I" in *Troilus and Criseyde* is the author's dueling anticipations of his dual roles as script-reciter and text-writer. Chaucer distinguishes the products of these two stages of composition in the Prologue to *The Legend of Good Women* when he confronts the (supposedly unexpected) negative responses of Love and his court to *Troilus and Criseyde* and the *Romaunt*. The offended (because obtuse) God objects that Chaucer "mysseyest" (F 323; G 249) but refers to two quite distinct types of publication. Chaucer's *Romaunt* seems to have been circulating exclusively as a manuscript: "For in pleyn text, withouten nede of glose, / Thou hast translated the Romaunce of the Rose" (F 328–29; G 254–55). Although Love similarly notes in the G-version that Chaucer made "the bok" (G 264), the F-version remembers Chaucer's presentation of *Troilus and Criseyde* primarily as a recital event: "thou hast seyd as the lyste" (F 332). The G-version, I still contend, was the product of revision for manuscript circulation; the F-version, Chaucer's recital script—which most readers prefer.

Seeking the voice of the author in the text admittedly chases a sort of hermeneutic Möbius strip. Till the very end of his career,

---

2. Spearing, *Textual Subjectivity*, 95; whereas textual indicators of subjectivity in much Middle English literature can be diffused or disunified, comprising a "'subjectless subjectivity'... in Chaucer and some of his successors there is an important movement towards a conception of the literary text as 'the product of a particular consciousness'" (*Textual Subjectivity*, 33). Spearing concedes that the narrative "I" can approximate the characterization of a persona: "I do not wish to deny that such encoding can amount to the creation of a narrator as part of the narrative fiction, but we should not suppose that it must work like that" (*Textual Subjectivity*, 77).

POSTSCRIPT

Chaucer wrote primarily in terms of "speche." Even in his "Retraction" to *The Canterbury Tales*, Chaucer addresses future readers who may "herkne ... or rede" (CT 10, 1) his little treatise. Conversely, Chaucer frequently envisions his "I" as the product of other writings. For example, Chaucer introduces himself in the *Parliament of Fowls* primarily as a reader of texts (PF, 10)—"as I yow tolde" (PF, 16). Chaucer recites a book report on Macrobius's *Commentary on the Dream of Scipio* written "with lettres olde" (PF, 19). Solitary, silent Chaucer had read this book all day till deprived of sufficient light. Both Chaucer and his book now tell (PF, 30, 36, 39, 43) the purpose of this matter (PF, 26), though both Scipio's and Chaucer's dreams are reported in the past tense. At the entrance to a phantom reading experience, Chaucer sees an inscription on the portal of dreams, a gate that also serves as the *accessus* to such narratives: "And over the gate , with lettres large iwroughte, / There were vers iwriten ... than spak that other side.... These vers of gold and blak iwriten were" (PF, 123–41).

Right in the middle of his reading, Chaucer recites what the text says: "Be glad, thow redere" (PF, 132; cf. T&C V, 267). The dream-gate is here quoting *Dante*—sort of. The dreamer reads this second-person pronoun as directly addressed to himself, but the quoted text simultaneously speaks indirectly to Chaucer's reader.[3] This "Story" within Chaucer's *Book* then pictures its author as a text to be read himself. Scipio sees the hesitancy of Chaucer's body language: "It stondeth writen in thy face, / Thyn errour, though thow telle it not to me" (PF, 155–56). Scipio perceives (because conjured to do so by a self-deprecating author) that Chaucer is misreading "the pleyn sentence" (PF, 126); Chaucer has read the text as personally relevant although "this writyng

---

3. Muscatine, *Riverside*, 997, n. 132.

POSTSCRIPT

nys nothyng ment bi the" (PF, 158). As for love, Chaucer may look but not touch: "And if thow haddest connyng for t'endite, / I shal the shewe mater of to wryte" (167–68).

And, truly, Chaucer seems to have started writing "The Clerk's Tale" (like "The Knight's Tale" or *Troilus and Criseyde*) as a matter of rather straightforward translation. It too may have once been recited in a stand-alone context. But its extant conclusion with the *Tales* presents a decomposing "I" because too many voices can lay claim to the one text.[4] The tone of the envoy to "The Clerk's Tale" (CT 4, 1177–1212) still looks clearly sarcastic.[5] But whose point of view does the text represent? The Clerk's? Some unidentified intruder's? Chaucer-the-pilgrim/narrator/poet's? The modern reader's confusion—itself a legitimate tonal response—actually begins two stanzas earlier with some exiting minstrel's remark: "But o word, lordynges, herkneth er I go" (CT 4, 1163). Unlike the "Envoy's" ballade stanzas, this text-linking comment maintains the tale's rhyme-royal format, but where would the Clerk be going upon completion of his turn? What "I" is demanding whose attention? In print, the ending of "The Clerk's Tale" now reads like an interpretive controversy unto itself. The Clerk (as prelector) seems to be usurping Petrarch's "I"; alternatively or simultaneously, Chaucer (as the not-dead-yet author) adds another of his own "Short Poems" to subvert Petrarch's *moralitas*.

The tale's "Envoy" is normally read as "de Chaucer" precisely because it sounds so inconsistent with (the Host's prior joke

---

4. Warren S. Ginsberg notes, "Whether any considerable time elapsed between the writing of the tale and the addition of this ending (or for that matter, the addition of the ClPro), is unknown" (*Riverside*, 883, n. 1170).

5. Howell Chickering has found the interminable rhyming of this double ballade so excessive that Chaucer's intent must have been to make his ironic viewpoint indeterminable ("Form and Interpretation in the Envoy to the Clerk's Tale," *The Chaucer Review* 29 [1995]: 352–72).

POSTSCRIPT

about) the Clerk's maidenly coyness: "This day ne herde I of youre tonge a word" (CT 4, 4).[6] This final voice prepares to sing "with lusty herte, fressh and grene" (CT 4, 1173), however. These prefatory remarks presume a male voice—"Herkneth my song that seith in this manere" (CT 4, 1176),[7] but the envoy sounds far more like the call-to-arms of a harridan.[8] Its "I" cries "in open audience" (CT 4, 1179). Outraged (and outrageously), the text reads, "Ne lat no clerk ... write of yow a storie" (CT 4, 1185–86; cf. CT 4, 935, and 3, 688–92). The anonymous speaker commands all women present: "Folweth Ekko, that holdeth no silence" (CT 4, 1189).

Though attempting to quiet critical disagreement, F. N. Robinson acknowledges this cacophony of voices in the text: "The song, as the scribe's heading ... indicates, is Chaucer's independent composition. But it belongs dramatically to the Clerk and is entirely appropriate."[9] This opinion is quoted verbatim by Warren S. Ginsberg;[10] a full colon invites the reader to imagine the Clerk reciting (perhaps, indeed singing) this lyric from memory.[11] Baugh and Fisher likewise introduce the envoy with a full colon.[12]

---

6. Ginsberg notes that such a clerk's "demeanor ought to be maidenly" (*Riverside*, 879, nn. 2–3).

7. Chickering takes "seith" as indicative of the envoy's being "not a song to be sung to music" ("Form and Interpretation," 358).

8. This envoy's allusions to Wife of Bath (CT 4, 1170 and perhaps 1195) can be explained within the Clerk's fictional frame of reference. Chaucer's recommendation that Bukton go read the Wife of Bath ("L'Envoy a Bukton") presupposes that some version of the text was already accessible in manuscript, perhaps pamphlet form.

9. Robinson acknowledges possible contradiction: "(For the opposing view see Koch. *Angl.*, L, 65f.)" (*Works*, 712, n. 1177).

10. Benson, *Riverside*, 883, n. 1177.

11. Ganim sees that the envoy's very singable double ballade form, which uses only three rhymes through six stanzas, "immediately assumes the quality of epistolary lyric, akin to the casual and witty performances of Chaucer's own lyrics" (*Theatricality*, 81). Ganim focuses on the Clerk's (Chaucer's) ironic ambivalence and chooses not to be "sidetracked ... by further arguments about persona, performance, and who is speaking where and when" (90).

12. John H. Fisher then includes the "Merry Words" of the Host as a supernumer-

Donaldson also introduces the envoy with a full colon, and Donaldson also provides a disambiguated title: "The Clerk's Envoy." Fisher and Donaldson both omit, or refuse to insert, Skeat's final exclamation point and so mute the envoy's intensity—relatively speaking. In short, all of these editors strive to incorporate the text of the envoy into an ongoing act of narration performed by the pilgrim-persona.

However, the text as presented by Adam Pinkhurst and the Rev. W. W. Skeat does not concur with this prevailing critical consensus. Thomas J. Farrell provides an extensive review of the critical debate and, based on the evidence of manuscript rubrication, concludes that the envoy should be presented as a discrete reading entity: "the dramatic question" of attribution to the Squire or Chaucer-the-narrator "is, in this case, simply a false issue."[13] Both the Hengwrt and the Ellesmere manuscripts provide a marginal citation of Petrarch's Latin moral next to lines 1156–62; as quoted, Petrarch's "nos" means all of us patient Christians.[14] This marginal citation of the source text's conclusion suggests that the Clerk has here completed "hanc historiam"—that is, his announced intent to "telle a tale" (CT 4, 26) learned from the clerk of Padua.[15] In the Ellesmere manuscript, this marginal yet

---

ary (1212a–g) part of the text proper (*The Complete Poetry and Prose of Geoffrey Chaucer*, 2nd ed. [New York: Holt, Rinehart and Winston, 1989]). E. Talbot Donaldson too incorporates "The Host's Comment" (*Chaucer's Poetry*, 2nd ed. [New York: John Wiley and Sons, 1958], 305). But Albert C. Baugh ends the envoy and the tale together with an exclamation point, sending the Host's stanza to a footnote (*Chaucer's Major Poetry* [New York: Appleton-Century-Crofts, 1963], 440).

13. Thomas J. Farrell provides a review of the critical debate regarding the integrity and the integral-ity of the "Envoy" to the Clerk's tale. (See "The 'Envoy de Chaucer' and the 'Clerk's Tale,'" *The Chaucer Review* 24 [1990]: 329–36, 333).

14. Germaine Dempster, "Chaucer's Manuscript of Petrarch's Version of the Griselda Story," *Modern Philology* 41 (1943): 6–16, 6, n. 3. Ellesmere alone has twenty-eight glosses; other MSS. have two to twenty-seven.

15. Petrarch's *Epistolae Seniles* XVII. 3.

POSTSCRIPT

concluding comment occurs (perhaps fortuitously) at the bottom of a page. In his note to line E [IV] 1162, Skeat claims: "It seems to have been Chaucer's intention, in the first instance, to end this Tale here."[16] Both manuscripts specify the envoy is "de Chaucer"—that is, that it was written, not here fictionally recited by Chaucer. The Ellesmere somewhat reinforces this implication with its marginal decoration (also used to mark the *partes* of the tale) but obscures the stand-alone quality of the inserted envoy by placing its explicit after the "merry words" of the Host. The Hengwrt manuscript more clearly divorces the envoy from the Clerk's "I" by declaring, "Here endeth" his voice after line 1176, and by giving the "Envoy" its own explicit as a stand-alone insert. This lyric may have once been enacted with mock enthusiasm, but it here seems inserted as a tonal antidote to the preceding lugubrious tale (like the copying of "To Rosemounde" after *Troilus and Criseyde* in BL MS Rawlinson Poet. 163). The text of the envoy may be genuinely Chaucer's but its inclusion, in this context, only scribal—a textual gesture that disrupts the framing fiction.

The authenticity of the "murye words" of the Host in response to the Clerk's recital of his "storie" (CT 4, 1142) has also been called into question. These lines do not provide an explicit link to "The Merchant's Tale" (cf. CT 4, 1224). In most modern editions, Herry wishes that his wife had heard the *legend* (CT 4, 1212c) of Griselda—not the envoy. He hopes that Goodelief will be moved thereby to become patient. But Herry himself has completely failed to hear the tone of lines 1163 to 1212 and ignores Petrarch's intentions. Herry thus embodies Chaucer's worst fear as an au-

---

16. Walter W. Skeat, *Works*, vol. IV, 424. Skeat adds: "Hence we find in MSS. E. [Ellesemere] Hn. [Hengwrt] Cm. [Cambridge UL Gg. 4. 27] Dd. [Cambridge UL 4. 24], the following genuine, but rejected stanza, suitable for insertion at this point:—"; Skeat is referring to "the merry words" that follow the (allegedly intrusive) envoy.

thor: the completely self-centered audience member. Accordingly, Herry has no hope that his absent, belligerent wife would welcome such an interpretation of the Clerk's "gentil" exemplum: "As to my purpos, wiste ye my wille; / But thyng that wol nat be, lat it be stille" (CT 4, 1212f–g). Even if spurious, this moment sounds truly Chaucerian. There is a certain perfect irony to the fact that this fictional listener's statement of doubt should be so doubted as textually legitimate. Nevertheless, unlike modern novelists on whose work so much theory is based, Chaucer, though he feared becoming invisible, did not deliberately hide.

Assigning specific dates to Chaucer's compositions—including *Troilus and Criseyde*—remains another ongoing critical controversy that, unlike Chaucer's "I," most modern readers can blithely ignore more often than not. Nevertheless, we read each text within *The Complete Works of Geoffrey Chaucer* corralled into some order, usually chronological after yielding priority of reading place to *The Canterbury Tales*. Even though most editors and literary biographers emphatically warn that their putative chronologies are only most tentative, each composition so positioned presents itself to the modern reader with certain evaluative assumptions ready-made. Kathryn Lynch targets the primary interpretive danger of the unavoidable placement of Chaucer's compositions in some textual sequence—an oversimplification of the significance of their serial appearance: "The most thorny and vigorously contested problems of dating seem to settle into an orthodoxy whose inertia is almost impossible to disturb."[17] The most persistent and widespread template for ordering Chaucer's works remains an "old, not altogether mistaken" notion that Chaucer's career is divisible into three phases: his French, Italian, and English peri-

---

17. Kathryn L. Lynch, "Dating Chaucer," *The Chaucer Review* 42 (2007): 1–22, 10.

ods.[18] Although "as early as 1963 Wolfgang Clemen securely assumed the demise of the tripartite theory of influence," the appeal of this scheme remains strong, probably because it so neatly suggests the progress of Chaucer's career from apprentice through journeyman to master poet.[19]

Kathryn Lynch especially objects to "the effect of petrifying" Chaucer's compositions in a presumed sequence that delimits intertextual analyses.[20] To legitimize optional orderings, the reader must "discard, or at any rate bracket, our sense of his work as having unfolded in a linear chronology."[21] Arguing from effect to cause, Lynch understands the "braided complexity" of Chaucer's sequence of projects exclusively in terms of his practice as a author.[22] Granting the possibility of a public recital then manuscript circulation for any one of Chaucer's compositions makes the question of its chronological ordering even more complicated.

Chaucer may be imagined as rewriting everything in his atelier intermittently yet continuously until he died. If so, Chaucer's texts never fully escaped his desk till granted posthumous publication by scribes. Only the habit of thinking in terms of the fixity of printed publication makes us think that Chaucer progressed from one discrete writing project to another. Yet, almost all of

---

18. L. Benson, *Riverside*, xxix. Richard H. Osberg also affirms the usefulness of this tripartite division of Chaucer's poetic career, in Preminger and. Brogan, eds., *The New Princeton Encyclopedia of Poetry and Poetics*, 336. According to Lynch, this tripartite division was popularized (though not invented) by Bernhard ten Brink as early as 1870 ("Dating Chaucer," 21, n. 66).

19. Lynch, "Dating Chaucer," 13.

20. Ibid., 14.

21. Ibid., 17.

22. Ibid., 16. For example, reconsidering the normative dating of *Anelida and Arcite* prior to the Squire's tale, Lynch writes: "More likely Chaucer worked on these different poems in stages ... always with his characteristic distrust of a firmly settled and authoritative point of view ... as related poetic experiments that Chaucer was imagining in tandem, and probably working on in overlapping time period" (ibid., 16).

Chaucer's extant texts can be considered "unfinished" or "works in progress" to a certain extent.[23]

At best, Chaucer's compositions can now be assigned an earliest *terminus ab quo* and a latest *terminus ad quem*.[24] More informative, in a number of cases, would be a twin pinpointing of the putative dates of each work's recital presentation and then of its manuscript publication. The most curious cases in the putative chronology of Chaucer's career are not those compositions that have no discernible datability, nor those that retain a very plausible occasionality, but those that suggest such a slippage between two key moments of probable presentation. Chaucer's "To his Purse," for example, may present the simple case of recycled complaint. Chaucer rededicates his jocular text by adding a sincerely sycophantic (or secretly sarcastic) envoy to Henry IV; "this song to yow I sende" (l. 24) in the hope of winning favor.[25]

The Book of the Duchess has been dated to sometime between 1369 and 1372—a span that permits quite different tonal presumptions depending on its being read as occasioned by the death of the Duchess Blanche (1368), or the Duke of Lancaster's marriage to Princess Costanza of Castile (1371), or the birth of Gaunt's son by Katherine Swynford (1372).[26] Similarly, "Anelida

---

23. See, for example, Larry Sklute, *Virtue of Necessity: Inconclusiveness and Narrative Form in Chaucer's Poetry* (Columbus: Ohio State University Press, 1984), and Rosemary McGerr, *Chaucer's Open Books: Resistance to Closure in Medieval Discourse* (Gainesville: University of Florida Press, 1998).

24. Lynch finds "'facts' external to the poems ... useful only for establishing a terminus *a quo*.... Chaucer's death constitutes the only certain *terminus ad quem*" ("Dating Chaucer," 1–2).

25. R. F. Yeager reads Chaucer's envoy as intended to subvert Lancastrian claims to legitimacy ("Chaucer's 'To His Purse': Begging, or Begging Off?" *Viator* 36 [2005]: 373–414).

26. Edward I. Condren argues that Chaucer originally composed an "ur-*Duchess*, one might say" to commemorate the death of Queen Phillippa, but revised it almost a decade later to win favor during the regency of John of Gaunt (*Chaucer from Prentice to*

211

and Arcite" is often thought to be an aborted formal experiment begun rather early in Chaucer's career (1373–74), though finally abandoned only much later, on the threshold of his Italian period. So, too, metrical form and a plausible occasion place Chaucer's initial composition of The House of Fame sometime between 1377 and 1381, probably 1380; its pervasive allusiveness to Dante, however, suggests that Chaucer returned to some core text of this dream vision somewhat later in his Italian period, perhaps while preparing to start Troilus and Criseyde.[27]

The two extant versions of the Prologue to The Legend of Good Women present what may be the surest evidence that Chaucer revised a perfectly adequate recital script for subsequent manuscript circulation. But, even in this instance, the case is hardly certain. It seems likely that the F-prologue was composed sometime between 1386 at the earliest and 1388 at the very latest.[28] Chaucer probably revised the G-version sometime after the death of Queen Anne (June 7, 1394), and so well after his composition of much of The Canterbury Tales.

It is generally taken for granted that "The Knight's Tale" circulated as a stand-alone romance prior to inclusion in The Canterbury Tales. Chaucer may have started to translate its source, Boccaccio's il Teseide delle nozze d'Emelia, as early as the mid-1370s. Internal evidence indicates 1380 or 1381 or 1386 or 1387 as its date of composition. I would suggest consideration of the possibility that Chaucer

---

Poet [Gainesville: University Press of Florida, 2008], 32). Michael Foster sees alternative datings of Chaucer's composition of the Book of the Duchess (i.e., before or after Gaunt's affair with Katherine Swynford) as a determining factor informing conflicting assessments of the poem's representation of its narrator and the Black Knight ("On Dating the Duchess: The Personal and Social Context of Book of the Duchess," Review of English Studies 59 [2008]: 185–96).

27. Helen Cooper suggests 1384 as a more likely date ("The Four Last Things in Dante and Chaucer: Hugolino and the House of Rumour," New Medieval Literatures 3 [1999]: 39–66).

28. M. C. E. Shaner and A. S. G. Edwards, Riverside, 1060b.

composed a recital version of "The Knight's Tale" in the early 1380s which he then revised for inclusion in the Canterbury frame and manuscript circulation.[29] It was during such revision that Chaucer invented the surrogate of a fictional persona for his recital "I"—but not with absolute rigor. Nor was Chaucer the first to do so.[30]

As a reader of old clerks himself, Chaucer had heard Ovid complain about his enforced separation from a real audience—that is, his expulsion from Rome to Tomis. Ovid's topos of authorial separation from future readers thus " originated in ... the absence of exile."[31] Ovid's *Tristia* begins with an elaborate envoy.[32] The poet envisions his book traveling unadorned, as befits this text's mournful content. Ovid trusts that his blotted tears on the page will convey the genuine tone of his words. Ovid tells the messenger text: "vade, liber, verbisque meis loca grata saluta: contingam certe quo licet illa pede" (Go, my book, and in my name greet the loved places: I will tread them at least with what foot I may).[33] Ovid's pun on *pede* desperately hopes his metrical

---

29. Bernhard ten Brink's speculation that Chaucer had written an earlier rhyme-royal version of the tale now seems implausible, but the more general notion that a stand-alone version of this romance circulated before its inclusion as a tale in the Canterbury frame remains a common assumption.

30. For Robert R. Edwards, "To make a claim for textuality and literary relations as historical context is to follow the lead of Chaucer's first readers, his fourteenth-century poetic contemporaries and fifteenth-century writers who established his place in English literary history. But ... more ... Chaucer engages classical and vernacular writers under the rubric of cultural analysis and criticism" (*Chaucer and Boccaccio: Antiquity and Modernity* [New York: Palgrave, 2002], xii).

31. Spearing notes that Tatlock ("Epilog," 1920/1921) traced Chaucer's "Go little book" topos at the conclusion of *Troilus and Criseyde* to Ovid (*Textual Subjectivity*, 15 and n. 12). Chaucer may recall Ovid's *Tristia* in his "Retraction" to *The Canterbury Tales* as well; see too Anita Obermeier, "Chaucer's Retraction," in *Sources and Analogues of The Canterbury Tales*, 2 vols., ed. Robert M. Correale and Mary Hamel, vol. II, 775–808, 784–85 (Woodbridge: D.S. Brewer, 2002 [vol. I], 2005 [vol. II]).

32. Cf. Edmund Spenser's "Happy ye leaves" (*Amoretti*, Sonnet 1).

33. *Tristia*, Bk. I, i, 15–16, in Arthur Leslie Wheeler, ed. and trans., *Ovid*, vol. VI; 2nd rev. ed., edited by G. P Gould (Cambridge, Mass.: Harvard University Press, 1924, 1988).

feet can preserve some print of his voice. In a later poem, Ovid must say farewell to his reader because "scribere plura libet: sed vox mihi fessa loquendo/dictandi vires siccaque lingua negat" (more could I write, but my voice worn out with speaking and my parched tongue deny dictation).[34] This statement of compositional surrender indicates that in fact (or in act) *dictation* fails to distinguish *speaking* from *writing*. On a less literal level as well, Chaucer would fully concur with Ovid that the process of producing a text inevitably exhausts its author's voice.

Ovid desperately hopes that his transcribed words would make him immortal—that is, alive to future readers. He composed an epitaph to preserve his name; he published texts as enduring monuments of his fame. Yet, Ovid—as was typical for his time too—wrote primarily to recite because "all classic literature, it may be said, is conceived of as a conversation with, or an address to, an audience."[35] And Chaucer believed he could hear Ovid still. For Chaucer, any renunciation of such confidence in writing would seem narcissistic. Had the very idea of "reading to oneself" with its full modern force occurred to Chaucer, he would have found it both terrifying and immoral because fruitless.

Medieval authors acknowledged the autonomy of subjectivity only in admonitory tales. For example, at the end of Fragment A of the Middle English *Romaunt of the Rose* (the section most plausi-

---

34. *Tristia*, Bk. III, iii, 85–86, trans. by Wheeler. Ovid explains that he cannot write in his own hand because he is so ill. He asks the reader (originally his wife) to receive the last word from his lips—"vale!"—which he glosses as not literally true of the sender (i.e., because he is not "well").

35. Hadas, *Ancilla*, 50. Hadas adds, "Among the Greeks, the regular method of publication was by public recitation, at first, significantly, by the author himself, and then by professional readers or actors, and public recitation continued to be the regular method of publication even after books and the art of reading had become common" (50); among the Romans, "the practice of *recitationes* continued in full flower until Hadrian's day, and survived thereafter" (64).

bly but still only tentatively attributable to Chaucer), the dreamer Guillaume discovers the dangerous Well of Love (*Romaunt*, 1455–1705). The poet specifically addresses his female readers: "Ladyes, I preye ensample takith" (*Romaunt*, 1539). But the text's lesson relates far more to the education of the author himself: "this lettre of which I telle / Hadde taught me" (*Romaunt*, 1543–44).

Lest he be mistaken, Guillaume provides a punning gloss of his own specific interpretation of his own *descriptio*:

> The *welle* is clepid, as *well* is knowen,
> The Welle of Love, of verray right,
> Of which ther hath ful many a wight
> Spoken in bookis dyversely. (*Romaunt*, 1626–29)

Guillaume then boasts that his readers can hear no better reading of the scene than his own:

> But they shull never so verily
> Descripcioun of the welle heere,
> Ne eke of the sothe of this matere,
> As ye shull, whanne I have undo
> The craft that hir bilongith too. (*Romaunt*, 1630–34)

Guillaume de Lorris sounds a bit self-celebratory here as he presents his rendition as an improvement over prior texts. And, indeed, the Middle English translation of the tale of Narcissus is a good deal more faithful to its Middle French source than Guillaume had been to Ovid.

In the *Metamorphoses*, Echo, who had herself been cursed by Juno for talking too much, can only repeat what others say. But she can do so to suit her own intentions. In a sense, Ovid's Echo personifies the much-dreaded misuse of "oral performance" as an excuse to interpret the tone of a text any which way the reader pleases. Ovid's Echo superimposes her own desires on her reiteration of the speaker's words. In the *Romaunt*, however, Echo does not so cleverly restate Narcissus's syntax to voice her own wishes. Instead, a plainspoken Lady Echo curses Narcissus; she wishes him to feel the same frustration as she. And Guillaume explicitly approves the rightness of this nemesis or *contrapasso*: "This prayer was but resonable" (*Romaunt*, 1499).[36] Staring at the "mirrour perilous" (*Romaunt*, 1601), Narcissus loves only his own self-projection in vain, "His owne shadowe had hym bytrasshed" (*Romaunt*, 1520). The tale of Narcissus and Echo (in addition to all its other meanings) warns against such solipsistic scrutiny—that is, against refusing to listen. Narcissus was simply deceived "shortly for to telle," "shortly all the sothe to telle" (*Romaunt*, 1501, 1528).

When Guillaume himself recognizes the Well of Love for what it is, he fears that he too may fall into the same self-infatuation, but then—for some unstated reason—he claims that he is not personally at risk (*Romaunt*, 1549–52). Frederick Goldin explains that Guillaume apparently feels immune "because he knows the story."[37] Nevertheless, Guillaume is entranced by his perception of the beauty of another, "That mirrour hath me now entriked" (*Romaunt*, 1642). Guillaume as narrator has warned his audience, but as dreamer he still falls for a reflection of the Rose—itself yet another type of imaginative self-projection that the poet did not live long enough to renounce as an illusion.[38]

Guillaume (in Fragment B) bluntly blames the reader disin-

36. In Ovid, however, it was not Echo but another anonymously frustrated lover who cursed Narcissus. In the twelfth-century Norman-French *Narcisus*, Lady Dané and Narcissus die together. Curiously, Guillaume himself becomes distracted by optics. He is especially fascinated by the Well's "two cristall stonys" (*Romaunt*, 1568), prisms that divide white light into "blew, yelow, and red" (*Romaunt*, 1578) and images that reflect the eyes of the Rose herself.

37. Frederick Goldin, *The Mirror of Narcissus in the Courtly Love Lyric* (Ithaca, N.Y.: Cornell University Press, 1967), 54.

38. John Fleming links Troilus's "spectacular inamoration" to the Ovidian topos of narcissism via Boccaccio and Benôit (*Classical Imitation*, 135).

clined to hear his "new" reading of an allegorical dream as truly pleasing:

> For a reder that poyntith ille
> A good sentence may ofte spille.
> The book is good at the eendyng,
> Maad of newe and lusty thyng. (Romaunt, 2161–64)

The patient reader will attend till the completion of the text and thereby discover his true intentions:

> For whoso wol the eendyng here,
> The craft of love he shall mowe lere,
> If that he wol so long abide,
> Til I this Romance may unhide,
> And undo the signifiance
> Of this drem into Romance. (Romaunt, 2165–70)

In good faith, Guillaume promises to be candid with the reader of good faith:

> The sothfastnesse that now is hid,
> Without coverture shal be kid
> Whanne I undon have this dremyng,
> Wherynne no word is of lesyng. (Romaunt, 2171–74)

As a young lover and author, Guillaume here affirms an almost blind confidence in complete transparency.

With far less sympathy than Guillaume de Lorris (and much less irony than Jean de Meun), the more moralistic John Gower, in *The Confessio Amantis*, reads and so rewrites the tale of Narcissus as an exemplum of deep self-deception:

> Which torneth wisdom into wenynge
> And sothfastnesse into lesynge
> Thurgh fol ymaginacioun. (CA I, 2268–70)

Gower reads what Ovid wrote "for thin enformacion" (CA I, 2274) with little irony and less compassion. Gower silences Echo entirely. Rather, solitary Narcissus, who has been left behind while a hunt of the hart goes on without him, is drawn to the fatal well by natural appetite (that is, thirst). Narcissus perceives his own reflection as that of a nymph. Gower thus makes the "sotie" of Narcissus superficially heterosexual because Narcissus supposes "it were a woman that he syh" (CA I, 2320–21). In the *Confessio*, Narcissus hears only himself although his own voice sounds like a woman's: "the same word she cride also" (CA I, 2327). For his "surquiderie" (CA I, 2358), for his certainty in his own isolated imagination's perception of reality "as he caste his lok ... and hiede tok" (CA I, 2314–15), Narcissus drowns in self-referentiality.

Like Narcissus, Troilus seems a victim of amorous vanity (T&C V, 1817). Enthralled at the first sight of Criseyde, Troilus misreads her as "the idealized image of the man who consecrates himself to serving her."[39] But Criseyde can exist outside Troilus's imagination and so seems a broken mirror. Chaucer warns young lovers (and readers) to attend to his negative narrative that demonstrates the dangers of false faith rather than false women. And, in light of *The Metamorphoses*, the *Roman de la rose*, and the *Confessio Amantis*, it is easy to see the validity of R. A. Shoaf's reading of Chaucer's admonition:

> Maturity will consist partly in the recognition that, while each of us is a Narcissus, none of us ought or needs to be a narcissist: the Narcissus in each of us seeks his image, but he is not necessarily condemned to find his *own* image.[40]

This idea per se is not Chaucer's—that is, there is nothing identifiably personal to his authorship of this truth. But what is unique

---

39. Goldin, *Mirror*, 40–41.
40. R. A. Shoaf, *Dante, Chaucer, and the Currency of the Word* (Norman, Okla.: Pilgrim, 1983), 144.

POSTSCRIPT

about this statement at the end of *Troilus and Criseyde* is its tonal moment: the expression of authorial consent to an emotion that is shared again by young readers now—or not. I feel that Chaucer in this final address to his audience should sound more pastoral than magisterial, more concerned about the future than contemptuous of the past, more worried about his present listeners than confident that anyone will truly listen. It is not impossible to say; it is only impossible to say with complete certainty. The only completely dead modern reading, however, is simply not caring about Chaucer's caring so much.

BIBLIOGRAPHY

Ackroyd, Peter. *Chaucer: Brief Lives*. London: Chatto and Windus, 2004.
Amtower, Laurel. "Authorizing the Reader in Chaucer's 'House of Fame.'" *Philological Quarterly* 79 (2000): 273–91.
———. *Engaging Words: The Culture of Reading in the Later Middle Ages*. New York: Palgrave, 2000.
Amodio, Mark C., *Writing the Oral Tradition*. Notre Dame, Ind.: University of Notre Dame Press, 2004.
———, ed. *New Directions in Oral Theory*. Tempe: Arizona Center for Medieval and Renaissance Studies, 2005.
———, ed.,with Sarah Gray Miller. *Oral Poetics in Middle English Poetry*. New York: Garland, 1994.
Augustine. *Confessions*. Translated by R. S. Pine-Coffin. New York: Dorset, 1986.
Austin, J. L. *How to Do Things With Words*. Cambridge, Mass.: Harvard University Press, 1962.
Axton, Richard. "Chaucer and the Idea of the Theatrical Performance." In *"Divers toyes mengled": Études sur la culture européenne au Moyen Age à la Renaissance en hommage à André Lascombes*, edited by Michel Bitot, with Roberta Mullini and Peter Happé, 83–100. Tours: l'Univeristé François Rabelais, 1996.
Barney, Stephen A., ed. *Chaucer's Troilus: Essays in Criticism*. London: Scolar Press, 1980.
———. *Studies in "Troilus": Text, Meter, and Diction*. East Lansing, Mich.: Colleagues Press, 1993.
———. "Troilus Bound." *Speculum* 47 (1972): 445–58.
———, ed. *Troilus and Criseyde, with Facing-Page il Filostrato*. New York: W. W. Norton, 2006.
Baugh, Albert C. "Improvisation in the Middle English Romance." *Proceedings of the American Philosophical Society* 103 (1959): 418–54.

BIBLIOGRAPHY

———. *Chaucer's Major Poetry*. New York: Appleton-Century-Crofts, 1963.
———. "The Middle English Romance: Some Questions of Creation, Presentation, and Preservation." *Speculum* 42 (1967): 1–31.
Beadle, Richard, and Jeremy Griffiths. *St. John's College Cambridge, Manuscript L.1, A Facsimile*. Norman, Okla.: Pilgrim, 1983.
Bennett, H. S. "The Production and Dissemination of Vernacular Manuscripts in the Fifteenth Century." *The Library* 1 (1946–47): 167–78.
Bennett, Michael. "The Court of Richard II and the Promotion of Literature." In *Chaucer's England: Literature in Historical Context*, edited by Barbara Hanawalt, 3–22. Medieval Studies at Minnesota 4. Minneapolis: University of Minnesota. 1992.
Benson, C. David. *Chaucer's Troilus and Criseyde*. London: Unwin Hyman, 1990.
Benson, Larry D., gen. ed. *The Riverside Chaucer*, 3rd ed. Boston: Houghton Mifflin, 1987.
Benveniste, Emile. *Problèmes de linguistique générale*. Paris: Gallimard, 1966–74.
Berry, Craig A. "The King's Business: Negotiating Chivalry in Troilus and Criseyde." *The Chaucer Review* 26 (1992): 237–65.
Besserman, Lawrence. "A Note on the Sources of Chaucer's Troilus V, 540–613." *The Chaucer Review* 24 (1990): 306–8.
———. "'Priest' and 'Pope,' 'Sire and Madame': Anachronistic Diction and Social Conflict in Chaucer's Troilus." *Studies in the Age of Chaucer* 23 (2001): 181–224.
Blake, N. F. "Geoffrey Chaucer: Textual Transmission and Editing." In Minnis and Brewer, *Crux and Controversy*, 19–38.
———. "Speech and Writing: An Historical Overview." *The Yearbook of English Studies* 25 (1995): 6–21.
Bloomfield, Morton. "Distance and Predestination in Troilus and Criseyde." *PMLA* 72 (1957): 14–26.
———. "Troilus' Paraclausithyron and Its Setting: Troilus and Criseyde V, 519–602." *Neuphilogische Mitteilungen* 73 (1972): 15–24.
Boffey, Julia. "Annotation in Some Manuscripts of Troilus and Criseyde." *English Manuscript Studies, 1100–1700* 5 (1995): 1–17.
———. "Bodleian MS Arch. Selden B. 24 and the 'Scotticization' of Middle English Verse." In Prendergast and Kline, *Rewriting Chaucer*, 166–85.
———. "Manuscripts and Audience." In Saunders, *Concise Companion*, 34–50.
——— and A. S. G. Edwards. *The Works of Geoffrey Chaucer and The Kingis Quair: A Facsimile of Bodleian Library, Oxford, MS Arch. Selden. B. 24*. Introduction and an Appendix by B. C. Barker-Benfield. Cambridge: D.S. Brewer, 1997.

BIBLIOGRAPHY

———. *A New Index of Middle English Verse* [NIMEV]. London: The British Library, 2005.

Boitani, Piero, and Jill Mann, eds. *The Cambridge Chaucer Companion*. Cambridge: Cambridge University Press, 1986.

Børch, Marianne. "Poet and Persona: Writing the Reader in Troilus." *The Chaucer Review* 30 (1996): 215–28.

Borthwick, M.C. "Antigone's Song as 'Mirror' in Chaucer's *Troilus and Criseyde*." *Modern Language Quarterly* 22 (1961): 227–35.

Bowden, Betsy. *Chaucer Aloud: The Varieties of Textual Interpretation*. Philadelphia: University of Pennsylvania Press, 1987.

Bowers, John. "Two Professional Readers of Chaucer and Langland: Scribe D and the HM 114 Scribe." *Studies in the Age of Chaucer* 26 (2004): 113–46.

Boyd, Beverly. *Chaucer and the Medieval Book*. San Marino, Calif.: Huntington Library, 1973.

Bradbury, Nancy Mason. *Writing Aloud: Storytelling in Late Medieval England*. Urbana: University of Illinois Press, 1998.

———. "Literacy, Orality, and the Poetics of Middle English Romance." In Amodio, *Oral Poetics*, 39–69.

Branca, Vittore. *Il cantare trecentesco e il Boccaccio del Filostrato e del Teseida*. Florence: G. C. Sansoni, 1936.

Brewer, Derek S. *Chaucer*. 2nd ed. London: Longmans, 1960.

———. *Chaucer in His Time*. London: Longmans, 1973.

———. "Chaucer's Poetic Style." In Boitani and Mann, *The Cambridge Chaucer Companion*, 227–42.

———. "Orality and Literacy in Chaucer." In *Mündlichkeit und Schriftlichkeit in englischen Mittelalter*, edited by Willi Erzgräber and Sabine Volk, 85–119. Tübingen: G. Narr, 1988.

———. "The History of a Shady Character: The Narrator of *Troilus and Criseyde*." In *Modes of Narrative: Approaches to American, Canadian, and British Fiction*, edited by Reingard M. Nischik and Barbara Korte, 166–78. Würzburg: Königshausen & Neumann, 1990.

———. *The World of Chaucer*, 2nd ed. Cambridge: D.S. Brewer, 1992.

———. "Some Aspects of the Post-War Reception of Chaucer: A Key Passage, Troilus II 666–679." In *Expedition nach der Wahrheit: Poems, Essays, and Papers in Honour of Theo Stemmler, Festschrift zum 60*, edited by Stefan Korlacher and Marion Islinger, 513–24. Heidelberg: C. Winter, 1996.

Brody, Saul N. "Making a Play for Criseyde: The Staging of Pandarus's House in Chaucer's *Troilus and Criseyde*." *Speculum* 73 (1998): 115–40.

Bronson, Bertrand H. "Chaucer's Art in Relation to His Audience." In *Five Studies in Literature*, edited by Bertrand H. Bronson, J. R. Caldwell,

BIBLIOGRAPHY

J. M. Cline, Gordon McKenzie, and J. F. Ross, 1–53. Berkeley: University of California Press, 1940.

Brown, Carleton. "Another Contemporary Allusion in Chaucer's Troilus." *Modern Language Notes* 26 (1911): 208–11.

Brown, Peter, ed. *A Companion to Chaucer*. Oxford: Blackwell, 2000.

Brusendorff, Aage. *The Chaucer Tradition*. London: Oxford University Press, 1925.

Bühler, Curt F. *The Fifteenth-Century Book: The Scribes, The Printers, The Decorators*. Philadelphia: University Pennsylvania Press, 1960.

Burrow, John A. *Medieval Writers and Their Work*. Oxford: Oxford University Press, 1982.

———. "The Poet and the Book." In *Genres, Themes and Images in English Literature: The J. A. W. Bennett Memorial Lectures, Peruguia, 1986*, edited by Piero Boitani and Anna Torti, 230–45. Tübingen: G. Narr, 1988.

———. *Gestures and Looks in Medieval Narrative*. Cambridge: Cambridge University Press, 2002.

Butler, Judith. *Gender Trouble: Feminism and the Subversion of Identity*. New York: Routledge, 1990.

———. *Bodies That Matter: On the Discursive Limits of "Sex."* New York: Routledge, 1993.

Butterfield, Ardis. "Mise-en-page in the Troilus Manuscripts: Chaucer and French Manuscript Culture." *Huntington Library Quarterly* 58 (1996): 49–80.

———. "French Culture and the Ricardian Court." In *Essays on Ricardian Literature: In Honour of J. A. Burrow*, edited by A. J. Minnis, Charlotte C. Morse, and Thorlac Turville-Petre, 82–120. Oxford: Clarendon Press, 1997.

Campbell, Jackson J. "A New Troilus Fragment." *PMLA* 73 (1958): 305–8.

Cannon, Christopher. "Raptus in the Chaumpiegne Release and a Newly Discovered Document Concerning the Life of Geoffrey Chaucer." *Speculum* 68 (1993): 79–94.

———. "Chaucer and Rape: Uncertainty's Certainties." *Studies in the Age of Chaucer* 22 (2000): 67–92.

Carruthers, Mary. *The Book of Memory: A Study of Memory in Medieval Culture*. Cambridge: Cambridge University Press, 1990.

Catalogue of Additions to the Manuscripts in the British Museum in the Years MDCCCXLI–MDCCCXLV. London, 1850.

Catalogue of the Harleain Manuscripts in the British Museum. Vols. I–III. London, 1808.

Chartier, Roger. *Forms and Meanings: Texts, Performances, and Audiences from Codex to Computer*. Philadelphia: University of Pennsylvania Press, 1995.

Chaytor, H. J. *From Script to Print*. Cambridge: Cambridge University Press, 1945.

Cherniss, Michael D. "The Clerk's Tale and Envoy, the Wife of Bath's Purgatory, and the Merchant's Tale." *The Chaucer Review* 6 (1972): 235–54.
Chickering, Howell. "Unpunctuating Chaucer." *The Chaucer Review* 25 (1990): 96–109.
———. "Form and Interpretation in the Envoy to the Clerk's Tale." *The Chaucer Review* 29 (1995): 352–72.
Clanchy, M. T. *From Memory to Written Record: England 1066–1307*. Cambridge, Mass.: Harvard University Press, 1979.
Cohen, Jeffrey J. *Medieval Identity Machines*. Minneapolis: University of Minnesota Press, 2003.
Coleman, Janet. *Medieval Readers and Writers, 1350–1400*. New York: Columbia University Press, 1981.
Coleman, Joyce. *Public Reading and the Reading Public in Late Medieval England and France*. Cambridge: Cambridge University Press, 1996.
———, producer. *Troilus: Reading in a paved parlor*. University of Oklahoma, 2006. http://www.nyu.edu/projects/mednar/file.php?id=1027.
———. "Where Chaucer Got His Pulpit: Audience and Intervisuality in the Troilus and Criseyde Frontispiece." *Studies in the Age of Chaucer* 32 (2010): 103–28.
Collette, Carolyn. "Criseyde's Honor: Interiority and Public Identity in Chaucer's Courtly Romance." In *Literary Aspects of Courtly Culture: Selected Papers from the Seventh Triennial Congress of the International Courtly Literature Society*, edited by Donald Maddox and Sara Sturm-Maddox, 47–55. Woodbridge: D.S. Brewer, 1994.
Condren, Edward I. *Chaucer from Prentice to Poet*. Gainesville: University Press of Florida, 2008.
Connolly, Margaret. *John Shirley: Book Production and the Noble Household in Fifteenth-Century England*. Aldershot: Ashgate, 1998.
Cooper, Helen. "The Four Last Things in Dante and Chaucer: Hugolino and the House of Rumour." *New Medieval Literatures* 3 (1999): 39–66.
Copeland, Rita. *Rhetoric, Hermeneutics, and Translation in the Middle Ages*. Cambridge: Cambridge University Press, 1991.
Correale, Robert M., and Mary Hamel, eds. *Sources and Analogues of The Canterbury Tales*. 2 vols. Woodbridge: D.S. Brewer, 2002 (vol. I), 2005 (vol. II).
Cox, Catherine Stallworth. "Mirroring Language: Narcissus in Late Middle English Poetry." *DAI* 52 (1992): 2930A.
Crosby, Ruth. "Oral Delivery in the Middle Ages." *Speculum* 11 (1936): 88–110.
———. "Chaucer and the Custom of Oral Delivery." *Speculum* 13 (1938): 413–32.

BIBLIOGRAPHY

Cureton, Kevin K. "Chaucer's Revision of Troilus and Criseyde." Studies in Bibliography 42 (1989): 153–84.

Dahlberg, Charles. "The Poet of Unlikeness: Chaucer." Chap. 6 in The Literature of Unlikeness. Hanover, N.H.: University Press of New England, 1988. 125–48.

Dane, Joseph A. Who Is Buried in Chaucer's Tomb? Studies in the Reception of Chaucer's Book. East Lansing: Michigan State University Press, 1998.

———. The Myth of Print Culture: Essays on Evidence, Textuality and Bibliographical Method. Toronto: University of Toronto Press, 2003.

Davis, Norman, ed. Paston Letters and Papers of the Fifteenth Century, Part I. Oxford: Clarendon Press, 1971.

Dean, James M., and Christian Zacher, eds. The Idea of Medieval Literature: New Essays on Chaucer and Medieval Culture in Honor of Donald R. Howard. Newark: University of Delaware Press, 1992.

Delany, Sheila. Chaucer's House of Fame: The Poetics of Skeptical Fideism. Chicago: University of Chicago Press, 1972.

———. "Techniques of Alienation in Troilus and Criseyde." In Shoaf, Chaucer's Troilus and Criseyde "Subgit to alle Poesye," 29–46.

Dempster, Germaine. "Chaucer's Manuscript of Petrarch's Version of the Griselda Story." Modern Philology 41 (1943): 6–16.

"Descriptions of Medieval and Renaissance Manuscripts." CORSAIR: The Online Research Resource of The Pierpont Morgan Library. <http://corsair.morganlibrary.org/msdescr/msdescriptions.htm>

Devereux, James A., S.J. "A Note on Troilus and Criseyde, Book III, Line 1309." Philological Quarterly 44 (1965): 550–52.

Dickens, Charles. Christmas Carol; The Public Reading Version. A Facsimile of the Author's Prompt-Copy with Introduction and Notes by Philip Collins. New York: New York Public Library, 1971.

Dinshaw, Carolyn. "Readers in/of Troilus and Criseyde." Yale Journal of Criticism (1988): 81–105.

———. Chaucer's Sexual Poetics. Madison: University of Wisconsin Press, 1989.

———. Getting Medieval: Sexualities and Communities, Pre- and Postmodern. Durham, N.C.: Duke University Press, 1999.

Doane, A. N., and Carol Braun Pasternack, eds. Vox Intexta. Madison: University of Wisconsin Press, 1991.

Donaldson, E. Talbot. "Chaucer the Pilgrim." PMLA 69 (1954): 928–36.

———. Chaucer's Poetry. 2nd ed. New York: John Wiley and Sons, 1958.

———. Speaking of Chaucer. New York: Norton, 1970.

Donoghue, Denis. The Practice of Reading. New Haven, Conn.: Yale University Press, 1998.

BIBLIOGRAPHY

Donovan, Claire. "The Mise-en-Page of Early Books of Hours in England." In *Medieval Book Production: Assessing the Evidence*, edited by L. L. Brownrigg, 147–61. Proceedings of the Second Conference of the Seminar in the History of the Book to 1500, Oxford, July 1988. Los Altos, Calif.: Anderson-Lovelace, 1990.

Doyle, A. I., and A. J. Piper. "Description of Durham University MS Cosin V. ii. 13." In "Notes and Drafts of Descriptions of Medieval Manuscripts in Durham University Library," amended November 2003, <http://www.dur.ac.uk/library/asc/theme/medmss/apviii3/>.

Dutschke, C. W. *Guide to Medieval and Renaissance Manuscripts in the Huntington Library*. 2 vols. San Marino, Calif.: Huntington Library, 1989.

Economou, George D. "The Two Venuses and Courtly Love." In *In Pursuit of Perfection: Courtly Love in Medieval Literature*, edited by Joan M. Ferrante and G. D. Economou, 17–50. Port Washington, N.Y.: Kennikat Press, 1975.

Edwards, A. S. G. "Chaucer from Manuscript to Print: The Social Text and the Critical Text." *Mosaic* 28, no. 4 (1995): 1–12. Retrieved from http://0-search.proquest.com.library.uark.edu/docview/205366701?accountid=8361.

———. "John Shirley and the Emulation of Courtly Culture." In *The Court and Cultural Diversity: Selected Papers from the Eighth Triennial Meeting of the International Courtly Literature Society, 1995*, edited by E. Mullaly and J. Thompson, 309–17. Cambridge: D.S. Brewer, 1997.

———. "Manuscript and Text." In McCarren and Moffat, *A Guide to Editing*, 159–68.

Edwards, Robert R. *Chaucer and Boccaccio: Antiquity and Modernity*. New York: Palgrave, 2002.

Eisenstein, Elizabeth L. *The Printing Press as an Agent of Change*. Cambridge: Cambridge University Press, 1979.

———. *The Printing Revolution in Early Modern Europe*. Cambridge: Cambridge University Press, 1983.

Ellis, Roger, et al., eds. *The Medieval Translator: Theory and Practice of Translation in the Middle Ages*. Cambridge: D.S. Brewer, 1989.

Emmerson, Richard K. "Text and Image in the Ellesmere Portraits of the Tale-Tellers." In Stevens and Woodward, *The Ellesmere Chaucer*, 143–70.

Erasmus [Desiderius]. *Libellus de conscrinbendis epistolis* (1521). In *The Collected Works of Erasmus*, edited by J. Kelley Sowards. Toronto: University of Toronto Press, 1985.

Evans, Murray J. "'Making Strange': The Narrator (?), the Ending (?), and Chaucer's 'Troilus.'" *Neuphilologische Mitteilungen* 87 (1986): 218–28.

Farrell, Thomas J. "The 'Envoy de Chaucer' and the 'Clerk's Tale.'" *The Chaucer Review* 24 (1990): 329–36.

BIBLIOGRAPHY

———. "The Griselda Story in Italy." In Correale and Hamel, *Sources and Analogues of The Canterbury Tales*, vol. I, 103–29.

Fergusson, Francis. *The Idea of a Theater, A Study of Ten Plays*. Princeton, N.J.: Princeton University Press, 1949.

Fisher, John H. "Animadversions on the Text of Chaucer, 1988." *Speculum* 63 (1988): 799–93.

———. *The Complete Poetry and Prose of Geoffrey Chaucer*. 2nd ed. New York: Holt, Rinehart and Winston, 1989.

Fleming, John V. *Classical Imitation and Interpretation in Chaucer's Troilus*. Lincoln: University of Nebraska Press, 1990.

Foster, Michael. "On Dating the Duchess: The Personal and Social Context of Book of the Duchess." *Review of English Studies* 59 (2008): 185–96.

Foucault, Michel. "Qu'est-ce qu'un auteur?" *Bulletin de la Société Française de Philosophie* 22 (1969): 73–95. Translated by Donald F. Bouchard and Sherry Simon in *Michel Foucault, Language, Counter-Memory, Practice*. Ithaca, N.Y.: Cornell University Press, 1977, 113–38.

Fradenburg, L. O. Aranye. "'Voice Memorial': Loss and Reparation in Chaucer's Poetry." *Exemplaria* 2 (1990): 169–202.

———. *Sacrifice Your Love: Psychoanalysis, Historicism, Chaucer*. Minneapolis: University of Minnesota Press, 2002.

Frantzen, Allen J. *Troilus and Criseyde: The Poem and the Frame*. New York: Twayne, 1993.

Frese, Dolores Warwick, and Katherine O'Brien O'Keefe, eds. *The Book and the Body*. Notre Dame, Ind.: University of Notre Dame Press, 1997.

Fries, Maureen. "(Almost) Without a Song: Criseyde and Lyric in Chaucer's Troilus." *The Chaucer Yearbook* 1 (1992): 47–63.

Fyler, John M. *Chaucer and Ovid*. New Haven, Conn.: Yale University Press, 1979.

———. *Language and the Declining World in Chaucer, Dante, and Jean de Meun*. Cambridge: Cambridge University Press, 2007.

Ganim, John M. "Tone and Time in Chaucer's Troilus." *ELH* 43 (1976): 141–53.

———. *Style and Consciousness in Middle English Narrative*. Princeton, N.J.: Princeton University Press, 1983.

———. "Carnival Voices and the Envoy to the Clerk's Tale." *The Chaucer Review* 22 (1987): 112–27.

———. "Chaucerian Performance." *Envoi: A Review Journal of Medieval Literature* 1 (1989): 266–75.

———. *Chaucerian Theatricality*. Princeton, N.J.: Princeton University Press, 1990.

Gaylord, Alan. "The Lesson of the Troilus: Chastisement and Correction." In Salu, *Essays*, 23–42.

———. "Reading Chaucer: What's Allowed in 'Aloud'?" *Chaucer Yearbook* 1 (1992): 87–109.

Gellrich, Jesse. *The Idea of the Book in the Middle Ages: Language, Theory, Mythology, and Fiction.* Ithaca, N.Y.: Cornell University Press, 1985.

Genette, Gérard. *Paratexts: Thresholds of Interpretation.* Cambridge: Cambridge University Press, 1997.

Gibson, Jonathan. "Letters." In *A Companion to English Renaissance Literature and Culture*, edited by Michael Hathaway, 615–19. Oxford: Blackwell, 2000.

Giffin, Mary. *Studies on Chaucer and His Audience.* Hull, Quebec: Éditions L'Éclair, 1956.

Goldin, Frederick. *The Mirror of Narcissus in the Courtly Love Lyric.* Ithaca, N.Y.: Cornell University Press, 1967.

Gravdal, Kathryn. *Ravishing Maidens: Writing Rape in Medieval French Literature and Law.* Philadelphia: University of Pennsylvania Press, 1991.

Green, Richard Firth. *Poets and Princepleasers.* Toronto: University of Toronto Press, 1980.

———. *A Crisis of Truth: Literature and Law in Ricardian England.* Philadelphia: University of Pennsylvania Press, 1999.

Griffiths, J. J., and Derek Pearsall, eds. *Book Production and Publishing in Britain, 1375–1475.* Cambridge: Cambridge University Press, 1989.

Gumbrecht, Hans Ulrich. *Production of Presence.* Stanford, Calif.: Stanford University Press, 2004.

Hadas, Moses. *Ancilla to Classical Reading.* New York: Columbia University Press, 1961.

Hagedorn, Suzanne C. *Abandoned Women: Rewriting the Classics in Dante, Boccaccio, and Chaucer.* Ann Arbor: University of Michigan Press, 2004.

Halm, Carolus. *Rhetores Latini Minores.* Leipzig: Teubner, 1863.

Hanna, Ralph, III. "Robert K. Root." In *Editing Chaucer: The Great Tradition*, edited by Paul G. Ruggiers, 191–205. Norman, Okla.: Pilgrim, 1984.

———. "The Scribe of Huntington HM 114." *Studies in Bibliography* 42 (1989): 120–33.

———. "The Manuscripts and Transmission of Chaucer's Troilus." In Dean and Zacher, *The Idea of Medieval Literature*, 173–88.

———. "Producing Manuscripts and Editions." In Minnis and Brewer, *Crux and Controversy*, 109–30.

———. *Pursuing History: Middle English Manuscripts and Their Texts.* Stanford, Calif.: Stanford University Press, 1996.

———. "Reconsidering the Auchinleck Manuscript." In *New Directions in Later Medieval Manuscript Studies* (Essays from the 1998 Harvard Conference), edited by Derek Pearsall, 91–102. Woodbridge: Boydell for York Medieval Press, 2000.

BIBLIOGRAPHY

———. *London Literature, 1300–1380*. Cambridge: Cambridge University Press, 2005.

Hanning, Robert W. "The Crisis of Mediation in Chaucer's *Troilus and Criseyde*." In *The Performance of Middle English Culture*, edited by James J. Paxson, Lawrence M. Clopper, and Sylvia Tomasch, 143–59. Cambridge: D.S. Brewer, 1998.

Harari, Josué V., ed. *Textual Strategies: Perspectives in Post-Structuralist Criticism*. Ithaca, N.Y.: Cornell University Press, 1979.

Hardmann, Phillipa. "Interpreting the Incomplete Scheme of Illustration in Cambridge, Corpus Christi College MS 61." *English Manuscript Studies, 1100–1700* 6 (1996): 52–69.

Hardwick, C. *A Catalogue of the Manuscripts Preserved in the Library of the University of Cambridge*. Vol. III. [Cambridge]: Cambridge University Press, 1858.

Harvey, Nancy Lenz. "Chaucer's *Troilus and Criseyde* and the Idea of 'Pleye.'" In *The Work of Dissimilitude: Essays from the Sixth Citadel Conference on Medieval and Renaissance Literature*, edited by David G. Allen and Robert A. White, 48–56. Newark: University of Delaware Press, 1992.

Havely, N. R., ed. and trans. *Chaucer's Boccaccio: Sources of Troilus and the Knight's and Franklin's Tales*. Cambridge: D.S. Brewer, 1980.

Hellinger, Lotte, and J. B. Trapp, eds. *Cambridge History of the Book in Britain*. Vol. III. Cambridge: Cambridge University Press, 1998.

Helmbold, Anita. "Chaucer Appropriated: The Troilus Frontispiece as Lancastrian Propaganda." *Studies in the Age of Chaucer* 30 (2008): 205–34.

Hermann, John. "Gesture and Seduction in *Troilus and Criseyde*." In Shoaf, *Chaucer's Troilus and Criseyde "Subgit to alle Poesye*, 138–60.

Hodapp, William F. "The Visual Presentation of Chaucer's *Troilus and Criseyde* in Three Fifteenth-Century Manuscripts." *Manuscripta* 38 (1994): 237–52.

Hollander, Robert. *Boccaccio's Two Venuses*. New York: Columbia University Press, 1977.

Howard, Donald R. *The Idea of the Canterbury Tales*. Berkeley: University of California Press, 1976.

———. *Chaucer and the Medieval World*. London: Weidenfeld and Nicolson, 1987.

Huot, Sylvia. *From Song to Book*. Ithaca, N.Y.: Cornell University Press, 1987.

Hutson, Arthur E. "Troilus' Confession." *Modern Language Notes* 69 (1954): 468–70.

Irvine, Martin. "'Both text and gloss': Manuscript Form, the Textuality of Commentary, and Chaucer's Dream Poems." In *The Uses of Manuscripts* in *Literary Studies: Essays in Memory of Judson Boyce Allen*, edited by Charlotte Cook Morse, Penelope Reed Doob, and Marjorie Curry Woods, 81–119. Kalamazoo: Western Michigan University Press, 1992.

———. *The Making of Textual Culture*. Cambridge: Cambridge University Press, 1994.

———, with David Thomson. "Chapter One: *Grammatica* and Literary Theory." In *Cambridge History of Literary Criticism, Vol. II: The Middle Ages*, edited by A. J. Minnis and Ian Johnson, 15–41. Cambridge: Cambridge University Press, 2005.

Ives, Carolyn, and David Parkinson. "Scottish Chaucer, Misogynist Chaucer." In Prendergast and Kline, *Rewriting Chaucer*, 186–202.

James, Montague Rhodes. *A Descriptive Catalogue of the Manuscripts in the Library of St. John's College*. [Cambridge]: Cambridge University Press, 1913.

Jenkins, T. Atkinson. "Deschamps' Ballade to Chaucer." *Modern Language Notes* 33 (1918): 268–78.

Jennings, Margaret, C.S.J. "To *Pryke* or to *Prye*: Scribal Delights in the *Troilus*, Book III." In *Chaucer in the Eighties*, edited by Julian N. Wasserman and Robert J. Blanch, 121–33. Syracuse, N.Y.: Syracuse University Press, 1986.

Jones, E. A., ed. *The "Exhortacion" from Disce Mori Edited from Oxford, Jesus College, MS 39*. Middle English Texts 36. Heidelberg: Universitätsverlag Winter, 2006.

Jordan, Robert M. *Chaucer's Poetics and the Modern Reader*. Berkeley: University of California Press, 1987.

Kaminsky, Alice R. *Chaucer's Troilus and Criseyde and the Critics*. [Athens]: Ohio University Press, 1980.

Kamowski, William. "A Suggestion for Emending the Epilogue of *Troilus and Criseyde*." *The Chaucer Review* 21 (1987): 406–18.

Kaylor, Noel Harold, Jr. "Boethian Resonance in Chaucer's 'Canticus Troili.'" *The Chaucer Review* 27 (1993): 219–27.

Kelly, Henry Ansgar. *Ideas and Forms of Tragedy from Aristotle to the Middle Ages*. Cambridge: Cambridge University Press, 1993.

———. *Chaucerian Tragedy*. Cambridge: D.S. Brewer, 1997.

Kendrick, Laura. "The Troilus Frontispiece and the Dramatization of Chaucer's Troilus." *The Chaucer Review* 22 (1987): 81–92.

Kimmelman, Burt. *The Poetics of Authorship in the Later Middle Ages*. New York: Lang, 1996.

Kimpel, Ben. "The Narrator of the Canterbury Tales." *ELH* 20 (1953): 77–86.

Kindrick, Robert L., ed. *The Poems of Robert Henryson*. Kalamazoo, Mich.: Medieval Institute Publications, 1997.

Kinney, Clare Regan. "'Who Made This Song?': The Engendering of

Lyric Counterplots in Troilus and Criseyde." *Studies in Philology* 89 (1992): 272–92.
Kiser, Lisa J. *Truth and Textuality in Chaucer's Poetry*. Hanover, N.H.: University Press of New England, 1991.
Kittredge, George Lyman. *Chaucer and His Poetry*. Cambridge, Mass.: Harvard University Press, 1970 [1915].
Knight, Stephen. *Rymyng Craftily*. London: Angus and Robertson, 1973.
Koff, Leonard Michael. *Chaucer and the Art of Storytelling*. Berkeley: University of California Press, 1988.
———. "Ending a Poem Before Beginning It, or The 'Cas' of Troilus." In Shoaf, *Chaucer's Troilus and Criseyde "Subgit to Alle Poesye,"* 161–78.
Kolve, V. A. "God-Denying Fools and the Medieval 'Religion of Love.'" *Studies in the Age of Chaucer* 19 (1997): 3–59.
Korte, Barbara. *Body Language in Literature*. Toronto: University of Toronto Press, 1997.
Krochalis, Jeanne. *The Pierpont Morgan Library Manuscript M. 817, A Facsimile, with Introduction*. Norman, Okla.: Pilgrim, 1986.
Laskaya, Anne. *Chaucer's Approach to Gender in the Canterbury Tales*. Chaucer Studies 23. Cambridge: D.S. Brewer, 1995.
Lawton, David. *Chaucer's Narrators*. Cambridge: D.S. Brewer, 1985.
Leicester, H. Marshall, Jr. "Oure Tonges Différance: Textuality and Deconstruction in Chaucer." In *Medieval Texts and Contemporary Readers*, edited by Laurie A. Finke and Martin B. Schichtman, 15–26. Ithaca, N.Y.: Cornell University Press, 1987.
———. *The Disenchanted Self: Representing the Subject in the Canterbury Tales*. Berkeley: University of California Press, 1990.
Lerer, Seth, ed. *Chaucer and His Readers*. Princeton, N.J.: Princeton University Press, 1993.
———. "'Now holde youre mouth': The Romance of Orality in the Thopas-Melibee Section of the Canterbury Tales." In Amodio, *Oral Poetics*, 181–205.
———, ed. *Readings from the Margins: Textual Studies, Chaucer, and Medieval Literature*. San Marino, Calif.: Huntington Library, 1996.
———. *Courtly Letters in the Age of Henry VIII*. Cambridge: Cambridge University Press, 1997.
———, ed. *The Yale Companion to Chaucer*. New Haven, Conn: Yale University Press, 2006.
Lewis, C. S. "What Chaucer Really Did to Il Filostrato." *Essays and Studies by Members of the English Association* 17 (1932): 56–75.
———. *The Allegory of Love*. Oxford: Oxford University Press, 1936.
Lindahl, Carl. *Earnest Games*. Bloomington: Indiana University Press, 1987.

BIBLIOGRAPHY

Loxley, James. *Performativity (New Critical Idiom)*. New York: Routledge, 2007.
Lucas, Peter J. *From Author to Audience: John Capgrave and Medieval Publication*. Dublin: University College Dublin Press, 1997.
Ludlum, Charles. "Chaucer's Criseyde: 'Hire Name, Allas! Is Published So Wyde.'" *Pacific Coast Philology* 21 (1986): 37–41.
Lumiansky, R. M. *Of sondry folk; the Dramatic Principle in the Canterbury Tales*. Austin: University of Texas Press, 1955.
Lynch, Kathryn L. "Dating Chaucer." *The Chaucer Review* 42 (2007): 1–22.
Machan, Tim William. "Texts." In Brown, *Companion*, 428–42.
Madan, F., and H. H. E. Craster. *Summary Catalogue of Western MSS. in the Bodleian Library*, Nos. 2354–3490. Oxford: Clarendon Press, 1922.
———. *Summary Catalogue of Western MSS. in the Bodleian Library*, Nos. 8717–14671. Oxford: Clarendon Press, 1922.
Maguire, John B. "The Clandestine Marriage of Troilus and Criseyde." *The Chaucer Review* 8 (1974): 262–78.
Manly, John Matthews. *Some New Light on Chaucer*. London: Henry Holt, 1926.
Mann, Jill. "Shakespeare and Chaucer: 'What Is Criseyde Worth?'" In *The European Tragedy of Troilus*, edited by Piero Boitani, 219–42. Oxford: Clarendon Press, 1989.
Mathew, Gervase. *The Court of Richard II*. London: John Murray, 1968.
McAlpine, Monica E. *The Genre of Troilus and Criseyde*. Ithaca, N.Y.: Cornell University Press, 1978.
McCall, John. "The Parliament of 1386 and Chaucer's Trojan Parliament." *JEGP* 58 (1959): 276–88.
———. *Chaucer Among the Gods*. University Park: Pennsylvania State University Press, 1979.
———. "Troilus and Criseyde." In *Companion to Chaucer Studies*, rev. ed., edited by Beryl Rowland, 446–63. Oxford: Oxford University Press, 1979.
McCarren, Vincent, and Douglas Moffat, eds. *A Guide to Editing Middle English*. Ann Arbor: University of Michigan Press, 1998.
McGerr, Rosemary. *Chaucer's Open Books: Resistance to Closure in Medieval Discourse*. Gainesville: University of Florida Press, 1998.
McKim, Anne, ed. *The Laste Epistle of Creseyd to Troyalus*. Kalamazoo, Mich.: Medieval Institute Publications, 1997.
McKinnell, John. "Letters as a Type of the Formal Level in Troilus and Criseyde." In Salu, *Essays*, 73–89.
McKitterick, David. *Print, Manuscript, and the Search for Order, 1450–1830*. Cambridge: Cambridge University Press, 2005.
Meech, Sanford B. *Design in Chaucer's Troilus*. Syracuse, N.Y.: Syracuse University Press, 1959.

BIBLIOGRAPHY

Mehl, Dieter. "The Audience of Chaucer's Troilus and Criseyde." In Rowland, Chaucer and Middle English Studies in Honour of Rossell Hope Robbins, 173–89.

———. "Chaucer's Audience." Leeds Studies in English, n.s. 10 (1978): 58–73.

———. "Chaucer's Narrator: Troilus and Criseyde and the Canterbury Tales." In Boitani and Mann, eds., The Cambridge Chaucer Companion, 213–26.

Middleton, Anne. "The Idea of Public Poetry in the Reign of Richard II." Speculum 53 (1978): 94–114.

Mieszkowski, Gretchen. "Chaucer's Much Loved Criseyde." The Chaucer Review 26 (1991): 109–32.

Minnis, A. J. The Medieval Theory of Authorship. Philadelphia: University Pennsylvania Press, 1988.

——— and Charlotte Brewer, eds. Crux and Controversy in Middle English Textual Criticism. Woodbridge: D.S. Brewer, 1992.

Miskimin, Alice S. The Renaissance Chaucer. New York: Yale University Press, 1975.

Mooney, Linne R. "Chaucer's Scribe." Speculum 81 (2006): 97–138.

Moore, Arthur K. "Chaucer's Use of Lyric as an Ornament of Style." Comparative Literature 3 (1951): 32–46.

Moore, Marilyn Reppa. "Who's Solipsistic Now? The Character of Chaucer's Troilus." The Chaucer Review 33 (1998): 43–59.

Mosser, D. W. "A New Collation for Bodleian Digby MS. 181." Papers of the Bibliographical Society of America 82 (1988): 604–11.

———. "The Scribe of Chaucer Manuscripts Rylands 113 and Bodleian Digby 181." Manuscripta 34 (1990): 129–47.

Murphy, James J. Rhetoric in the Middle Ages. Berkeley: University of California Press, 1974.

Nelson, William. "From 'Listen, Lordings' to 'Dear Reader.'" University of Toronto Quarterly 46, no. 2 (1976/7): 110–24.

Neufeld, Christine. "Speakerly Women and Scribal Men." Oral Tradition 14 (1999): 420–29.

Nicolaisen, W. F. H., ed. Oral Tradition in the Middle Ages. Binghamton: Medieval and Renaissance Texts and Studies, 1995.

Nolan, Barbara. "'A Poet Ther Was': Chaucer's Voices in the General Prologue to the Canterbury Tales." PMLA 101 (1986): 154–69.

Nolan, Maura. John Lydgate and the Making of Popular Culture. Cambridge: Cambridge University Press, 2005.

Obermeier, Anita. "Chaucer's Retraction." In Correale and Hamel, Sources and Analogues of The Canterbury Tales, vol. II, 775–808.

Olsen, Alexandra Hennessey. "In Defense of Diomede: 'Moral Gower' and Troilus and Criseyde." In Geardagum 8 (1987): 1–12.

BIBLIOGRAPHY

Olson, Clair C., and Martin M. Crow, eds., with illustrations selected by Margaret Rickert. *Chaucer's World*. New York: Columbia University Press, 1948.

Olson, Glending. *Literature as Recreation in the Later Middle Ages*. Ithaca, N.Y.: Cornell University Press, 1982.

———. "Geoffrey Chaucer." In *The Cambridge History of Medieval English Literature*, ed. David Wallace, 566–88. Cambridge: Cambridge University Press, 1999.

Olson, Mary C. *Fair and Varied Forms: Visual Textuality in Medieval Illuminated Manuscripts*. Studies in Medieval History and Culture. New York: Routledge, 2003.

Ong, Walter J., S.J. *The Presence of the Word*. New Haven, Conn.: Yale University Press, 1967.

———. "The Writer's Audience Is Always a Fiction." PMLA 90 (1975): 9–22.

Ovid. Vol. VI, edited and translated by Arthur Leslie Wheeler; 2nd rev. ed., edited by G. P Gould. Cambridge, Mass.: Harvard University Press, 1924, 1988.

Owen, Charles A., Jr. "The Significance of Chaucer's Revisions of *Troilus and Criseyde*." Modern Philology 55 (1957–58): 1–5.

———. "Mimetic Form in the Central Love Scene of *Troilus and Criseyde*." Modern Philology 67 (1969): 125–32.

———. "Minor Changes in Chaucer's *Troilus and Criseyde*." In Rowland, *Chaucer and Middle English Studies in Honour of Rossell Hope Robbins*, 303–19.

———. "*Troilus and Criseyde*: The Question of Chaucer's Revisions." Studies in the Age of Chaucer 9 (1987): 155–72.

———. *The Manuscripts of The Canterbury Tales*. Cambridge: D.S. Brewer, 1991.

Parkes, M. B. *Pause and Effect: An Introduction to the History of Punctuation in the West*. Berkeley: University of California Press, 1993.

———. "The Planning and Construction of the Ellesmere Manuscript." In Stevens and Woodward, *The Ellesmere Chaucer*, 41–47.

——— and Elizabeth Salter. *Troilus and Criseyde, Geoffrey Chaucer, A Facsimile of Corpus Christi College MS 61*. Cambridge: D.S. Brewer, 1978.

——— and Andrew G. Watson, eds. *Medieval Scribes, Manuscripts and Libraries: Essays Presented to N. R. Ker*. London: Scolar Press, 1978.

——— and Richard Beadle. *Poetical Works Geoffrey Chaucer, A Facsimile of Cambridge University Library MS GG. 4. 27*, with Introductions. 3 vols. Cambridge: D.S. Brewer, 1979.

Patterson, Lee W. *Negotiating the Past*. Madison: University of Wisconsin Press, 1987.

———. *Chaucer and the Subject of History*. Madison: University of Wisconsin Press, 1991.
Pearsall, Derek, ed. *Manuscripts and Readers in Fifteenth-Century England*. Cambridge: D.S. Brewer, 1983.
———. "Editing Medieval Texts: Some Developments and Some Problems." In *Textual Criticism and Literary Interpretation*, edited by Jerome J. McGann, 92–106. Chicago: Chicago University Press, 1985.
———. "Authorial Revision in Some Late-Medieval English Texts." In Minnis and Brewer, *Crux and Controversy*, 39–48.
———. *The Life of Geoffrey Chaucer*. Oxford: Blackwell, 1992.
Pedersen, Frederik. "Did the Medieval Laity Know the Canon Law Rules on Marriage? Some Evidence from Fourteenth-Century York." *Mediaeval Studies* 56 (1994): 111–52.
Prendergast, T. A., and B. Kline, eds. *Rewriting Chaucer: Culture, Authority and the Idea of the Authentic Text, 1400–1602*. Columbus: Ohio State University Press, 1999.
Price, T. R. "A Study of Chaucer's Method of Narrative Construction." *PMLA* 2 (1896): 307–22.
Provost, William. *The Structure of Chaucer's Troilus and Criseyde*. Copenhagen: Rosenkilde and Bagger, 1974.
Pulsiano, Phillip. "Redeemed Language and the Ending of *Troilus and Criseyde*." In *Sign, Sentence, Discourse: Language in Medieval Thought and Literature*, edited by Julian N. Wasserman and Lois Roney, 153–74. Syracuse, N.Y.: Syracuse University Press, 1989.
Quinn, William A. "Chaucer's Janglerye." *Viator* 18 (1987): 309–20.
———. *Chaucer's Rehersynges: The Performability of the Legend of Good Women*. Washington, D.C.: The Catholic University of America Press, 1994.
———. "The Rapes of Chaucer." *The Chaucer Yearbook* 5 (1998): 1–17.
———. "Henryson's 'ballet schort.'" *Studies in Scottish Literature* 32 (1999): 232–44.
———. "Presenting 'the' *Legend of Good Women*." In *New Approaches to Chaucer's Legend of Good Women*, edited by Carolyn Collette, 1–32. Cambridge: D.S. Brewer, 2005.
———. "Chaucer's *House of Fame* and the Embodiment of Authority." *The Chaucer Review* 43 (2008): 169–94.
———. "Red-Lining and Blue-Penciling *The Kingis Quair*." *Studies in Philology* 108, no. 2 (Spring 2011): 189–214.
Reed, Teresa. "Overcoming Performance Anxiety: Chaucer Studio Products Reviewed." *Exemplaria* 15 (2003): 245–61.
Riddy, Felicity, ed. *Regionalism in Late Medieval Manuscripts and Texts*. Cambridge: D.S. Brewer, 1991.
Robinson, F. N. *The Works of Geoffrey Chaucer*. 2nd ed. Boston: Houghton Mifflin, 1957.

Robinson, Peter M. W. "The Computer and the Making of Editions." In McCarren and Moffat, *A Guide to Editing*, 249–261.

Root, Robert Kilburn. "Publication before Printing." PMLA 28 (1913): 417–31.

———. *The Textual Tradition of Chaucer's Troilus*. London: Oxford University Press, 1916.

———. *Troilus and Criseyde*. Princeton, N.J.: Princeton University Press, 1926.

———, ed. *The Book of Troilus and Criseyde by Geoffrey Chaucer*. Princeton, N.J.: Princeton University Press, 1945.

Ross, Thomas. "Troilus and Criseyde, ii, 582–587: A Note." *The Chaucer Review* 5 (1970): 137–39.

Rothman, Irving N. "Humility and Obedience in the Clerk's Tale, with the Envoy Considered as an Ironic Affirmation." *Papers on Language and Literature* 9 (1973): 115–27.

Rowe, Donald W. *"O Love, O Charite!": Contraries Harmonized in Chaucer's Troilus*. Carbondale: Southern Illinois University Press, 1976.

Rowland, Beryl, ed. *Chaucer and Middle English Studies in Honour of Rossell Hope Robbins*. Kent, Ohio: Kent State University Press, 1974.

———. "Chaucer's Speaking Voice and Its Effect on His Listeners' Perception of Criseyde." *English Studies in Canada* 7 (1981): 129–40.

———. "Pronuntiatio and its Effect on Chaucer's Audience." *Studies in the Age of Chaucer* 4 (1982): 33–51.

Saenger, Paul. "Silent Reading: Its Impact on Late Medieval Script and Society." *Viator* 13 (1982): 367–414.

———. "Books of Hours and the Reading Habits of the Late Middle Ages." In *The Culture of Print*, edited by Roger Chartier, translated by Lydia G. Cochrane, 141–73. Princeton, N.J.: Princeton University Press, 1989.

———. *The Space Between Words*. Stanford, Calif.: Stanford University Press, 1997.

———. "Reading in the Later Middle Ages." In *A History of Reading in the West*, edited by Guiglielmo Cavallo and Roger Chartier, translated by Lydia G. Cochrane, 120–48. Amherst: University of Massachusetts Press, 1999.

Salter, Elizabeth. "The 'Troilus Frontispiece.'" In Parkes and Salter, *Troilus and Criseyde, Geoffrey Chaucer*, 15–23.

Salu, Mary, ed. *Essays on Troilus and Criseyde*. Cambridge: D.S. Brewer/Rowman & Littlefield, 1979.

Sams, Henry W. "The Dual Time-Scheme in Chaucer's Troilus." *Modern Language Notes* 56 (1941): 94–100.

Sato, Tsutomu. "The Narrative-Audience Relationship in Chaucer's

Troilus and Criseyde." *Studies in Medieval Language and Literature* 2 (1987): 31–53.

———. *The Narrative Technique in "Troilus and Criseyde."* Tokyo: Seibido, 1989.

Saunders, Corinne J. *Rape and Ravishment in the Literature of Medieval England.* Cambridge: D.S. Brewer, 2001.

———, ed. *A Concise Companion to Chaucer.* Oxford: Blackwell, 2006.

Scattergood, V. J. "Literary Culture at the Court of Richard II." In *English Court Culture in the Later Middle Ages*, edited by V. J. Scattergood and J. W. Sherbourne, 29–43. New York: St. Martin's, 1983.

Schechner, Richard. *Performance Theory.* New York: Routledge, 2003.

Schless, Howard. *Chaucer and Dante.* Norman, Okla.: Pilgrim, 1984.

Schoeck, R. J. "Chaucerian Irony Revisited: A Rhetorical Perspective." *Florilegium* 11 (1992): 124–40.

——— and Jerome Taylor, eds. *Chaucer Criticism.* Vol. II. Notre Dame, Ind.: University of Notre Dame Press, 1961.

Searle, John R. *Speech Acts: An Essay in the Philosophy of Language.* Cambridge: Cambridge University Press, 1969.

———. "The Logical Status of Fictional Discourse." *New Literary History* 6 (1974–75): 319–32.

———. "How Performatives Work." *Linguistics and Philosophy* 12 (1989): 535–58.

Severs, J. Burke. "Did Chaucer Rearrange the Clerk's Envoy?" *Modern Language Notes* 69 (1954): 472–78.

Seymour, M. C. "The Manuscripts of Chaucer's Troilus." *Scriptorium* 46 (1992): 107–21.

———. *A Catalogue of Chaucer Manuscripts: Volume I: Works before the Canterbury Tales.* Aldershot: Scolar Press, 1995.

Shepherd, Geoffrey T. "Troilus and Criseyde." In *Chaucer and the Chaucerians*, edited by Derek S. Brewer, 65–87. University: University of Alabama Press, 1966.

Shillingsburg, Peter. *From Gutenberg to Google.* Cambridge: Cambridge University Press, 2006.

Shoaf, R. A. *Dante, Chaucer, and the Currency of the Word.* Norman, Okla.: Pilgrim, 1983.

———, ed. *Geoffrey Chaucer, Troilus and Criseyde.* East Lansing, Mich.: Colleagues Press, 1989.

———, ed., with the assistance of Catherin S. Cox. *Chaucer's Troilus and Criseyde "Subgit to Alle Poesye": Essays in Criticism.* Binghamton, N.Y.: Medieval and Renaissance Studies and Texts, 1992.

Skeat, Walter W. *The Complete Works of Geoffrey Chaucer.* 2nd ed. 7 vols. Oxford: Clarendon Press, 1899. Reprint 1972.

BIBLIOGRAPHY

Sklute, Larry. *Virtue of Necessity: Inconclusiveness and Narrative Form in Chaucer's Poetry*. Columbus: Ohio State University Press, 1984.

Solopova, Elizabeth. "The Survival of Chaucer's Punctuation in the Early Manuscripts of the *Canterbury Tales*." In *Middle English Poetry: Texts and Traditions*, edited by A. J. Minnis, 27–40. York: York Medieval Press, 2001.

Sobecki, Sebastian. "'And to the Herte She Hireselven Smot': The Loveris Maladye and the Legitimate Suicides of Chaucer's and Gower's Exemplary Lovers." *Mediaevalia* 25 (2004): 107–21.

Spearing, A. C. "Troilus and Criseyde: The Illusion of Allusion." *Exemplaria* 2 (1990): 263–77.

———. *Medieval Poet as Voyeur*. Cambridge: Cambridge University Press, 1993.

———. *Textual Subjectivity: The Encoding of Subjectivity in Medieval Narratives and Lyrics*. Oxford: Oxford University Press, 2005.

Stanbury, Sarah, ed. *Geoffrey Chaucer, Troilus and Criseyde*. East Lansing, Mich.: Colleagues Press, 1989.

———. "The Voyeur and the Private Life in *Troilus and Criseyde*." *Studies in the Age of Chaucer* 13 (1991): 141–58.

———. "The Lover's Gaze in *Troilus and Criseyde*." In Shoaf, *Chaucer's Troilus and Criseyde "Subgit to alle Poesye,"* 224–38.

Steiner, George. *Real Presences*. Chicago: University of Chicago Press, 1989.

Stevens, John E. *Music and Poetry in the Early Tudor Court*. London: Methuen, 1961.

Stevens, Martin. "The Ellesmere Miniatures as Illustrations of Chaucer's *Canterbury Tales*." *Studies in Iconography* 7–8 (1981–82): 113–34.

——— and Daniel Woodward, eds. *The Ellesmere Chaucer: Essays in Interpretation*. San Marino, Calif.: Huntington Library, 1995.

Stillinger, Thomas C. *The Song of Troilus: Lyric Authority in the Medieval Book*. Philadelphia: University of Pennsylvania Press, 1992.

Strohm, Paul. *Social Chaucer*. Cambridge, Mass.: Harvard University Press, 1989.

Stroud, T. A. "The Palinode, the Narrator, and Pandarus's Alleged Incest." *The Chaucer Review* 27 (1992): 16–30.

Summit, Jennifer. "Troilus and Criseyde." In Lerer, *The Yale Companion*, 213–42.

Takano, Hidekuni. "The Audience of *Troilus and Criseyde*." *Bulletin of the Faculty of Humanities* 8 (1972): 1–9.

Tatlock, J. S. P. "The Epilog of Chaucer's *Troilus*." *Modern Philology* 18 (1920/1921): 625–59.

Taylor, Karla. *Chaucer Reads "The Divine Comedy."* Stanford, Calif.: Stanford University Press, 1989.

BIBLIOGRAPHY

Taylor, Paul Beekman, with Sophie Bordier. "Chaucer and the Latin Muses." *Traditio* 47 (1992): 215–32.

Thomson, Patricia. "The 'Canticus Troili': Chaucer and Petrarch." *Comparative Literature* 11 (1959): 313–28.

Trigg, Stephanie, ed. *Medieval English Poetry*. Harlow: Longmans, 1993.

———. *Congenial Souls : Reading Chaucer from Medieval to Postmodern*. Minneapolis: University of Minnesota Press, 2002.

Wallace, David. *Chaucer and the Early Writings of Boccaccio*. Woodbridge: D.S. Brewer, 1985.

———. "Troilus and the Filostrato: Chaucer as Translator of Boccaccio." In Shoaf, *Chaucer's Troilus and Criseyde "Subgit to alle Poesye,"* 257–67.

———. *Chaucerian Polity*. Stanford, Calif.: Stanford University Press, 1997.

———. "Italy." In Brown, *Companion*, 218–34.

Watts, William. "Translations of Boethius and the Making of Chaucer's Second 'Canticus Troili.'" *The Chaucer Yearbook* 3 (1996): 129–41.

Wentersdorf, Karl. "Some Observations on the Concept of Clandestine Marriage in Troilus and Criseyde." *The Chaucer Review* (15) 1980: 101–26.

Wetherbee, Winthrop. *Chaucer and the Poets: An Essay on Troilus and Criseyde*. Ithaca, N.Y.: Cornell University Press, 1984.

Wheeler, Bonnie. "Dante, Chaucer, and the Ending of Troilus and Criseyde." *Philological Quarterly* 61 (1982): 105–23.

Whiting, Bartlett Jere. *Chaucer's Use of Proverbs*. Cambridge, Mass.: Harvard University Press, 1934.

Wilkins, Ernest H. "Cantus Troili." *ELH* 16 (1949): 167–73.

Williams, Deanne. "The Dream Visions." In Lerer, *The Yale Companion*, 147–78.

Wimsatt, James I. *Chaucer and His French Contemporaries: Natural Music in the Fourteenth Century*. Toronto: University of Toronto Press, 1991.

Windeatt, Barry A. "The Scribes as Chaucer's Early Critics." *Studies in the Age of Chaucer* 1 (1979): 119–41.

———. "The Text of the Troilus." In Salu, *Essays*, 1–22.

———, ed. *Geoffrey Chaucer, Troilus and Criseyde*. New York: Longmans, 1984.

———. *Troilus and Criseyde, Oxford Guides to Chaucer*. Oxford: Clarendon, 1992.

———. "Courtly Writing." In Saunders, *Concise Companion*, 90–110.

Wood, Chauncey. *The Elements of Chaucer's Troilus*. Durham, N.C.: Duke University Press, 1984.

Worthen, W. B. "Drama, Performativity, and Performance." *PMLA* 113 (1998): 1093–1107.

Yates, Frances A. *The Art of Memory*. Chicago: University of Chicago Press, 1966.

BIBLIOGRAPHY

Yeager, R. F. "Chaucer's 'To His Purse': Begging, or Begging Off?" *Viator* 36 (2005): 373–414.

Zaerr, Linda Marie. "*The Weddynge of Sir Gawen and Dame Ragnell*: Performance and Intertextuality in Middle English Popular Romance." In *Performing Medieval Narrative*, edited by Evelyn Birge Vitz, Nancy Freeman Regaldo, and Marilyn Lawrence, 193–208. Woodbridge: D.S. Brewer, 2005.

Zumthor, Paul. *Essai de poétique médiévale*. Paris, Seuil, 1972.

———. "Body and Performance." In *Materialities of Communication*, edited by Hans Ulrich Gumbrecht and K. Ludwig Pfeiffer, translated by William Whobrey, 217–26. Stanford, Calif.: Stanford University Press, 1994.

INDEX

References to *Troilus and Criseyde* in subentries have been
shortened to *Troilus* to save space.

absence: authorial, 7, 25–26, 138, 159–60, 171n22, 202; textual, 14n30, 15, 25n64. *See also* "I", narrating
Ackroyd, Peter, 18
Aeneas, Dido's relationship to, 111n16
Amodio, Mark C., 14n30
Amtower, Laurel, 24, 27
Anelida and Arcite, 210n22, 211–2
Anglicana Formata handwriting script, 180
Anima, references to, 94
Anne, queen, death of, 212
Ariadne, references to, 156n9
Aristotle, 47
assimilation, orthographic, 184n32
atheism, 132n14
audiences: courtly, 23n57; for early print material, 176n7; literary, 214; Ovid's, 213
audiences, Chaucer's: anticipated, 10, 16, 23, 25, 141, 155; for *Canterbury Tales*, 9n21, 16n36, 209; eliciting reactions from, 49, 66, 82, 118; intended, 10, 41; involvement in recital, 91, 96–97, 102, 103, 120n6, 128, 149; listening, 20, 33, 61n1, 63–64, 122n7, 170; literacy levels of, 8n17, 13n30; men in, 17, 24, 183; mood of, 68, 69, 155; social standings in, 24, 80; for

Troilus, 16, 17n39, 18n40, 34, 84, 182; women in, 17, 94n3, 133, 169, 182, 183n29, 215
Augustine, Saint: hermeneutics of, 26n67; prayer of, 171–72
Austin, J. L., 6n11
authorial intent, Chaucer's, 2, 5, 16, 77n16, 166, 175, 177. *See also* readers, responses to authorial intent; tonal intent, Chaucer's
authorial recital, 4, 13, 168, 174; readers' relationship to, 25–26, 31–32, 213. *See also* voice, authorial
authorial recital, Chaucer's, 2–36; anaphora in, 108, 171; body language in, 13n29, 74, 121, 204; of *Cantus/Canticus Troili*, 38–44; Chaucer identified with Pandarus in, 55–56, 58, 66n8, 68, 97; composition for, 37, 159, 202; despair sounding in, 53, 121, 126, 132, 137, 146, 158, 200; emotions expressed in, 40, 42, 69–70, 83, 89, 123, 125, 219; *ennaratio* in, 27, 37–38; errors in, 54, 75n13; evidence of, 32–33; experience of, 64; impersonations in, 103, 105, 112, 128; improvisation in, 86; interpretive implications of, 28–32; invocations in, 45; manuscript versions of,

INDEX

authorial recital *(cont.)*
  31–33, 46, 173–77, 203, 210–11; pace of, 99, 108; pronuntiatio in, 37–38, 161; quasi-liturgical, 109n13, 109n15; reactions to characters' actions, 71, 84, 96, 108, 130, 140, 153, 166; readers' involvement in, 82, 141, 149–50; revisions of, 30, 62, 177, 178; script for, 15, 19, 114, 173, 203, 212; self-referential comments in, 46–47, 56n30, 128, 145, 168–71, 201; tonal intent, 2, 5, 8, 27–28, 33–38, 41, 48–49, 54–55, 59, 98, 163; voice in, 30, 32, 46–47, 49, 56–57, 100, 128; as work in progress, 62, 110. *See also* "I", narrating; tonal intent, Chaucer's
Axton, Richard, 12n26

Barney, Stephen A.: on Book I, 41, 43n19, 59n32; on Book II, 87n23; on Book III, 43n19, 64n6, 75n13, 78n18, 98n5, 98n6, 109n15; on Book IV, 119n4, 125n8, 128n11; on Book V, 164n15; on Chaucerian revisions of Troilus, 29, 30–31; comparing Troilus with il Filostrato, 117n3; Troilus edition by, 62n5, 108n11, 178, 198n66
Barthes, Roland, 25–26
Baugh, Albert C., 14n30, 178, 206, 207n12
Beadle, Richard, on St. John's Manuscript, 181, 182
Bédier, Joseph, 29n76
Benoît de Sainte-Maure, 117n3, 216n38
Benson, C. David, 2, 10n21, 19n41, 25–26, 151
Benveniste, Emile, 21n49
Besserman, Lawrence, 57n31
Blake, N. F., 11n24, 29
Blanche, duchess, death of, 211
Boccaccio, Giovanni, 24n58, 216n38; narrating "I" in, 3n5, 20–21; Proemio, 20, 6n1; il Teseide delle nozze d'Emelia, 156n9, 212. *See also* Filostrato, il (Boccaccio)
Boece (Chaucer), 14, 32

Boëthius, Anicius Manlius Severinus: Consolation of Philosophy, 9n20, 20, 43n18, 127n10; metrum by, 38–39, 43n18
Boffey, Julia, 183n32
Book of Hours, 177
Book of the Duchess (Chaucer), 13n28, 52; dating, 211, 212n26
Booth, Wayne, Rhetoric of Fiction, 20
Borthwick, M. C., 77n16
Bowden, Betsy, 36n94
Bowers, John, 197n62
Boyd, Beverly, 33
Bradbury, Nancy Mason, 14n30
Branca, Vittore, 39n7
Brewer, Derek S., 9, 13–14, 18n40, 24n61, 39n7
Brink, Bernhard ten, 210n18, 213n29
Brode, John, Jr., 195n58
Brody, Saul N., 12n26
Brown, Carleton, 119n6
Browne, William, 188n45
Burley, Sir Simon, 24n61
Butler, Judith, 6n11

Calliope, references to, 45, 94
Cambridge CD-ROM Project, 10n24
Campbell, Jackson J., 33n92, 173n1
"Canon's Yeoman's Tale, The" (Chaucer), 17n38
Canterbury Tales, The (Chaucer): authorial absence/presence in, 7, 202; dating, 184, 209, 212, 213; manuscript versions of, 9n21, 23n56, 33n92, 34, 193, 207–8; orality of, 16n36, 23n56, 25; print versions of, 198–99; Retraction to, 204, 213n31
Cassiodorus, 6n1
Cavell, Stanley, 6n11
Caxton, William, 197–98
Ceffons, Peter, Epistola Luciferi ad Cleros, 197
Chaucer, Geoffrey: career phases, 209–10, 211, 212; as court performer, 12–13, 17–18, 23–24, 37, 59, 197; dating writings of, 209–13; death

of, 211n24; ennaratio of, 27, 37; fifteenth-century image of, 26; narrating "I" in works of, 3–4, 19, 21–22, 30; oral performances by, 8, 17n59, 24–25, 27, 36n94, 203; poetry of, 12n26, 14, 51n26, 77n7, 93–94; prayers of, 171–72; pronuntiatio of, 16, 27, 37, 38n2, 94, 161; prose of, 14; publication strategies, 18n40; rhetorical art of, 4–5, 6n11, 170–71; self-consciousness of, 63, 116–17, 130; silences in works of, 21n49, 21n50; singing by, 42n16, 43–44; social standing of, 6n11, 17n39, 24; sources drawn on, 20, 28, 30n85, 153, 154–55; Speght's edition of Works, 182; as storyteller, 12n26, 100n8, 177; tributes to, 1–2; voice of, 19–20, 32, 57, 75, 103, 125, 170, 194, 203–4; as writer, 14–15, 137–38, 141, 142, 168, 175n4, 203, 210–11. *See also* authorial intent, Chaucer's; authorial recital, Chaucer's; revisions, Chaucer's; tonal intent, Chaucer's; tonal presence, Chaucer's; translations, Chaucer's; *and individual works*
Chickering, Howell, 5n9, 205n5, 206n7
Christian references, 45, 46, 57n31, 143, 169n17, 170–72, 189n49, 200
Clemen, Wolfgang, 210
Cleo, references to, 45, 62
"Clerk's Tale, The" (Chaucer): Ellesmere manuscript, 207, 208; envoy in, 205–9, 211n25; Hengwrt manuscript, 207, 208; manuscript versions of, 193, 207–8; Prologue, 6n1
clichés, 48, 50, 62, 71, 159
Cohen, Jeffrey J., 172n24
Coleman, Joyce, 9n21, 14n30, 15n34, 16n35, 22n54, 65
"Complaint of Venus" (Chaucer), 42n16
Condren, Edward I., 211n26
confabulation, 75n14, 92, 112, 145, 155, 178. *See also* speech; storytelling
Connolly, Margaret, 182n27
Cooper, Helen, 212n27

Creed, Robert, 14n30
criticism, expressive, 201, 202. *See also* New Criticism
Crosby, Ruth, 8
Crow, Martin M., 13n28
Cupid, references to, 46, 47, 50, 99, 143, 145. *See also* Hoccleve, Thomas, "Epistle of Cupid"
Cureton, Kevin K., 30, 31
Curschmann, Michael, 14n30

Dahlberg, Charles, 20n47
Dane, Joseph A., 10n24, 27
Dante, 21n49, 62; Chaucer's homage to, 112, 141, 171n23, 212; *Purgatorio*, 62n4; *La Vita Nuova*, 170n20
David, Alfred, 210n19
Davis, Norman, 82n21
declamation. *See* authorial recital; authorial recital, Chaucer's; performance, oral
deficiency theory, 8
deixis, 7n12, 195
Delany, Sheila, 170n20
Derrida, Jacques, 25
Destiny, references to, 136
Devereux, James A., 109n15
Dickens, Charles, *A Christmas Carol*, prompt copy of, 38n4
dictation, 214. *See also* speech; writing
Dido, Aeneas's relationship to, 111n16
Dinshaw, Carolyn, 27
Disce Mori, 183n29
Donaldson, E. Talbot, 12n26, 171n21, 207; on narrator in Troilus, 18, 19n41, 27; Troilus edition by, 178
Donoghue, Denis, 201n1
Donovan, Claire, 177
drama. *See* theater
Dryden, John, 7, 12n26, 27

Echo, references to, 215–16, 218
Economou, George D., 94n2
editing, 5n9, 175; electic school of, 29n76; optimist school of, 29n76; recensionist school of, 11n24, 28n76,

245

INDEX

editing (cont.)
  29n77; of Troilus, 28–32, 171. See also revisions
Edwards, A. S. G., 31, 174, 176, 182n27, 183n32, 196n60
Edwards, Robert R., 213n30
emotions, 47, 79. See also authorial recital, Chaucer's, emotions expressed in
entertainment, medieval, 13n30, 75n14. See also theater
"entremette," use of term, 59n32
Epicurean references, 132n14, 154
Erasmus, 158
Eurydice, references to, 125

Farrell, Thomas J., 207
Fergusson, Francis, 12n26
fiction, 7, 9, 18n41; narrative, 128, 203n2; oral, 23n56, 25
Filostrato, il (Boccaccio): as basis for Troilus, 2–3, 8n15, 20; portrait of Boccaccio as illustration, 22n54, 61n1; proem, 62n2, 94n2; Troilus compared with, 43n18, 46, 55n29, 62n2, 65n8, 76, 109n13, 111n16, 117n3, 157
Finnegan, Ruth, 14n30
Fisher, John H., 206, 207
Fleming, John V., 2, 19n41, 41, 74n11, 216n38
Foley, John Miles, 14n30
"Fortune" (Chaucer), 42n16
Foster, Michael, 212n26
Foucault, Michel, 25
Fradenburg, L. O. Aranye, 14n30, 108
"Franklin's Tale, The" (Chaucer), 12n25, 193
Frese, Dolores Warwick, 14n30
Froissart, Jean, 9n19, 14n30
Fry, Donald K., 14n30
Furies, references to, 44–45, 117

Ganim, John M., 12n26, 120n6, 206n11
Gaylord, Alan, 5n9
Gellrich, Jesse., 27
gender, 6n11, 149, 176. See also men; women
gesture. See authorial recital, Chaucer's, body language in; kinesics (gesture)
Gibson, Jonathan, 79n20
Ginsberg, Warren S., 205n4, 206
gloss(es), 87n23, 142, 215; scribal, 174, 175, 181n21
Goldin, Frederick, 216
Gower, John: The Confessio Amantis, 75n13, 217–18; as first reader of Troilus, 110, 171; oral performances by, 24–25; "Tale of Florent," 9n18
Greece, drama in, 12n26, 214n35
Green, Richard Firth, 12n27, 13n30, 51n26
Griffiths, Jeremy, 181, 182
Guido delle Colonne, 117n3
Guillaume de Deguilleville, Pèlerinage de la vie humaine, 22n54
Guillaume de Lorris, 215, 216, 217
Gumbrecht, Hans Ulrich, 3

Hadas, Moses, 8n18
Hagedorn, Suzanne C., 156n9
Hall, Audley, 14n30
Hanna, Ralph, III, 29
Hanning, Robert W., 3n5
Harari, Josué V., 25n64
Harvey, Nancy Lenz, 12n26
Havely, Nicholas R., 24n58
Helmbold, Anita, 23n56
Henry IV, king, envoy to, 211
Henryson, Robert, Testament of Cresseid, 161n13, 182–83, 187, 199
Hermann, John, 13n29
Hoccleve, Thomas, 197; "Epistle of Cupid," 187, 188
Hodapp, William F., 179
Hollander, Robert, 109n14
House of Fame, The (Chaucer), 212
Howard, Donald R., 7, 18n40, 18n41, 26, 27
humanists, 24, 189
Hutson, Arthur E., 57n31
hylomorphism, 94n2, 159n11

"I," narrating: Boccaccio's, 3n5, 20–21; Chaucer's role as, 3–4, 19, 21–22,

INDEX

75n4, 78n19, 99, 202–4, 209, 213; in "The Clerk's Tale," 205, 206, 208; omniscience of, 7–8, 97; Petrarchian, 205; pilgrim persona, 207; scribal, 176; subjectivity of, 30. *See also* narrator; *Troilus and Criseyde* (Chaucer), narrator persona in
in-eching, 110; use of term, 30n85
intentionality, 15, 98, 116; authorial, 34, 35, 115, 153, 200, 208–9; recital, 2, 5–6, 8, 18, 176; tonal, 27, 39, 138, 201–2
intertextuality, 38n6, 210. *See also* textuality

James, Montague Rhodes, 22n54
Jean de Meun, 217
Jennings, Margaret, 175n4
Jesus Christ, 41–42, 172
John of Gaunt, 211, 212n26
John of Salisbury, 15n34
Jordan, Robert M., 27

Kamowski, William, 169n18
Kane, George, 29n76
Kelly, Henry Ansgar, 111n16
Kendrick, Laura, 22n54
Kimpel, Ben, 18n41
kinesics (gesture), 13, 95, 118, 145, 175, 193, 208
Kinney, Clare Regan, 169n17
Kiser, Lisa J., 28, 100n8
Kittredge, George Lyman, 12n26, 26
Knight, Stephen, 77n16
"Knight's Tale, The" (Chaucer), 50, 205; dating, 212–13; manuscript versions of, 193; orality of, 21n49, 26n68; print version of, 198n66
Koff, Leonard Michael, 4, 7, 12n26, 176
Kolve, V. A., 132n14

Lachmann, Ludwig, 11n24, 28n76
Lamb, Charles, 38n1
Lancaster, duke of, marriage, 211
Langland, William, oral performances by, 24–25
language, use of, 2n3, 4, 6n11

Laskaya, Anne, 24n58
Lawton, David, 18n41, 21
Legend of Good Women, The (Chaucer), 17, 156n9; dating, 184; print version of, 199; Prologue to, 30, 78n19, 164n14, 203, 212
Leicester, H. Marshall, Jr., 26, 27
Leland, Virginia, 13n28
Lerer, Seth, 26, 27, 79n20, 175
letters, 165n16; Criseyde's, 83, 85, 159n11, 161, 165–66; sewn, 82n21; Troilus', 79, 80–82, 100, 158–61, 164–65
Lewis, C. S., 111n16
Lindahl, Carl, 16n36
literacy, 8, 13n30, 24
literature: as conversation, 214; medieval, 75n14, 203. *See also* fiction
Lord, Albert B., 13n30
Lucas, Peter J., 32n91
Lumainsky, R. M., 12n26
Lydgate, John, 164n15, 195–96, 197
Lynch, Kathryn L., 209–10
lyrics: in "The Clerk's Tale," 206n, 208; complaint as type of, 54n28; embedded, 38–44, 54, 77, 85, 112, 182, 189, 191; stand-alone, 42, 43n18

Maas, Paul, 28n76
Macrobius, *Commentary on the Dream of Scipio*, 204
Magoun, Francis Peabody, 14n30
Man, Paul de, 25
Manly, John Matthews, 17n38
"Man of Law's Prologue and Tale, The" (Chaucer), manuscript versions of, 193
manuscripts: circulation of, 13–14, 21; of "The Clerk's Tale," 193, 207–8; commissions for, 179n14, 185; public performances contrasted with, 3–4; reading unedited versions of, 5, 9; variations related to scribal practice, 28n75, 29. *See also Canterbury Tales, The* (Chaucer), manuscript versions of

247

INDEX

manuscript versions, *Troilus and Criseyde*: Additional, 188, 190; best reading copies, 5–6, 28, 173–74, 175, 178–79, 186; Cambridge University Library (Gg), 184–85, 186, 194; Campsall (Morgan), 178n12; Cecil Fragment, 30, 33n92, 173n1; circulation of, 13, 32–33, 46, 117n2, 173–74, 202, 210–11; Corpus Christi College, Cambridge, 22–23, 29n81, 178–79, 180, 182, 186; Cosin, 187–88; Devonshire, 174n2; Digby, 195–96; East Anglian, 185; Ellesmere, 22n54; errors in, 169–70; Findern, 174n2; Harley, 43n17, 45, 188–93, 197n62; Hoccleve, 22n54; Huntington Library, 43n17, 196–97; illustrations on, 179, 180, 184–85, 187–88; marginalia on, 180–81, 183, 189, 192, 193n54, 195, 208; Phillips, 197n61; Pierpont Morgan Library, 29n81, 180, 185–87; Rawlinson, 29n81, 174n2, 194, 208; recital copies, 31–33, 46, 173–77, 203, 210–11; revisions of, 28–29; Rylands, 196n58; Scribe, 197n62; Selden, 183–84, 194; Selden Supra, 193–94; for silent reading, 30; St. John's College, Cambridge, 179–83; stand-alone, 183, 187, 188, 190, 194; Trinity, 174n2

Mathew, Gervase, 17
McAlpine, Monica E., 12n25, 21
McCall, John, 45n22, 120n6
McCormick, William S., 28
McGillivray, Murray, 14n30
Machan, Tim William, 23n57
McKim, Anne, 138n2, 148n4, 155n8
McKinnell, John, 165
Mehl, Dieter, 19–20
men: in Chaucer's audiences, 17, 24, 183; new, 24, 182
"Merchant's Tale, The" (Chaucer), 208
"Merciles Beaute" (Chaucer), 42n16
metonymy, 149n5, 171
Middleton, Anne, 24
"Miller's Tale, The" (Chaucer), Prologue, 198n69

minstrels, 13n30
Miskimin, Alice, 8n17, 198n65
misogynist references, 155, 167, 183
Möbius strip, 203–4
Mooney, Linne R., 33n92
mouvance, Zumthor's theory of, 29n78
Murphy, James J., 61n1
mystics, medieval female, 28

narcissism: Ovidian, 216n38; in Troilus, 49–50
Narcissus, tale of, 41–42, 215–16, 217–18
narrative, 12n25, 19, 20n46, 99, 128, 203n2. See also storytelling
narrator, 7–8, 18n41, 26n66. See also "I", narrating; storytelling; *Troilus and Criseyde* (Chaucer), narrator persona in
Natura, 94n2
Nelson, William, 9–10
New Criticism, 10, 19. See also criticism, expressive
New Men, 24, 182
Nicolaisen, W. F. H., 14n30
NIMEV 2297. See Hennyson, Robert, *Testament of Cresseid*
Nolan, Barbara, 27
Nolan, Maura, 23n57

O'Keefe, Katherine O'Brien, 14n30
Olsen, Alexandra Hennessey, 139n3
Olson, Glending, 12–13, 13n28, 75n14
Olson, Mary C., 23n56
omnipresence, 7, 65, 75
omniscience, 7–8, 75, 97, 102
Ong, Walter J., 9, 15n33
oral, use of term, 10, 13–14. See also performance, oral; presence, oral; *Troilus and Criseyde* (Chaucer), orality of
Orpheus, references to, 125
Osberg, Richard H., 210n18
Ovid, 54n28; *Amores*, 74n11; *Metamorphoses*, 215–16, 218; *Tristia*, 213–14
Owen, Charles A., Jr., 29

pagan references, 42, 45
"Pardoner's Tale, The" (Chaucer), 26n68

INDEX

Parkes, M. B., 22
Parks, Ward, 14n30
Parliament of 1386, 120n6
Parliament of Fowls (Chaucer), 204
parody, use of term, 164n15
Parry, Milman, 13n30
"Parson's Tale, The" (Chaucer), 14
Pasternak, Carol, 14n30
Pater, Walter, 201
patronage: manuscript commissions, 179n14, 185; royal, 13, 94
Patterson, Lee W., 10, 26n67, 27
Payne, Robert, 10n21
Pearsall, Derek, 18n40, 28n75, 31n88
Pedersen, Frederik, 111n16
performance, oral, 2n3, 3–4, 6–7, 7–8, 215–16
persona, 203n2, 206n11; of Boëthius, 20; Chaucerian, 12n26, 18, 26; fictional, 213; narrator, 3n5, 14–15, 19n41, 21–22, 28, 203; pilgrim, 207; *in propria*, 43n18, 115, 169; Troilus's, 43n18
Petrarch, 6n1, 208–9; *Canzoniere*, 43n18; *moralitas*, 205, 207; sonnets, 38–42
Phillippa, queen, 211n26
Pinkhurst, Adam: "The Clerk's Tale" transcriptions, 207; Troilus transcriptions, 30, 32, 33, 173
poetry: audience for, 17; development of narrators in, 21–22; novelists contrasted with, 3n5; in old clerk's speech, 14n30, 171n21, 204; Ricardian, 25; Silver Age Latin, 8n18. *See also individual titles*
poetry, Chaucer's: experiments in, 210n22; orality of, 12n26, 14; publication strategies for, 18n40; scribal glosses of, 174, 175, 181n21; self-visibility in, 77n17, 204. *See also individual titles*
Pointed Style, 9n18
punctuation, 5, 53, 202
prayers, 171–72, 189n49
prelection: literacy and, 8; manuscript versions for, 175–76, 179; of Troilus, 15, 37, 39, 43, 170, 193; use of term,

15n34. *See also* oral, use of term; *Troilus and Criseyde* (Chaucer), orality of
presence: authorial, 4, 7, 12n26, 13, 64, 202; oral, 3, 14n30, 15, 26, 201n1, 202. *See also* real presence
presence effect, 3
Price, T. R., 11n25
print versions: circulation of, 13–14, 198; early, 176n7; effects of, 8, 161
print versions, *Troilus and Criseyde*, 31–32, 174, 177, 197–200; Caxton's, 197–98; Pynson's, 198n66; Thynne's, 198–99; Worde's, 198
proems, function of, 6n1. *See also individual Books of Troilus and Criseyde*
prose: Chaucer's, 14; Silver Age Latin, 8n18
Provost, William, 9n20, 38n5
puns, 47, 62n2, 64, 69–70, 94n3, 97, 125; examples of, 74n11, 83, 100, 101
Pynson, Richard, print version of Troilus, 198n66

Quinn, William A., 14n30

raptus (rape), use of term, 107n10, 122
readers: Chaucer's address to, 141, 176–77; empowering, 25–26; fifteenth-century, 163; proto-humanist, 189; responses to authorial intent, 21–22, 150, 158, 159–60, 170, 201n1, 205, 213; scribes as, 175, 176. *See also* literacy
reading, 27, 34–35; aloud, 171n22, 179, 185, 186; of Chaucer's extant texts, 17–18, 21n49; as courtly entertainment, 13n30, 18n40; group recital, 16, 182; histrionic, 9, 12n26, 27, 36n94, 80, 192; performance-based, 5, 10n21, 12n26, 27, 36; public recital, 183, 190, 191, 198; scribal, 174; silent, 14n30, 30, 66, 168, 170, 180–81, 186, 190, 193, 198; solitary, 74, 82, 122n7, 144, 182, 183, 188, 191, 194, 195, 214; writing's relationship to, 159–60, 174, 202. *See also* authorial recital, Chaucer's; manuscript

249

INDEX

reading (cont.)
  versions, Troilus and Criseyde, best reading copies; prelection
real presence, 4, 64, 113, 124, 160, 176
revisions: Chaucer's, 65n8, 138, 141, 164n14, 177, 210–11, 213; for manuscript circulation, 46, 181, 202; of Troilus, 37, 62, 116, 169n18, 173. See also editing
rhetoric: Chaucer's art of, 4–5, 6n11, 9n20, 170–71; medieval, 6n10, 25
Richard II, king, 23n56; court of, 17n39, 115; literacy of, 14n30, 24n61; references to in Troilus, 65
Rising of 1381, 120n6
Robertson, D. W., 74n11
Robertsonians, 10
Robinson, F. N., 206
Robinson, Peter M. W., 11n24, 197n61; Troilus edition by, 178
Roman de la Rose (Romaunt), 22n54, 203, 216, 218; Fragment A, 214–15; print version of, 199
Rome, public recitation in, 214n35
Root, Robert Kilburn: on Book IV, 128n11; on Chaucer's revisions of Troilus, 30, 43n17; on manuscript versions of Troilus, 28–29, 32n90, 181–82, 197n61
Ross, Thomas, 74n11
Rossetti, 55n29
Rowe, Donald W., 93
Rowland, Beryl, 38n2

Saenger, Paul, 14n30
Salter, Elizabeth, 22
sarcasm: in "The Clerk's Tale," 205, 211; in Troilus, 48–49, 51–52, 59, 76, 105, 119, 144, 157
Schechner, Richard, 6n11
Schoaf, R. A., 77n17
Scipio, 204
scoping, use of term, 48n25
scribes: fifteenth-century, 175, 180; manuscript variants attributable to, 28n75, 29, 62, 163, 174, 175n4, 184n33, 210; and readings of Troilus, 178, 180–81, 185, 194. See also manuscript versions, Troilus and Criseyde; Pinkhurst, Adam
script(s), 34, 176, 177; recital, 15, 19, 114, 173, 203, 212
Scylla, references to, 155n9
Searle, John R., 6n11
Seymour, M. C., 29, 178n11
Shakespeare, William, 17n37
Shepherd, Geoffrey T., 19
Shirley, John, 178n12; circle of, 24, 182
Shoaf, R. A., 218
silences, literary, purposes of, 14n30, 21n49, 21n50, 49
Silver Age Latin poetry and prose, 8n18
Sinclair, Henry, 183
singing, use of term, 39n7. See also lyrics
Skeat, Walter W., transcriptions of "The Clerk's Tale" by, 207, 208
skepticism, Epicurean, 132n14
Sobecki, Sebastian, 12n17
Solopova, Elizabeth, 11n24
Spearing, A. C., 3n5, 7n12, 8n15; on Chaucer's poetic style, 93–94, 213n21; on "I" narrator, 18–19, 25n66, 176, 203; on narrator in Troilus and Criseyde, 19n41, 20n46, 171n22; on oral readings of texts, 18–19
speech, 47, 54–55, 171, 204; written text and, 15n33, 165, 214. See also authorial recital; authorial recital, Chaucer's; Chaucer, Geoffrey, voice of; confabulation
"Squire's Tale, The" (Chaucer), 35–36, 210n22
Stanbury, Sarah, 48n25
Statius, Thebaid, 156n9, 163
Steiner, George, 4
Stillinger, Thomas C., 38n6, 41n12, 44n20, 94n2
storytelling, 12n26, 38n1, 100n8, 177. See also confabulation
Straw, Jack, and Rising of 1381, 120n6
Strode, Ralph, as first reader of Troilus, 110, 171

INDEX

Strohm, Paul, 23, 25
subjectivity, 203n2n, 214
suicide, references to, 51, 70–72, 120, 121n7, 125–26, 129, 158
Summit, Jennifer, 28, 149n6
Swynford, Katherine, 211, 212n26

Takano, Hidekuni, 17n39
"Tale of Melibee" (Chaucer), 14
Tasso, Bernardo, 9n18
Tatlock, J. S., 213n31
Taylor, Karla, 21n49, 172n25
Tereus, story of, 160n12
texts, 3n5; embedded, 38–44, 159, 188, 191; oral interpretations of, 15, 18; reading, 2n3, 171n22, 215–16; tone of, 10, 21–22, 35, 36, 202; use of term, 2n3. *See also* manuscripts; print versions
textual, use of term, 13–14
textuality, 8–9, 176, 213n30. *See also* absence, textual; intertextuality
theater: Greek, 12n26, 214n35; medieval, 11n25, 11n26
Thomson, Patricia, 38n6
Thynne, William, 198–99
Tisiphone, references to, 44–45
"To his Purse" (Chaucer), 211
tonal intent, 12n25, 16–17; textual, 21–22, 215–16
tonal intent, Chaucer's, 2–3, 8, 27–28, 53, 76, 201–2; audience responses to, 68, 80, 91, 149, 205; comprehending, 138, 141, 195, 211; conveying conversations, 55, 65–67, 72–74, 82, 84, 86, 88–89, 99, 104, 116; empathy shown by, 144–45, 155, 166; interpretations of, 93–94; manuscript versions conveying, 175–76; mirroring characters' tones, 72, 120; in Troilus, 27–28, 37–39, 151, 219. *See also* authorial intent, Chaucer's; authorial recital, Chaucer's; tonal intent
tonal presence, Chaucer's, 2–4, 12n26, 15–16. *See also* "I", narrating; presence, oral

"Tongue, The" (Chaucer), 174n2
"To Rosemounde" (Chaucer), 195, 208
tragedy, definitions of, 12n25, 47
transcriptions: accuracy of, 175n4, 178, 181; handwriting scripts for, 180, 186; limitations of, 31–32; of Troilus, 184, 188–89, 196–97. *See also* manuscript versions, Troilus and Criseyde
translations, 3n5, 115, 171; Chaucer's, 39, 40, 42, 44, 63, 76, 205
travesty, use of term, 164n15
Treatise on the Astrolabe, A (Chaucer), 40n8
Trevisa, references to, 56n30
Tristan and Isolde, love potion scene in, 75n13, 76
Troilus and Criseyde (Chaucer): audiences for, 16, 17n39, 18n40, 34, 84, 182; based on il Filostrato, 2–3, 8n15, 20, 61n1; Chaucer's voice in, 2, 5, 30, 77n17; composition of, 2–3, 13, 33, 179; dating, 184, 212; dialects in, 194, 199n79; editing of, 28–32, 171; editions of, 32n91, 173–74; expressions of characters' flaws, 149n5; homosocial bonds in, 24n58, 79n20; love-making in, 109n13; narrator persona in, 3n5, 14–15, 19n41, 21–22, 28, 203; orality of, 9, 13n30, 15, 18; palinode to, 164n14; performances of, 15–16, 33–34, 38–39, 176–77; Pinkhurst's transcriptions of, 30, 32, 33, 173; readings of, 10–11, 17–18, 27–28, 33–35, 37–38, 182; revisions of, 37, 62, 116, 169n18, 173; scene summary, 11n25; selections copied from, 174n2; settings of, 33; structural devices in, 38n5; textuality of, 8–9, 26, 169–70; tonal features of, 4, 33–34, 36, 37–39; transcriptions of, 184, 188–89, 196–97; tributes to, 1–2; written versions of, 168, 171n22. *See also* authorial recital, Chaucer's; Filostrato, il (Boccaccio), Troilus compared with; manuscript versions, Troilus and Criseyde; print versions, Troilus and Criseyde; sarcasm, in Troilus

INDEX

Troilus and Criseyde (Chaucer), Book I, 37–60; audience for, 43; beginning, 44, 45–46; Cantus, 38, 39–43, 49–50; Chaucer identified with Pandarus in, 55–56; embedded lyrics, 38–44, 54; ending, 59–60; lack of proem, 61; length of, 46; narrative "I" in, 50; performance notes, 38–39; sarcasm in, 48, 49, 52, 59; time-frame, 64; tonal intent, 39–44

Troilus and Criseyde (Chaucer), Book II, 57n31, 61–92; embedded lyrics in, 77, 85; ending of, 87, 92, 93; invocations in, 45; proem, 61, 62–64, 92; sarcasm in, 76; time-frame, 64

Troilus and Criseyde (Chaucer), Book III, 93–115; adultery vs. marriage in, 111n16; Canticus in, 38, 39, 41n12, 43–44, 190; embedded lyrics in, 112; ending, 115; invocations in, 45; proem, 43, 62, 93–94, 109n15; shipwreck motif, 62n4; stanzas extracted from, 174n2

Troilus and Criseyde (Chaucer), Book IV, 116–36; ending, 135–36; proem, 45, 62, 116–17; satire in, 119n4

Troilus and Criseyde (Chaucer), Book V, 76, 137–72; beginning, 136, 137; embedded text in, 159; ending, 48, 213n31, 219; epilogue, 170–72; lack of proem, 61, 137; revisions of, 169n18; sarcasm in, 144, 157; scene summary, 137; tonal intent, 151, 153; as written composition, 137–38

Venus (goddess), references to, 43, 58, 68, 94, 109n14, 115
Virgil, Aeneid, 111n16, 116
voice, 26, 27, 44; authorial, 21–22, 201n1; recital, 30, 32, 46–47, 49, 56–57, 100, 128. See also Chaucer, Geoffrey, voice of
vulture, use of term, 56n30

Waldron, Ronald A., 14n30
Wallace, David, 39n7, 40
Wedding of Sir Gawain and Dame Ragnelle, The, 9n18
Wentersdorf, Karl, 111n16
Wetherbee, Winthrop, III, 21n48
"Wife of Bath's Tale, The" (Chaucer), 9n18, 26n68, 206n8; manuscript versions of, 193
Williams, Deanne, 40n9
Wimsatt, James I., 38n5, 111n16
Windeatt, Barry A.: on Book II, 65, 85n22, 87n23; on Book III, 98n5, 98n6, 109n13, 112n17; on Book V, 137; on Chaucer, 3n5, 22; comparing Troilus and il Filostrato, 20n48; Troilus edition by, 31n88, 62n5, 178; on variations in manuscript versions of Troilus, 29, 30, 108n11, 174, 185n36
women, 28, 130; in Chaucer's audiences, 17, 24n58, 94n3, 133, 169, 182, 183n29
Wood, Chauncey, 38
word, spoken. See speech
Worde, Wynkyn de, 198
Worthen, W. B., 17n37
writing, 25n64, 62, 171, 214; reading's relationship to, 159–60, 174, 202; teleology of, 68–69. See also Chaucer, Geoffrey, as writer; letters; scribes

Yeager, R. F., 211n25

Zaerr, Linda Marie, 9n18
Zumthor, Paul, 2n3, 29n78

www.ingramcontent.com/pod-product-compliance
Lightning Source LLC
Chambersburg PA
CBHW020318010526
44107CB00054B/1888